NONE MORE BRAVE
THE INSIDE STORY OF TT LEGEND
WAL HANDLEY

NONE
MORE BRAVE

THE INSIDE STORY
OF TT LEGEND
WAL HANDLEY

JOHN HANDLEY
FOREWORD BY MURRAY WALKER, OBE

None More Brave
John L. Handley

Published by Aspect Design 2012
Malvern, Worcestershire, United Kingdom.
Designed, printed and bound by Aspect Design
89 Newtown Road, Malvern, Worcs. WR14 1PD
United Kingdom
Tel: 01684 561567
E-mail: books@aspect-design.net
Website: www.aspect-design.net

ISBN 978-1-908832-13-9

*To Walter's brother, Tom, who did so much
to preserve the memory of one of Birmingham's
greatest sporting heroes.*

'None Ever Passed This Way More Bravely'.
*Inscription on the Walter Handley
Memorial Seat on the Isle of Man*

CONTENTS

FOREWORD
BY MURRAY WALKER, OBE

The motorcycle racing scene was very different in Wal Handley's time (he was, of course, Walter but everyone called him 'Wal'). So soon after World War One the bikes were unreliable and the times were hard when he started racing in 1922 at the age of twenty. There weren't events every weekend during the season in the UK and on the Continent as there are now but the camaraderie was great and the competition was fierce – especially at the fabled Isle of Man TT, which mattered more than all the rest put together to the British motorcycle manufacturers whose bikes dominated world markets and to whom TT publicity success was manna from heaven.

Handsome, modest, independent and apt to speak his mind Walter Handley electrified the TT aficionados when he made his TT debut on an OK Blackburne in the 1922 Lightweight (250cc) race and made the fastest lap. Clearly a man to watch!

I was a child of seven when he had his greatest triumph in 1930 and, in the close-knit racing community of the time, he was 'Uncle Wal' to me, just as the other greats of the day were my 'uncles' too. Motor cycle racing has always been a friendly sport and I've been lucky enough to see it at its best.

There were far more British manufacturers then and Walter rode for no less than seven of them: OK, Rex Acme, AJS, Rudge-Whitworth, Excelsior, Velocette and Norton, plus FN from Belgium. And he did them proud. In his time he was the only rider to win four different TT trophies, in the Ultra Lightweight, Lightweight, Junior and Senior categories, plus five more podium places and nine record or fastest laps, a brilliant achievement from just twenty-eight races over thirteen years of competition. And nor were his successes in the Isle of Man, at Brooklands and on the Continent achieved against a bunch of no-hopers. Walter took on and beat all of the very best of his era, including Alec Bennett, Charlie Dodson, Jimmie Guthrie, Tim Hunt, Jimmy Simpson and the great Stanley Woods.

Although I was there I was much too young to recall his incredible ride in the 1926 Senior TT on a Rex Acme Blackburne V-twin, when he finished second after having been delayed several *minutes* in the early stages, but I can dimly remember his storming ride to victory in the 1930 Senior TT on a Rudge, as a private entrant, taking on the might of the works team led by my father, Graham Walker and supported by Tyrell Smith and Ernie Nott. The race lasted for over three and half hours, with much of it in driving winds and lashing rain so typical of the Isle of Man in an ugly mood. Before a massive crowd Walter led from start to finish and shattered the lap record when he became the first rider in history to complete the ultra-demanding Mountain Course in less than thirty minutes. A magnificent ride which he typically shrugged off afterwards, saying that the bike was so good that all he had to do was sit on it. My father was second and little Murray wasn't best pleased!

But for the unpredictable reliability of the bikes in those days Walter's career would doubtless have been even more outstanding but, nevertheless, he goes down in history as one of the truly greats. In 1935 he transferred his brilliance from two-wheeled competition to four, only for his progress to be arrested by World War Two which, sadly, took his life as a pilot with the Air Transport Auxiliary. To honour his memory there is a wooden seat on the Quarter Bridge Road in Douglas where today's TT riders race by at the start of another lap, just as he did, and to this day Walter Handley is remembered with great liking and respect by those who were privileged to know him as a truly great competitor and a thoroughly decent man.

AUTHOR'S PREFACE

In the inter-war years Handley was one of a bunch of men who it can be said made the Isle of Man TT course forever famous. Each generation has its own heroes, but forget the likes of Alec Bennett, Howard Davies, Jimmy Guthrie, Wal Handley, Tim Hunt, Jimmy Simpson, and Stanley Woods and you run the risk of demeaning the sport itself. These men were idolised by the crowds who thronged the Island for the races round what Murray Walker has called the most demanding and challenging road race in the world.

When I came to do the research for this book I found that Walter's contemporaries had been in no doubt that he was outstanding, not only because of his road racing ability, but also because of his remarkable personality and character. By nature he was quiet, modest, unassuming and sometimes moody. On the racetrack it was a different story, of all the TT stars he will probably be best remembered as the born 'racer', a man who would never give up, a great favourite of the crowds who instinctively recognised his quality and his great will to win. Being the individualist he was, he much preferred to be independent and had no settled racing policy. Consequently he had to work hard for every success. It was one of his outstanding characteristics that if delayed by an unkind fate he would ride back into the race with superhuman brilliance. Businessman and self-educated engineer, this multi-talented man went on to race cars superbly and became a very experienced airman at a time when this was unusual; it's a story of courage in the face of adversity.

I concluded that Wal Handley had led such an active and adventurous life that this was a story that was just too good for it not to be told. And if this was so who better than myself, a nephew with access to information, much of it never before published, to tell it.

John Handley

THE ISLE OF MAN
MOUNTAIN TT COURSE

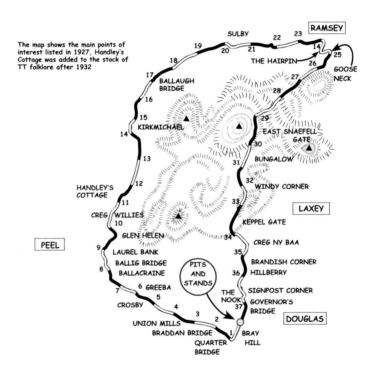

The map shows the main points of
interest listed in 1927, Handley's
Cottage was added to the stock of
TT folklore after 1932

RAMSEY

SULBY

THE HAIRPIN

GOOSE
NECK

BALLAUGH
BRIDGE

KIRKMICHAEL

EAST SNAEFELL
GATE

BUNGALOW

HANDLEY'S
COTTAGE

WINDY CORNER

CREG WILLIES

LAXEY

GLEN HELEN

KEPPEL GATE

PEEL

CREG NY BAA

LAUREL BANK

BALLIG BRIDGE

BRANDISH CORNER

BALLACRAINE

PITS
AND
STANDS

HILLBERRY

GREEBA

SIGNPOST CORNER

CROSBY

THE
NOOK

GOVERNOR'S
BRIDGE

UNION MILLS

BRADDAN BRIDGE

BRAY
HILL

DOUGLAS

QUARTER
BRIDGE

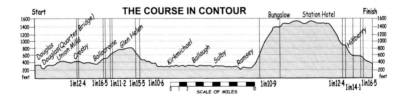

THE COURSE IN CONTOUR

Walter Handley shortly after winning the 1930 Senior TT in the Isle of Man.

CHAPTER 1
HARD TIMES

On Saturday, 15 November 1941, a single engine fighter took off
from Kirkbride Airfield in Cumberland on what should have been
a routine ferry flight. Shortly afterwards the plane caught fire
and crashed. The pilot, Captain Walter Handley of Air Transport
Auxiliary, was killed. Winner of TT races in the Isle of Man
and International Grand Prix races; holder of World Motor Cycle
Speed Records; the name Wal Handley was a name to conjure
with in the world of motor sport. The *Motor Cycle* said:

> Every war necessarily takes its sad toll of our
> motorcycling stars, because as a class motorcyclists are
> athletes, adventurers and courageous. Walter was one of
> our greatest aces. He occupies forever an honoured page
> in the history of our sport.

'With the passing of Wal Handley, motorcycling has lost not
only a brilliant rider but also an outstanding personality,' said
the journal *Motor Cycling*. 'It is hard to hear that Wal Handley
was killed last Saturday, he was always an enterprising driver, as
befitting his training,' wrote the *Autocar*. 'His Ferry Pool will
miss the inspiring presence of their much respected and fiery
little skipper for many moons to come,' said the *Aeroplane*.

Geoff Davison, a fellow TT winner and long-standing friend
took note of another obituary that read:

> Walter L. (Wally) Handley known, to motor racing

enthusiasts, as 'the man who would not be frightened,' was killed in an aeroplane crash on Saturday. One of the most dare-devil track motorcyclists and car drivers, Handley had several times escaped death.

Geoff, a journalist himself, commented, 'I can picture the expression on his face if he could have read that paragraph; he would have said, I think, just – "Ah, you Pressmen again!"'

The man about whom all these things were said was born on the 5 April 1902 at 14 Warwick Terrace in Bolton Road, Small Heath, Birmingham. This address no longer exists but Bolton Road is still there, near St Andrew's Football ground. Walter was the eldest of Jack and Clara Handley's three children. They were destined to have a hard childhood tinged with sadness. Walter, being the eldest, soon had responsibility thrust upon him and grew up quickly. He was only nine years old when an event took place which must have had a lasting effect upon his sensitive nature. He was present when, after a long illness his father died of cancer on 18 July 1911. The loss of this strong and handsome man, who was only forty years old, was a shattering blow to the family. It has been claimed that the early loss of a parent can cause a sense of deprivation that sets up certain drives and ambitions in gifted children. Whatever the cause, Walter's determination to win through to help his mother look after his young brother Tom and baby sister Doris cannot be doubted. In later life it became one of his outstanding qualities to win through no matter how hopeless his situation appeared.

Of one thing we can be sure, the Wal Handley of TT fame did not get his speed talent from his father, Jack Handley, who was known as the slowcoach of the local church's bicycling outings! Invariably the last to arrive home he would disarmingly explain, 'I only stopped to admire the scenery.' No-one could have begrudged him such simple pleasures for in truth Walter's father had led a hard life. Apart from the unhealthy nature of brass working, he had suffered several periods without work, reputedly walking on one occasion from Birmingham to

Coventry looking for employment. It was at a time when there was no adequate relief of temporary unemployment arising from the ups and downs of the trade cycle.

In such uncertain and hard times it was understandable that just over two years later Walter's mother should have decided to remarry. Unfortunately this marriage to a tool-maker, a man who was considerably older than herself, was not a success and resulted in many years of unhappiness. Walter must have been saddened by it all; throughout his life he remembered his own dear father, and the loyalty and affection he felt for his mother added poignancy to the situation. Truly it can be said that Walter Handley did not have a happy childhood. This probably helps to explain those mercurial switches of mood from gaiety to anger, from infectious humour to an almost morose sadness, that his friends came to recognise in later life.

After his father died Walter helped his mother by earning a few shillings as a lather boy in a local barber's shop. On Sunday mornings, while most of the other children were out playing or in church, Walter, around the age of ten, would go into the barbers to clear out the fire grate, and clean up. Walter's young brother Tom played his part by getting up early to serve the men with twist tobacco and cigarettes as they made their way to the factories in the cold dawn light. The takings helped a little to ease their poverty. This small tobacconist shop at 153 Cattell Road was situated within a few hundred yards of where there is now (on the opposite side of the road) the entrance to St Andrew's Football Ground. The shop had been inherited by Walter's mother from her sister Rose Causer and the family lived there.

The living conditions in Cattell Road were uncomfortable although they were probably typical of the 1900s in a working class district. Walter and his brother shared the top floor bedroom. Tom recalled that the roof sloped and it was very cold in winter. They had bare boards except for a strip of carpet each side of the bed. There was a round polished table and a couple of chairs. The walls showed unmistakeable signs of having been peppered with air rifle pellets and the two lads got into trouble over that! A small window faced the street below and rattled with the crash of trams over the points. It was hardly conducive to peace and quiet. The bedroom was reached by two flights of stairs; both were steep, narrow and winding. On the way down there was no landing outside the bedroom door, they were greeted by the first step which they missed at their peril. On the ground floor at the rear of the shop was a small living room and kitchen. They had no bathroom; they went to the local public baths for such luxuries!

Young people are however very resilient and Walter was no exception. At school he was always a personality, with excited boys following his latest escapade with keen interest. His adventurous nature was never far below the surface. On one occasion he built from scratch an old lady's cycle frame and fitted men's racing pattern handlebars. Eventually the proud day arrived when he wheeled it out and set off 'round the square' to see how quickly he could go. The youngsters would gather to watch the fun and, who knows, perhaps time him as Walter swung left round the hairpin from Templefield Street into Cattell Road, then left again into Camp Street and on into Garrison Lane before re-joining Templefield Street. It is tempting to speculate that even at this early age he probably clipped the corners and banked his cycle over more daringly than anyone else.

Tilton Road Council School was the only school he ever attended. He was an outstanding pupil and reached the seventh standard before he was twelve years old. He became 'top boy' at Tilton Road, having as one might expect in view of his subsequent career, wonderfully quick reflexes which showed to advantage in subjects like mental arithmetic. Not long after the outbreak of the Great War he entered the special Labour Examination. This examination had been introduced as a wartime measure to give suitably qualified boys the opportunity to leave school and start work, thus helping to fill vacancies caused by enlistments in the services. Having been in the top class for one year, Walter qualified to enter the examination which he passed and duly started work at the early age of twelve and a half years. The Local Education Committee officials were not happy to lose such an exceptional scholar and tried to persuade his mother to let his education progress further. However, with his stepfather having periods of unemployment, finances were stretched at home and Walter himself was probably anxious to help out.

During those war years, Walter would slip out of the blacked out shop at around 5.30 AM en-route for the Wisemann factory in Glover Street, where they were engaged in war work. In more normal times, Wisemanns were the manufacturers of Sirrah, Verus and Weaver motorcycles, the Sirrah name derived from one of their directors – Mr Harris. After the ending of hostilities war work stopped and with the return of the soldiers there came another period of unemployment. It was about this time that Walter suffered the experience of being out of work. He had several changes of job and when Bill Mewis, who later became one of the Norton mechanics, bought his first bike from Pilkington's Garage on the Lichfield Road, opposite the Waterworks Pub, he recalled seeing Walter working there, stripping down a bike and assisting in fitting a Sturmey Archer gearbox. Bill told me that he was convinced that Walter had a job at Pilkington's not long after the war.

He would have been about sixteen or seventeen years old, but looked younger, when he managed to get a job with the Dunlop Rubber Company at Erdington. Walter, who enjoyed telling a tale against himself, told his brother what had happened. They asked him if he could drive a Box Sidecar Outfit, so of course, seeing his chance of a job he said, 'Yes' even though he had never experienced three wheels at that time. He duly set off from Fort Dunlop with the box outfit loaded with tyres. He reached the main Lichfield Road somehow and then the fun began. Oh boy, you should have seen the alarming gyrations when the Box decided to take charge. The outfit mounted the dual carriageway and roared along in zigzag style with Walter struggling to regain control with the public at panic stations watching this young man perform. All must have ended well for he kept the job.

It would be after Walter left school that he took a keen interest in Syd Hutchinson's cycle and motorcycle shop at the corner of Green Lane in Small Heath. The shop was a regular meeting place for the enthusiasts. It was here that Walter first met Sammy James, who lived nearby in Wyndcliffe Road, and who became Walter's pal and subsequently his loyal mechanic in the Rex Acme and Rudge period of his racing career. It was Syd, an ex-dispatch rider, who lent Walter an old 6 hp BAT-JAP machine upon which it is believed that Walter taught himself to ride. If anyone reading this is a learner or possibly despairing of ever putting up a good show on two wheels, this story related by Walter to Peter Chamberlain, one of the motoring correspondents, should give encouragement. Towards the end of the Great War, Wal Handley thought he might be taken on by the army as a dispatch rider. Having by that time done some work in the trade and already sensing that he could ride a motorcycle as well as the next, he went along and applied. He was told to ride a motorcycle round a track and asked several questions about the 'cog wheels' and in due course was rejected, not because he was under age, which he was, but because he was considered as 'not being a suitable person to have anything to do with motorcycles!' Amazing as it may seem the Army had just rejected a man who was destined to become a TT legend!

CHAPTER 2
WAL JOINS THE ROARING TWENTIES

The spectacular start to Walter's TT career in 1922 came as a surprise only to those who had not been following motorcycle sport. He was already at that time employed in the motorcycle business and was getting known as a competent trials rider and he'd also taken part in a few speed events. Looking back on his career in 1930, Walter wrote, 'Like many other young men in the early years which followed the war, I looked upon the motorcycle trade as a most romantic profession.'

Early in 1919 he had joined Humphries and Dawes Limited, the Birmingham Manufacturers of OK motorcycles. Today, OK is an almost forgotten marque. However, before World War One, OK was the second largest producer of motorcycles in Britain. During the 1920s they were still strong competitors in the lightweight market. Walter's initial labours were rather vague, a sort of junior tester, as he explained:

> I did a little fetching and carrying and tried my hand at various processes in the different shops and was, naturally enough, attracted towards the technical department where work on competition machines was done.

It was here in the OK works at York Road, Hall Green, that another friendship was formed when Walter met Neville Hall, known to his pals as 'Sammy'. Ten years older than Walter, Hall had been riding motorcycles since before the war and the younger man proved an interested learner and spectator.

On Saturdays Walter would move out to the hills south of Birmingham, to watch those events called 'Trials' and liked what he saw. 'Bert Kershaw became my hero; he was riding New Imperials in those days and did a lot to encourage me,' wrote Walter. He needed very little encouragement and no-one really taught him how to ride, as Sammy Hall readily acknowledged. Years later; Graham Walker, a TT winner, journalist and broadcaster, added 'no-one taught Walter, he was a born natural.'

Walter's first chance to show what he could do arrived unexpectedly on 24 April 1920 not long after his eighteenth birthday. It was the occasion of the second Victory Cup Reliability Trial organised by the Birmingham Motor Cycle Club covering over 140 miles and routed across the South Midlands. The OK company had reverted to its earlier practice of buying engines and gearboxes and producing a range of two-stroke machines, the largest of which was 292cc. Neville Hall had been entered in the Victory on one of these machines known as the OK Union. However, Hall was unwell and so Walter took over his entry. Consequently you will not find the name of W. L. Handley mentioned in reports of the trial, but nonetheless this was his first competitive event. It was just the opportunity he needed. He took it superbly climbing Beacon Hill just beyond Rubery, heading up the Old Wyche Cutting at Malvern and climbing all the famous Cotswold Test Hills such as Birdlip, Leckhampton, Rising Sun, Winchcombe, Sudeley, Broadway and Willersey before returning to the start at Berkswell via Stratford, Warwick and Kenilworth.

Watching anxiously at the top of one of the hills was Walter's boss, Mr E. H. Humphries, the managing director of the OK Company. When Walter arrived he promptly took the hill at the top speed possible in the conditions, apparently Ernie Humphries got so excited that he threw his hat in the air – and Walter promptly ran over it! All's well that ends well, and the proud first entry in Walter's diary records quite simply that he was, 'on time at all checks, mileage 150, awarded silver medal,

An alert looking Wal Handley, aged eighteen, astride the 2¾hp OK Union.

highest except Specials.' After this Walter became quite the little competition rider and later that year he competed in the ACU Six Days Trial centred in the North of England, winning this time his first Gold Medal.

Pictures of him in this period show a slight, youthful looking figure. When seated astride his machine he gives an impression of eager alertness. His thick wavy hair, brushed back reveals an intelligent handsome face. The aquiline nose combined with the purposeful looking jaw already suggesting an air of determination and practicality. As Walter's trials life developed, he often brought his bike back to Cattell Road overnight on Fridays so that he could get off for an early start on Saturday morning. On Friday evening Walter would check over the machine, while his brother Tom would check the route card, taking care to note the time checks in capital letters. Tom wrote:

> Next morning, we would be up very early for Walter to give his bike a final check and help him on with his waterproofs and waders – checking that nothing was forgotten. Then he would be on his way to get to the start. After he had gone we could think of the shop being opened.

In such informal ways the quiet background partnership between the brothers began, long before Walter founded his motorcycle sales and service business in 1929.

An interruption to all this came in 1921 when Walter was one of a group lent by the OK Company to the Army to reclaim damaged tanks. He was stationed at Bovington Camp in Dorset. Here the OK men worked very hard on their unpleasant task but they also managed to enjoy themselves. There is a snapshot taken of an amused Walter, standing nonchalantly in the doorway of the officer's quarters, not long after he and Sammy Hall had been thrown out of their own hut for making too much noise. Never a great letter writer at the best of times it is easy to see why he was reputed to be a man of few words. In a brief letter home, he closes by commenting that he has got nothing further to say. Then pencilled in on the back of the letter is an afterthought:

> I nearly got gassed this morning, the tank I was working on caught fire and the chemical we used nearly killed us. After sticking it as long as I could I came out all of a rush.

A time to relax in the Highlands, near Inverness, during the 1921
Scottish Six Days Trial: Walter is in the foreground wearing a cap.

During the Sangster Cup Trial 1921, in southwest England;
Walter is riding an OK Union from Lands End to Birmingham.

In June they said goodbye to the Tank Corps and returned to the Midlands. In recognition of the firm's services to the Army, Ernie Humphries had been made a Major and the company decided to adopt as their official racing colours, the chocolate, red and green, of the Tank and Armoured Car Corps. The year 1921 turned out to be hectic, for in addition to the period of Army service in Dorset, Walter had managed to add further to his list of Trials successes. The most notable of which were; the Victory – Gold Medal; Birmingham to Lynmouth and return – Gold Medal; Scottish Six Days – Silver Medal having climbed all the hills except Glencoe; ACU Six Days – Gold Medal and the Bala Trial another Gold Medal. The Handley reputation for bad luck, which a few years later had become a bye-word in sports reports, was not apparent in these early efforts. That is unless you count the following incident, when in the North Wales Motor Cycle Club's Open Trial, Walter was motoring quite nicely on one of the Llangollen Hills when his coat tail got caught in the driving chain. After a series of somersaults, spectators were relieved to see the OK Union rider pick himself and his machine up and proceed to be among the finishers.

In the following year he had two notable trials successes. First, a Gold in the Colmore when only ten per cent managed first class awards; Walter was quietly proud of that one. Then in September he had the satisfaction of being a member of the OK team with Neville Hall and F. C. 'Charlie' North, that carried off the 350 class team award of the ACU Six Days Trial. They achieved this on their small 292cc two stroke machines and were delighted to find that over a distance of 830 miles encompassing Yorkshire, the Welsh mountains and the Thames valley; they had pipped an AJS team that included Jimmy Simpson by two marks. Trials riding was a challenge that they enjoyed. It was rough and demanding going up the hills, going over slippery tracks, rocks and streams. You had to negotiate tortuous sections non-stop without putting a foot down or touching a tape. It was highly competitive and great fun.

Walter continued to perform in trials after he had joined the

Rex Acme Company, using twin port JAP engines in preference to the Blackburne power units with which his name is usually associated. The reason for this being that the outside flywheel of the Blackburne engine rendered it unsuitable for work over uneven terrain. His diary reveals that his early experience at Wisemanns and the OK factory had given him a sound technical knowledge which was never to desert him. He prepared his

September 1921: Howard Davies (AJS) is followed by Bert Milner and Wal Handley (OK Junior) as they enter Bridgewater in the ACU Six Days Trial.

machines with care, altering the gearing, attending to the valve timing and the compression ratios to suit the type of event in the prevailing conditions.

As the months went by it was becoming clear to Walter that he wanted something speedier than trials work. On one occasion Walter said:

> I can quite appreciate why some people get so enthusiastic about hills and hairpins, ruts and route cards, but I should never have done so myself as my ambitions lay chiefly in the direction of road racing.

Nevertheless he continued to put in appearances in trials for some time. Even as late as 1926 Walter was only just thwarted from following his Victory Cup class win of the previous year, with an outright win in the same event. A choked jet on his 350 Rex Acme meant he had to be content with a silver medal.

When I asked Harry Perrey and Bert Perrigo, two famous trials riders for their assessment of Wal Handley as a trials exponent, they both agreed that he would have been very good if he had chosen to specialise.

CHAPTER 3
BATTLE FOR 'FIFTHS OF A SECOND'

In the light of subsequent events it's interesting that it was trials work that gave Walter an early opportunity to circle the famous Brooklands track going quickly. The occasion was the ACU Six Days Trial of 1921. It was held mainly in the West Country, but it began and ended at the famous Weybridge track – Brooklands. The conclusion of the trial included a speed test. On the fifth lap of the speed test, Walter caused a sensation by putting the OK on its stand right in the centre of the track and while other competitors roared past on either side of him, he coolly changed a plug! Unknown to him there was an interested spectator that day destined to play an important role in Walter's future racing career. The stalwart figure of Dougal Marchant went away impressed with the young Birmingham rider's handling of his machine, convinced that he had just seen an up and coming star. Walter had won his Gold Medal with ease. The 250cc two stroke OK models, weighing 205 lbs had averaged 95 mpg for the week's riding at an average speed of 36 mph, while the oil consumption had worked out at 2,920 mpg. Surely not a bad performance in economy terms at least despite all the development that has since taken place.

In view of his inclination to favour the excitement of going quickly, it is no surprise to learn that he entered his first outright speed trial later that same year on 13 August at Redditch. He entered his own machine – it may have been his first, a JAP-engined Armis 275cc. These little-known machines were manufactured in the period between 1920 and 1923 near

Dartmouth Street in Birmingham. Walter won the 350cc class at this meeting: he was nineteen years old.

The following year in Madresfield Court's Gloucester Drive, near Malvern, he really came into his own sweeping the board with fourteen firsts on his OK Junior machine. Madresfield was to prove a happy hunting ground for he returned here in 1925 to win the Severn Cup for the fastest time for solos up to 500cc. He achieved this on his 350cc Rex Acme, his head tucked down so low that his helmet appeared as a button on the end of his tank!

I was reminded not so long ago that some of these speed 'runs' were not always arranged with the blessing of the forces of law and order. On the Birmingham to Coventry Road there used to stand Ye Stonebridge Hotel which is no more. It was bulldozed to make way for the Stonebridge Roundabout. After the Great War the hotel became a popular venue for Midland motorcyclists situated as it was roughly half way between Birmingham and Coventry. Tom Handley could recall very clearly riding out from Birmingham along the main Coventry Road, which in those days could only be considered a country road, quite contrary to the tarmacadam dual carriageway of today:

> It was in the early 1920s when my brother's fame was growing that I recall there was always movement and a stir of excitement amongst the crowd outside the hotel when Walter arrived with a Rex Acme. Often Jack Parker would be there with his BSA. They were contrasting personalities, Walter very quiet while Jack was known for his volubility. Yet they got along together very well over the years. Jack Parker went on to become, in the view of many commentators, England's greatest speedway rider and a top star for over thirty years. At this rendezvous Walter and Jack would often have unofficial speed tests. We could always tell when this was due to happen because the lads would quietly start to drift off towards the Coleshill 'Straight', looking quite innocent.

Having arrived there, a half mile was measured out and lookouts were posted to alert traffic and watch out for 'coppers'. Then Walter and Jack would in turn fly down the road against a stop watch test.

As Geoff Davison once commented, if the law put in an unexpected appearance, a scarf over the front number plate, a coat tail over the back, a sudden swerve and the danger was past.

Despite these adventures along the way, Walter made his reputation in the official club events. Not long after the Madresfield success he entered his first hill climbs. One of the earliest was Chatcombe Pitch Hill, just four miles southeast of Cheltenham. Here Walter sent his 348cc OK twisting and roaring up the slope to gain three firsts and thus tie with the famous George Dance. In March 1923 he followed this up with nine firsts on the 902-yard, 1:8, fast winding ascent of the celebrated Kop Hill, situated just outside Princes Risborough in the beautiful Chiltern Hills. He did this with his OK Junior powered with 250 and 350 Blackburne engines. He returned to the Kop two years later to repeat this feat by that time using a Rex Acme Blackburne machine. This took place just before the Kop was closed to racing forever.

What had happened was that on 28 March 1925 firstly a big Zenith twin had crashed spectacularly into the roadside bank, followed later the same day by a Brescia Bugatti running amok amongst the spectators. Amazingly instead of the slaughter everyone expected, only one onlooker was injured. Yet this episode only served to underline what many people had been saying, that the Kop was dangerous. Of course the enthusiasts who lined one side of the slope loved every minute of it, but despite the protests an unconditional ban on speed events on public roads was imposed and has remained in force ever since. The Kop never heard the sound of racing engines again and today it is just a nostalgic memory associated with the names of Freddie Dixon, Wal Handley, Rex Judd, Bert Le Vack, and many others.

Just before the ACU withdrew permits for speed trials and hill climbs on public roads, the Wye Valley Club gained the distinction of holding the last such speed event before the ban became effective. A section of the main Hereford – Hay Road was used while ordinary traffic was diverted. An estimated crowd of 3,000 massed along one side of the course. The start was delayed so that only one, instead of the usual two runs along the half-mile course was permitted. By 1925 Walter was becoming known as the Rex Acme exponent having left OK to join the Coventry firm. For

At Kop Hill, near Princes Risborough, Wal comes first on his Rex Acme Blackburne 348cc, 28 March 1925.

this event he had prepared a 348cc Rex Acme Blackburne with a special thin tank using a Chater Lea frame for extra lightness. The specification featured Web forks, a Burman gearbox, Amac carburettor, Coventry chain, KLG plugs and Dunlop tyres. He was the first to go and covered the distance in an electrifying 22·4 seconds at 80·35 mph. The famous George Dance followed on his 347cc Sunbeam but to everyone's astonishment George's

April 1925, Wal Handley wins the 350 class of the Hereford Speed Trial at 80·35mph on a naked looking Rex Acme: it was the last speed trial on public roads.

time turned out to be no better than 23·8 seconds. Later in the day Dance swept along the half mile on his new 493cc overhead camshaft Sunbeam, but when the time went up at 23.4 seconds the record set by the 350cc Rex Acme still stood. So in the last event of its kind Wal Handley had made history by becoming the first man to beat the superb George Dance in a speed trial. He had won not only the Gloucester Cup for the fastest 350 solo but he had also the second fastest time in the 500cc class and third place in the 750cc class: he had done this with just one go on his 350 model.

The ban on speed events only applied to public roads. Off the highway it was a different matter and as late as 1927 Walter's 350 Rex Acme was recorded making the second fastest time of the day in a field of seventy starters at Gopsall Park in

Derbyshire. In the intervening period he had raced successfully on the sands at Pendine, also known as the Welsh TT and at Scarborough. The roar of his Rex Acme Blackburne had thrilled the crowds in speed trials at Clipstone, Doncaster, Worcester and at Stalybridge near Manchester. In those early days Walter would enter these events with zest and take them seriously. It did not matter how unusual or peculiar the race might be, he would say, 'that's all right it doesn't matter to me.'

With his liking for speed events it can come as no surprise to learn that his ambitions turned towards the Isle of Man. For it was on the Island, where racing on public roads was permitted, that the greatest road race in the world, the Tourist Trophy, awaited him.

CHAPTER 4
THE ISLE OF MAN BECKONS

Early in 1922 the ACU announced that the Isle of Man TT races were to have a new Lightweight Tourist Trophy. Hitherto there had not been a separate race for 250cc machines, simply a Lightweight Class run concurrently with the Junior Race. It was at this time that Humphries and Dawes Limited decided to make their first post-war TT appearance in the new Lightweight Race.

The new OK racing machines were the first four-strokes to be reintroduced into their programme. The engines were 248cc overhead valve Blackburnes with three-speed Burman gearboxes. The rear brake was internal and operated on either side giving parallel action. The bikes had chain transmission and the oil pump was operated by foot. The model was reputed to be quick and Walter must have been quietly hoping that his work in trials and speed events had been enough to earn him a place in the OK team.

While the OK chief, Ernie Humphries, was deliberating over his TT entries, a well-known TT rider called at his office. The visitor's name was Howard Davies, the man who the year before had become, as it turned out, the only man ever to win the Senior TT on a 350cc machine. Howard was one of the few men who had actually seen his own obituary! He carried with him a 1917 Press clipping which was headed 'Well-known Motor-cyclist in the RFC Killed in Action' – a report which, as he was fond of saying, was grossly exaggerated.

Howard found Humphries to be rather less than his customary ebullient self. He was undecided about his TT

The 1922 OK team for the Isle of Man TT. *Left to right:* Walter Handley, Neville Hall and Charlie North, the engines used were 248cc Blackburne.

entries. They were a man short in the OK team, who should he nominate to join his two very experienced men, Hall and North? He knew he had an up and coming star in Walter Handley, but was he ready for the most demanding road race in the world – the Isle of Man TT? Howard didn't hesitate, 'That lad is a born rider and a future winner given the chance.' It seems that this forthright expression of confidence from the stalwart HRD tipped the scales in Walter's favour and any lingering doubts were cast aside. Walter was told that he was going to the Isle of Man as a full member of the OK team. By late spring it was acknowledged by the rival New Imperial and Levis camps that the youngster was to spearhead the OK challenge and was the man they had to beat.

The Isle of Man; what visions the words raise for keen motorcyclists the world over and especially for the enthusiasts who, year after year, find themselves arriving in the Island for the June races. Those Manxland hills were to provide the setting for many memorable duels down the years to enhance the magic of those names: Bray Hill, Kirk Braddan, Union Mills, Greeba,

Ballacraine, Glen Helen, Ballaugh, Ramsey, the Gooseneck, the Bungalow, Keppel Gate, Creg-ny-Baa, Signpost Corner and many more.

Before going further we ought to say a few words about the development of the TT Course. The first motorcycle TT race took place in 1907 because the Island had no speed limit, on the mainland the limit was set at 20 mph and the Manx Government was able to close the roads. In those days the short anti-clockwise western circuit was used. It utilised the modern course from Ballacraine to Kirk Michael returning along the coast road to Peel and then back to the starting point at St Johns, close to the Tynwald Hill. However, the arrival of multi-gear transmission made it possible, just four years later, to use the mountain course for the first time. The only difference being that the course ran from Cronk-ny-Mona to the top of Bray Hill, thus omitting the section from Signpost Corner to Governor's Bridge used on the present day circuit. After World War One the TT series resumed in 1920; it was then that the course was increased to its present 37·75 miles by the inclusion of the Governor's Bridge section to finish on the Glencrutchery Road by the grandstand.

The course in the early 1920s had many more sharp corners on it than it has today and photographs, plus the testimony of veteran riders of that period, confirm that the roads were much narrower. The only stretches of tarmacadam road were the opening seven miles or so to Ballacraine and the bit through Ramsey. The rest of the course was plain macadam; that is earth and stones rolled together. In wet weather it was very muddy, while in dry conditions every bike raised clouds of dust that made visibility a problem and hence overtaking hazardous. When the riders came into close proximity with one another they could, and often did, suffer cuts and abrasions from flying stones. The mountain climb from near sea level at Ramsey to over 1,400 feet at the Bungalow was rough in the extreme, the road was mostly unfenced, and wandering sheep could be an additional danger for the unsuspecting rider out for an early morning practice. There was of course no rear springing on those early machines and it was not uncommon at the end of a race, that could have lasted well over four hours, to see riders literally lifted from the saddle and helped into the paddock.

Without quite knowing what awaited them three future stars came to the Island for the first time in 1922. They were to become legendary figures in the annals of the sport. This trio were Walter Handley, Jimmy Simpson and Stanley Woods. They were each entered in separate races and therefore did not compete against one another. As we shall see Wal Handley was entered in the newly introduced Lightweight event. Jimmy rode a Scott in the Senior Race but was forced to retire on his first lap with a split petrol tank, the sort of misfortune that Simpson was going to experience many times in the Island. In the Junior Race Woods rode a Cotton. The bike caught fire when refuelling but despite the delay and the burns, the young Dubliner managed to finish fifth. It was this accident which brought into being the rule which requires the stopping of engines while taking on fuel. It is a remarkable fact that these three men between them managed to win fifteen TT races and notch up 27 record laps at a time when there were far fewer TT races in the programme than today.

Meanwhile there was a bustling air of confidence at the OK Works in Birmingham. When Geoff Davison, the Levis star, called he was greeted by a now confident OK boss who introduced a somewhat embarrassed Wal Handley. 'I've got a boy here who can ride rings round you,' claimed Humphries, but Walter knew he had to prove himself on the Island course and remained diffident. Just approaching his twentieth birthday and looking younger, he looked down and quietly said, 'How do,' to Davison, his future friend.

The OK party arrived in Douglas during the first full two weeks of the practising period and put up at the Villiers Hotel. Walter's introduction to the famous course was certainly memorable. On the first morning he was up early, took out his OK Junior and promptly got into the news. Walter wrote:

I had never seen the TT course and when I arrived at the playing fields there was a heavy mist. I wheeled the OK out onto the Glencrutchery Road and was then told that I could go and did so at full speed into the murk. I had not gone half a mile before I was stopped by an agitated marshal at Governor's Bridge! I had set off in the wrong direction of the course.

Walter felt that this little episode was not entirely his own fault, might they not have had someone on hand to show a newcomer the right way. The Press of course loved this story and at home the local paper headed it 'Comedy of The Novice From Birmingham.' Continuing in a similar vein they spoke of Handley, a Birmingham youth, who being so raw and eager, had set off in the wrong direction giving the officials an anxious few minutes setting telephones into operation before bringing the 'flying terror' to a halt at the next control.

Of course the Handley temperament was aroused on seeing this and the reaction was swift. On the Saturday of the first week's practising he clipped nearly three minutes off Bert Kershaw's 1921 lap record and proceeded to increase this margin in the following week. It meant that his 250cc bike was lapping the Island at over 50 mph. A remarkable speed when it is borne in mind that the best lap speed he had managed on the OK when going for world records at Brooklands was 59 mph. This could only mean that Wal was certainly 'not hanging around on corners.'

On the race day the weather was good. The 250 class set off first followed by the 350cc riders. There was no warm up allowed and most riders applied paraffin injections before storing the bikes the previous day. Geoff Davison, the future founder of the *TT Special*, had taken pains to reduce the weight of his very reliable Levis two-stroke to only 147 lbs, much lower than any of his rivals. He came to the start wearing clothing intended to cut down wind resistance. He was rewarded with a very fast lap, clipping nearly five minutes off the existing record. Then

Walter, being one of the later starters at number 26, caused a hum of excitement by taking the lead with a record lap for the race in 44 mins, 24 secs at 51 mph. On his second lap Walter only got as far as Sulby where he had to retire with a broken inlet valve. Davison then took the lead and kept it to the end, winning the five-lap race at 49·89 mph. The winner collected £30, a gold medal and a replica of the trophy and in 1922 you could buy a good quality two-speed, two-stroke motorcycle for £30! It was the last occasion a two-stroke would triumph in the TT until the German DKW victory in 1938.

For Walter it was disappointing not to finish but he had the consolation of becoming the first rider to smash the existing lap record in a TT race from a standing start with a cold engine on his first ever appearance on the famous course. A performance that has never been equalled and now with the changes in race regulations will remain forever. After the race, Geoff sportingly commiserated with Walter on his bad luck. Always the man of few words, 'Ah,' he replied.

CHAPTER 5
NEVER GIVE UP!

Would Walter's luck change on the Continent? It was his first trip abroad and everything must have seemed possible. At that time the French and the Belgian Grand Prix Races were the two that really counted with British manufacturers. The French Grand Prix was held on the new triangular course near Strasbourg. It resulted in another win for Geoff Davison on his Levis. Wal Handley and Stanley Woods, both on OKs had to retire. So for most of the riders it was a case of transporting themselves and their machines to the Belgian town of Spa, not far from the German frontier, to be ready for the next big race on Sunday, 23 July 1922.

The course is situated in the wooded Ardennes region and is similarly demanding to the TT being hilly, with fast curves, sharp corners and hairpin bends. The main difference being that the Spa road circuit had a length of just under 10 miles. It was the kind of course that Walter liked because of the demands it made on the cornering ability of the rider. Would it be third time lucky for Walter?

It was to prove an unforgettable race for those who took part in it. There was fine weather at the start and Geoff Davison came to the line wearing as usual his dance shoes, stockings, drill breeches, cricket sweater and leather gloves – hardly the most suitable apparel for a four hour thunderstorm! Rain fell as the first batch of riders left and it soon became a downpour. Rain blew in on the Press stand ruining the scoring sheets. Then the stand began to collapse. The downpour became so heavy that the riders' visibility was at times no more than about 200 yards ahead. Being so inadequately clothed caused Geoff never to forget the 1922 Belgian. He described the event in terms of low cloud, a biting wind, and a red spray of mud continually thrown up by the machines. The object in everyone's mind must have been to complete those 20 laps as quickly as possible and to then get warm and dry again. Occasionally the rain would ease off and just as everyone was hoping it would stop, on it came again with renewed vigour. Virtually everyone was in trouble and those continuing were inclined to envy those who had retired, it was that sort of race. In the 250 class it was not long before Geoff and Walter were the only survivors. The Levis suffered from overheating due to mud clogged cylinders while the OK was troubled by water in the magneto.

The two passed and re-passed each other throughout the race. 'No matter which of us was on the move,' wrote Geoff, 'Walter gave me a cheery wave and that gay laugh which, as I came to know later, was characteristic of him in adversity.' At the end of the tenth lap Geoff stopped to fill up with 'petrol, oil and brandy.' Before he had half finished the cognac bottle, it was dashed from his lips by none other than Dougal Marchant – Walter's manager in the adjacent pit. It was a very sporting action, so typical of the men and the sport. However, poor Geoff was so numb with cold he no doubt believed he could have drunk the whole bottle with no ill effects. Geoff and Walter were the only two riders to finish in the Lightweight Class. Davison had completed the 'hat trick' by winning the Belgian race at 43.5 mph in 4 hrs, 18 mins, 43 secs. As the riders were helped off their machines and almost carried to the luxury of a hot bath, Walter had the satisfaction of knowing that he had gained his first 'podium position' in an international event.

If the Belgian Grand Prix had given Walter his first podium finish, it was in Northern Ireland on Saturday, 14 October 1922 that he scored his initial road race triumph. It was the occasion of the newly formed Ulster Motor Club's first Grand Prix. The 'Ulster' went on from this date to firmly establish itself in the racing calendar. The triangular shaped course was situated a few miles out of Belfast. It became known as the Clady Circuit after the punishing 7-mile straight of the same name, which in those days could be taken at full bore only by those with the endurance to hang on going over the bumps. Over the years the Ulster has been well supported by TT riders, but in 1922 it was a different story and only three famous TT riders crossed the Irish Sea – Wal Handley (OK) in the Lightweight Class, Stanley Woods (Cotton) in the Junior and Graham Walker (Norton) in the Senior.

Walter almost did not make it for he nearly missed the boat train for Ireland. He was held up at Brooklands and it was getting late on Friday afternoon when Walter announced that the OK was not to his satisfaction. 'Wouldn't pull the skin off a rice pudding,' he growled.

'So you don't reckon it has a chance?' queried Marchant.

'Hopeless,' snapped Walter, who by this time had decided to call it a day and went off to the clubhouse for a drink.

Dougal Marchant was a wily old campaigner and he was getting to understand his temperamental friend. Somehow he just knew he had to get Walter's 'dander up'.

Left alone in the shed he deliberately rammed the tag end of a file through the OK tank – result petrol everywhere. When later the pair returned to clear up before going home, Walter was amazed at the mess. 'Well we can surely fix up the tank, we're not going to let a small thing like this beat us!' Dougal's ploy had worked and Wal rushed over to Euston for the boat train to Ireland, travelling overnight, to arrive with his machine on the Saturday morning.

He was just in time for a quiet trip round the 20.5-mile course organised by the newly formed Ulster Club. On his return Wal pronounced the course to be 'sporting'. Actually it was by no means easy. Set in the hills towards Antrim, the narrow country lanes were terribly dusty and full of bumps, particularly the undulating seven miles of the notorious Clady Straight. Walter was heard to say that he would 'learn the course on the way round.' On the second lap he quickly learned the speed at which the bend at Aldergrove could not be taken! Despite a bent rib or two he continued on his way to such good effect that he completed the seven laps at 52·39 mph. This was nearly 3 mph faster than the 350cc winner and less than a mile per hour slower than the scratch man on a '1000' Brough Superior!

Even at this early stage in his career so much was his reputation growing that the race officials had put him on the fifteen minute mark so that his 250cc gave a 45 minutes start to the other 250s and 350s and as much as seventeen minutes to one of the 500s! The overall winner on handicap was Hubert Hassall on a 490cc Norton. Hassall had won at a speed only a fraction of a mile an hour slower than the fastest road race up to that time – the 1922 French Grand Prix won by Alec Bennett at 61 mph. The Ulster had only just missed earning its title of 'the fastest road race in the world' at the first attempt. It was to achieve this distinction in the following year and hold it for the next fourteen years.

After this success in Northern Ireland and an equally impressive high speed performance at Kop Hill in the following spring, Walter arrived in the Isle of Man buoyed up for the 1923 TT races. The first event was the 350cc Junior Race, which for Walter was destined to be something of a non-event. Walter wrote:

> Imagine waiting on the grid, all keyed up and ready, 'Five, four, three, two, one, go!' says Ebby [Mr Ebblethwaite, the time-keeper], off you push and nothing happens, except for a few dismal pops. Will it ever fire?

A situation like this is sheer agony for the rider after weeks of preparation and practice. Eventually Walter did get the OK machine to start only to get as far as Quarter Bridge where a valve rocker fractured, probably as a result of, to quote Walter, 'a particularly furious piece of riding down Bray Hill to make up for the delayed start.' All in the game but very disheartening especially as Walter had recorded some good practice times.

The race itself, increased to six laps, was won at record speed by the fourth and final race leader, none other than Stanley Woods. He rode a Cotton also powered by the Blackburne engine. The Cotton was noted for its triangulated frame design patented in 1914 which gave the bike superb steering qualities. In breaking the AJS monopoly in this event, which had held good since 1914, Stanley gained the first of his ten TT victories and it might be added splendid consolation for his misfortune in 1922.

Walter's hopes were now focused on the 250cc event. The race day dawned gusty, cloudy and miserably cold. With rain overnight the roads were wet in parts as the record entry of forty riders came to the start. This time Walter got away smartly and as the sun broke through it was seen on the scoreboard that he was gaining on his rivals. When the times were posted up it became clear that he had repeated his performance of the year before. There was another record lap in 41 min, 58 secs from a standing start, his average speed being 53.95 mph. Wal's lead over the twenty-nine year old motor agent from Edinburgh, Jock Porter, rider and manufacturer of his own New Gerrard, was nearly two minutes. At one stage Wal's lead had built up

A very determined-looking Wal Handley (OK)
is ready for his second TT race, the 1923 Lightweight TT.

to over three minutes but then on the third lap a tumble at Governor's Bridge caused him to lose time in straightening his footrests. Now Walter began one of those fights against adversity for which he was to become famous.

On the fourth lap of this six-lap contest the OK rider's brakes failed at Windy Corner. Walter fell heavily turning several somersaults. After picking himself up he examined the OK and found the machine had damaged footrests and the handlebar was badly bent. The magneto control had been swept away and the petrol filler cap was loose. Walter's troubles let Jock Porter into a lead that he never lost, winning at 51·93 mph nearly five minutes ahead of Bert Le Vack on his New Imperial.

The crash delayed Walter for four minutes but although his chance of a place had surely gone he remounted and set off undismayed. He now had to hold the magneto wire to keep it at full advance. He tried to tie the contact breaker at full advance but it went slack again. At the Bungalow he was seen to be steering with one hand. 'Handley still keeps going, despite his troubles, although how he can see through the fountains of fuel that spurt from his tank,' wrote the *Motor Cycling* journal, 'it is difficult to conceive.' Despite all the involuntary stops and two additional stops for petrol and oil, he managed to finish eighth in 4 hrs, 44 mins, 22 secs at 47·8 mph. It was his lowest position in a TT race, but one of which he could feel proud. It embodied his philosophy, 'Never Give Up.'

TT racing in these early years was a major test of physical endurance. Walter had been in the saddle for nearly five hours in the most trying conditions. It can have come as no surprise to discover that Wal Handley was awarded the Nisbet Shield. This award was inaugurated in 1920 in memory of a former Chairman of the ACU. It is awarded to competitors who in the opinion of the Stewards have exhibited such pluck or endurance as to deserve special recognition. However, with another record lap to his credit, he had the consolation of being the recipient of a gold cigarette case provided for TT lap record breakers by that sportsman, Mr P. J. Evans, the Birmingham motor agent.

CHAPTER 6
ENTER REX ACME

Walter's epic ride in the 1923 Lightweight TT had important consequences, for it was after this herculean performance that he was approached by the Rex Acme Company. George Hemingway, the managing director at the time, had been surprised to note that several of his employees had chosen to back Wal Handley on the OK rather than any of the Rex Acme riders. Although Walter did not win, the men from Coventry were so impressed that the matter did not end there and by July Walter had agreed to join Rex Acme. At the conclusion of the 1923 Lightweight Race it was reported that Ernie Humphries, the OK chief, had an altercation with his young star. If so his unsympathetic reaction to the young rider's sterling performance may have been a factor in Wal's decision to leave OK. What part Dougal Marchant may have played in the decision is not exactly known but the Blackburne tuner, whom Walter had met at Brooklands, almost certainly was an influence. The Osborne Road Repair Shop in Cheylesmore, Coventry would soon become familiar to the young Birmingham star and his mechanic, Sammy James, whom he had persuaded the company to recruit. The year before the two Coventry firms, Rex and the Acme Company (the machine of no regrets), had combined to form a name that was destined to achieve fame with Wal Handley.

Walter's first outing under the new racing colours brought a foretaste of what was to come. In 1923 the Belgian Grand Prix was held at Dinant, a hilly 8.75-mile course in the Ardennes. It was the only time in the inter-war years, apart from 1936, that the race was not held at Spa. At the outset it seemed that there was going to be a repeat of the bad weather of the previous year. Just before the start there was a terrific thunderstorm which brought down the huge scoreboard and lightning struck the timekeeper's box causing the inmates to pop out at speed! Fortunately no-one was hurt and the weather changed as the clouds passed over to allow the sun through.

For the first 80 miles or so Walter kept Geoff Davison company, the two men laughing and trying to talk to each other as they went. Considering Walter's Rex Acme was a faster machine than Geoff's Levis, this was for Walter a tremendous exercise in self restraint. Then Walter tucked his head down in that inimitable style of his and decided it was time to depart. Geoff wrote:

> I was not unduly worried by this, for Walter's bad luck was a byword and small overhead valve four-strokes were not very reliable in those days, but on this occasion his luck held and he won by about two minutes.

He would have won by a much greater margin had he not stopped at his pit believing he had completed his 22nd and final lap. Fortunately someone pointed out to him that the timekeeper's box, or what was left of it, was 100 yards further on and so Walter swiftly remounted and completed the course. He did so, much to the relief of the band leader, who had struck up 'God Save the King' in honour of young Walter as he was seen rounding the last corner. By the time Handley did cross the line the anthem was on its third lap!

Both Walter Handley and Geoff Davison were faster than the winner of the 350 class and also faster than the second man home in the 500 class. The latter race was won by Freddie Dixon (Indian) at about 58 mph. This was only marginally faster than the 56 mph average speed of the Rex Acme. Walter had achieved the only all British win in the 'Belgian' that year. He returned home in a jubilant mood feeling compensated for his disappointment in the Isle of Man.

Changing from one manufacturer to another in the middle of a race season is reckoned to be a risky business and not generally recommended but Walter's decision to switch to Rex Acme was to pay off with another success in 1923. After Dinant came the second Ulster Grand Prix. This time the race had been increased to 10 laps making 205 miles. The organisers were jubilant for the race had attracted one hundred entrants, the highest entry prior to that wettest of wet road races, the Ulster of 1948. There was tremendous interest in the event as an estimated 40,000 crowd streamed out of Belfast to make their way to the course, some on foot, others on bicycles, horseback, in cars, cabs, carts and charabancs.

The spectators were not going to find it an easy race to follow, although it became apparent that many of them followed the handicap times rather better than the race officials! In this race the limit man was under way for over an hour before the scratch man started. A few weeks earlier Walter had raised the 250cc world record for the flying kilometre to nearly 80 mph. The handicappers must have been aware of this for the race was 30 minutes old before the Rex Acme rider was allowed to go. He made his characteristic long run with a flying vault into the saddle to plunge into a trail of dust left by a 250 rider completing his first lap!

It was difficult for the riders, for while the dust made goggles essential, the localised stinging rain showers also made them impossible. The retirements came thick and fast, Stanley Woods, Alec Bennett and Jimmy Simpson were among those who were out of it. Just how punishing this race was is surely illustrated by the amazing fact that out of ninety-five actual starters only seventeen managed to finish.

The scenes at the end were remarkable. Roars of delight greeted the arrival of Jimmy Shaw on a 348cc Zenith-JAP, cries of 'Well done Belfast, well done Jimmy,' shook the air. Just

After winning the 1923 Ulster Grand Prix on his 248cc Rex Acme.
Rain fell during the race, hence the mudstains.

seconds later another Ulsterman, Joe Craig sped home on his 490cc Norton to be acclaimed as the runner-up. Meanwhile it was seen that an altercation was taking place. What had been posted as Walter's time for nine laps was actually his finishing time so that he was, in reality, an easy winner. Walter had been certain that he had done 10 laps but deeming it inadvisable to stand there arguing he had gone on to do a futile 11th lap, while the 'winner' and 'runner-up' were being cheered and presented to the Lord Mayor of Belfast. When Walter did come in 20 minutes or so afterwards, he scarcely got the notice he deserved.

Although many of the spectators in the grandstand were amazed when number 28, Handley/Rex Acme was posted as the winner, the mistake was not universal. Out on the course, where spectators do not have a scoreboard to distract them from their own calculations, many were puzzled to see number

28 roar round for the eleventh time! What had happened was that the timekeepers had completely missed Walter's second lap, which had been posted up 40 minutes after his first lap, roughly twice the length of time for a normal circuit of the Clady course at racing speed.

At the reception held later that evening at Thompsons Restaurant in Belfast, Walter was the subject of some characteristically generous tributes from the Ulster officials anxious to make amends for the earlier mix-up. Walter, for his part, was to retain affection for the people of Northern Ireland and for this event in which he was to record five wins before the end of his racing career. He could at least ruefully reflect that he had no need of a publicity agent, something always seemed to keep him in the news.

CHAPTER 7
WHEN THE LUCK'S AGAINST YOU

As the time for the Isle of Man TT races got nearer there was an air of expectation at Rex Acme's Coventry works. Would the Rex Acme bikes continue with the good form they had shown at Dinant, Clady and Brooklands? The Rex Acme Company's enterprising adoption of the Three Legs of Man as a motif on the fuel tank showed their intentions.

The 1924 TT programme consisted of five races. There was to be a sidecar event and four solo classes: 175, 250, 350 and 500. Walter was entered in three, the new Ultra Lightweight 175 class, the 250 and 350 races to match Rex Acme's sales programme. It is generally forgotten how the origins of the new Ultra Lightweight Race were connected with the proposals to do away with the 500cc class which some considered to have outgrown its usefulness. The idea was that the 250 and 350 races were to be the new Junior and Senior events respectively, while a new Lightweight race was to be introduced. Fortunately, the ACU sensibly decided to abandon any idea of jettisoning the 500 class in the uproar that greeted these proposals but nevertheless they retained the new Ultra Lightweight class.

If Walter had expected his Rex Acme machines to continue in the Isle of Man with the success he had experienced at Dinant and Clady, he was to be sadly disappointed. In not one of the races he entered was he able to complete three laps. There is no doubt that he felt his troubles keenly at this time. However he had, as usual, put some 'pep' into the series, having held the lead in the early stages of each race.

In the Junior race, Jimmy Simpson on the new 'big port' AJS was the favourite to win having made the fastest practice times. On the first lap three riders made TT history by being the first men to lap the mountain course at over 60 mph: they were Jimmy Simpson, Wal Handley and Len Horton (New Imperial). To Jimmy went the honour of being first to do this since he was leading on the roads, having been started earlier. It is a remarkable fact that they did this from a standing start on a day when misty conditions were reported on parts of the course. As anticipated Jimmy Simpson led the race in the early stages, closely followed by Walter.

There is an old adage in the race game that 'when two men fight, a third reaps the benefit,' and sure enough this is what happened. At Crosby on his third lap, Simpson had the valve seat of his AJS crack and so consequently lost all further interest in the proceedings. Wal Handley was now in the lead, but it proved short-lived. The Rex Acme champion's fight ended on the mountain descent of that eventful third lap with flywheel trouble. Out of fifty-eight starters only fifteen survived. The eventual winner was twenty-year-old Kenneth Twemlow riding a New Imperial to win at an average speed of 55.67 mph. He had been as lowly placed as seventeenth during that meteoric opening lap set by the pacemakers. This was a period when speed had outstripped reliability. Perhaps Twemlow had managed to ride at the speed that was just right for the machines of that time.

In the next two races Wal took the lead from the standing start only to retire each time on the third lap. The first of these, the Ultra Lightweight 175cc event was noteworthy for being the first massed start in a TT race. The seventeen riders got away cleanly despite dire predictions of calamity. Even so, the experiment of having a massed start was not repeated until the Lightweight race in 1949. Walter's race ended when his oil tank burst at the start of his third and final lap when lying second. It meant that he had a disconsolate walk back to the pits from Bray Hill. Jock Porter had won his second and as it turned out final TT race on his New Gerrard. He had completed the 3-lap race in 2 hrs, 12 mins, 40 secs at an average speed of 51·2 mph.

Walter's third race was the Lightweight 250 class held concurrently with the Senior event on Friday, the last day of race week. For the third year running Wal Handley led on the first lap. However, it was not very reassuring to learn that he led Porter by the slender margin of seven seconds. Sure enough he was not able to hold the lead for long. Walter's troubles ended again on that fateful third lap with a broken rocker just at the start of the mountain climb. In the closing stages of the race Porter had the misfortune to crash heavily at Glen Helen when leading comfortably. Then Harry Harris, the father of Pip Harris, the post-war sidecar exponent, riding a New Imperial ran out of fuel near the finish to let in Eddie Twemlow mounted on another JAP-engined New Imperial. Altogether quite a week for the Twemlow brothers who hailed from Sandbach in Cheshire. In their first TT appearance they had each won a TT trophy, having only sampled the TT Course for the first time in the amateur races, the previous year.

Slower riders sometimes won because of just being slower. 'It just happened,' as that well respected motorcycle journalist, 'Ixion' explained, 'that the speed which they (the slower men) could manage was the safety margin of the 1924 engines.'

In many respects 1924 must have been a year that Walter wanted to forget. Not only had he had no luck in the TT, but worse was to follow for he was also unable to finish in the Belgian Grand Prix, the Leinster 100 or the Ulster Grand Prix. It was an added frustration for Walter to know that in each of these events he was in an excellent position to win when forced to retire.

Having eclipsed the opposition in the 250 class of the Belgian Grand Prix, it was typical of Walter's racing instinct that he should then have tried to enliven the proceedings by 'taking on' some of the 500s. What a tremendous performance this must have been. Marchant, who was in charge of Blackburne interests, stated that Wal grounded his footrests on some corners despite an eight inch ground clearance; this meant he must have been heeling over at about 45 degrees! Afterwards he good-humouredly explained that he simply, 'couldn't bear to lose sight' of his pal Jim Whalley on his 498cc Douglas. All of this was too good to last, a burst tyre delayed Walter, and in trying to make up for lost time he crashed at Eau Rouge. The broken collar bone put him out of the French Grand Prix run two weeks later.

He had been the only English competitor in the Leinster event and had led the race in truly meteoric style when the 'gremlins' struck again. This time the front forks of his 248cc Rex Acme was damaged in crossing a culvert. Even a final consolation win right at the end of the season was to be denied him. He had been leading the Ulster Grand Prix after making an excellent getaway from the new starting position at Carnaughlis. The lap record was broken from a standing start and a repeat win looked likely when the oil pump on the Rex Acme failed.

It was a complete reversal of the good fortune that had greeted Walter's beginning with Rex Acme of Coventry. However, to keep this in perspective, we must remember that mechanical failures were on a scale scarcely imaginable to us now. It was certainly a problem for Walter who, in the three year period between 1922 to 1924, had led at some point in every TT race he had contested only to retire with various packets of trouble. People were beginning to notice this and soon the unenviable tag 'Unlucky Handley' was being used pretty freely by journalists. On one occasion a cartoon appeared showing Walter, with a large spanner in hand, peering round a corner in search of a black cat, who was anxiously looking back at Walter with a view to taking rapid evasive action!

Yet Walter was not easily discouraged and soon recognised that in the small, friendly Rex Acme concern he had found a niche for himself. The directors quickly rewarded his ability by giving him a free hand in managing the competitions department. It was a wise move for Handley, the individualist, was to remain loyal to Rex Acme for the next five years during which time he joined Mr Bramley and Mr Mills as a director of the Company. He now spent much more of his time at the Osborne Road works in Coventry and also at the Brooklands race track in Surrey where much of the testing took place. In 1925 Rex Acme moved to the Crown and Progress works on the Stoney Stanton Road and the Repairs and Racing Department soon followed. The scene was now set for Wal Handley to make a piece of TT history.

An early picture of Walter Handley (left) with the Rex Acme van in Coventry.

CHAPTER 8
THE TIDE TURNS

It has been said that Walter Handley entered the story of the Isle of Man TT like the 'demon king'. He certainly demonstrated his meteoric quality in the 1925 TT races as records tumbled like corn before the scythe of his Rex Acme. He became the first man to win two TT races in the same year. This had not been done before and at that time no-one had won more than two TT races. By 1925 only five riders could claim this distinction – Charlie Collier had done this on the Old St John's Course in 1907 and 1910; then on the mountain course we had Eric Williams in 1914 and 1921; Tom Sheard in 1922 and 1923; Alec Bennett in 1922 and 1924, and Jock Porter in 1923 and 1924.

Wal Handley's two TT wins were on successive race days, this remained unequalled until 1935 when the great Stanley Woods, on his way to ten TT wins, won the Lightweight and Senior events. In this same year of 1925 Walter made record laps in three TT races – a record that remained unequalled until 1967; it was then that the superb Mike Hailwood gained fastest laps in each of the three races in which he rode on to victory with those tremendous Honda machines.

It can come as no surprise to learn that Walter won both of his races at record speed. In the Junior TT he raised the average speed by over 9 mph; the biggest margin of increase ever known in a TT race from one year to the next, unless you count the 1929, 1955 and 1966 Senior TTs when the race speeds had dipped sharply in each of the previous years. In achieving this Walter had cut the 1925 race time by a prodigious 35 mins, 25 secs, this was equal to more than a whole lap of the mountain course.

Earlier in the year he had given an implicit warning of his intentions with some startling performances on his Rex Acme. He had won the Henley Cup in the Victory Trial for the best solo performance in the 275cc to 350cc category. This was encouraging after the earlier disappointment in the Colmore Trial when his front wheel had touched one of the tapes in the slow climb on Bushcombe Hill. The loss of one mark had not only debarred him from a premier award, but had also lost him a gold medal. Walter, commented, 'when I knew what had happened I admit that I felt rather downhearted, for it seemed as if fortune would never favour me.'

Yet he always knew that speed events were his preference and success now followed success in speed trials at Mansfield, Kop Hill, Hereford and Doncaster. His 250cc and 350cc Rex Acme models swept the board in their respective solo classes. Walter could now approach the start of the TT races with quiet confidence. The real question mark concerned the reliability of the Rex Acme over six laps of the toughest road race in the world. Speed trials were one thing but the TT was an entirely different proposition.

One wonders what Walter's thoughts were as he left his boarding house in Douglas on the morning of Monday, 15 June, making his way to the Glencrutchery Road for the start of the Junior TT. He must have been hoping for a clear run because in the previous three years he had been frustrated by ill luck when victory had seemed to be within his grasp. Perhaps on this sunny morning he sensed that it was to be his day.

This was one of the peak years in TT history with five separate races and a total of one hundred and forty-four entries. For the first race, the Junior TT, there were fifty-two starters. Walter was positioned for a late start at number 50. This was ideal for Walter who liked a late number because with forty-nine riders ahead of him he would have a good idea of how well he was going. A late start also gave his pit attendant, Sammy James, the chance to signal more confidently what was going on 'up front'.

On the first lap Wal's racing ability was zestfully employed in overtaking ten competitors, he knew therefore that he must be well in the picture. It turned out that he was just one second behind Freddie Dixon (HRD) at the end of that opening lap. As Wal passed his pit at the end of the second lap he learned that he was running second to Dixon but by this time, unknown to him, he had in reality a lead of 23 seconds. On receiving this signal the Rex Acme exponent went at it full bore. Afterwards, Walter wrote:

> I took Braddan rather too fast, skidded and hit the kerb, but managed to straighten up again. However, the thrill made me think seriously, for I realised that if I nearly had a crash in a mile and a half of this all out business I was not very likely to do the remaining four laps of it unscathed!

Walter decided to keep on at a speed a little below the maximum and continue cornering very fast. 'Later on,' wrote Walter, 'I saw Dixon at the roadside, and he very sportingly signalled me to go steady, showing me the thumbs up sign.'

Walter steadily increased his lead throughout the remainder of the race. As he passed his pit attendant for the fifth and last time at about 80 mph he was seen to incline his head slightly before a pleased looking Sammy James. The anxious eyes of his supporters followed the progress of his clock on the big grandstand Scoreboard as he swept round the course for the last time; would Handley's luck hold? It is easy to imagine Walter's anxiety on that last lap. The slightest hesitation or misfire of the engine and your heart misses a beat. Along comes that last gearbox testing climb from Ramsey up Snaefell. The small cheering crowd at the Bungalow is scarcely noticed. It is not long before the loosely surfaced track of over eighty years ago finally drops to the sharp right hand turn at the aptly named Windy Corner. The expectant crowd at Creg-ny-Baa look up the road, will the race leader be on schedule? Yes, there he is, the small figure crouching low over the tank of the lean looking Rex Acme whips round Kate's Cottage and dives down the 1:8 gradient towards the waiting crowd. Using the full width of the Creg-ny-Baa turn, the famous Keppel Hotel is left astern. From now on it is a series of fast bends on the approach to Governor's Bridge. The concentration must not be relaxed for a moment – Brandish, Hillberry, Signpost – and Wal knows he could push in now! At 2·52 PM Handley is signalled at Governor's Bridge and a few moments later he roars across the line to receive a standing ovation. This was the day on which he had beaten his 'Unlucky Handley' reputation in his fourth successive year of trying.

It was a popular win for the twenty-three-year-old as it was recognised that he had tried so often and the Rex Acme Company was not a powerful or influential manufacturer. The *Brooklands Gazette* wrote:

> He is just the type of rider whom we all like to see win a big race of this class. Quiet, unassuming, accepting defeat in the same spirit as he accepts victory; nothing spectacular about Handley, nothing but sheer grit and determination to place his firm's machine at the top of the list.

His race time was just under 3 hrs, 30 mins at an average speed of 65·02 mph. These figures may seem tame by today's standard until one remembers that Walter's top speed was only 80 mph. It is also interesting to note that the race speed would have been good enough to have given the Junior winner second place in Friday's TT had he been competing. No wonder it has been listed as one of the 'great TT races' by Mac McDiarmid. It was characteristic of Walter to attribute his achievement to the road improvements carried out by the Manx Government over the close season. Perhaps it is more significant that unlike 1924, when the slower riders had had their day, we had now seen one of the fast men finish.

By one of those strange ironies of sport, the runner up, nearly four minutes astern of Walter, was the man who had given

Second placed Howard Davies (HRD 344cc) congratulates
Walter Handley (Rex Acme 348cc) the winner of the 1925 Junior TT.

After his first TT victory in 1925, Walter joins (on his right) Mr Bramley, one of the Rex Acme
directors, followed by (on his left) Mr Bramley's son Len: they are behind the grandstand.

Ernie Humphries that tip, 'try young Handley, he's a future TT winner.' This was Howard Davies that remarkable rider, designer and manufacturer of the bike that bore his initials, HRD and it was typical of Howard to be among the first to congratulate the younger man. It was also turning out to be a good week for Howard who on Friday went on to win the Senior TT on his 490cc HRD at over 66 mph: a gain of nearly 5 mph over the previous best time in this class. The HRD design marked a turning point in motorcycling history. Howard had been able to house the tall long stroke JAP engine vertically in the duplex cradle frame, by virtue of an innovation so simple that it bore the stamp of genius. The answer was a single top tube with a flat-sided tank saddling it – this also enabled the

Walter watches expectantly as the Rex Acme 174cc
is hoisted and weighed for the Ultra-Lightweight TT in 1925.

saddle to be placed much lower. It was one of those concepts that caught on and is now taken for granted. In 1928 the HRD marque was sold on to Philip Vincent whose big V-twins gained a world-wide reputation.

The next race was the Ultra Lightweight 175cc class that had been introduced by the ACU in the previous year. It turned out that the ACU had decided that for this year there would be a weight limit of 150 lbs. This led some competitors to drill holes wherever possible in order to comply with the limit. As a result only seven competitors had met the weight limit. Wal was there in the number 7 position. In those early years of his career no race was too much trouble for Walter.

Somewhat surprisingly, in view of the size of the entry, the authorities decided to abandon the massed start of the previous year and revert to the usual practice of interval starts. Either way it made no difference to Walter and he proceeded to show his enthusiasm for the work in hand with a record lap from the standing start at 54·08 mph. It is interesting to note that according to Walter this same motorcycle had only just topped 60 mph flat out at Brooklands. This illustrates the point made by Nigel Spring, who had assisted Walter in making test runs at speed down the Island's Ballamodha Straight, that in the 1920s bikes had to be pushed to near capacity limits if you wanted to win a TT race.

Although Walter led the Ultra Lightweight throughout, he did not ease up until he had overtaken his old rival and the previous year's winner, Jock Porter. He had a 31 seconds lead at the end of lap 1. Conditions were not ideal, on reaching the pits, the riders were all complaining of fierce winds on the Mountain Road. At the end of lap 2 Walter's lead had slipped to only seven seconds, this was caused by his taking a 'toss' at Creg-ny-Baa when the twenty-four inch wheels and low slung exhaust pipe of the Rex Acme failed to clear the ground as he heeled over for the turn in the well known Handley style. Fortunately there was no damage and so he did not have to reach for the spanners or pliers, which competitors, in those days, often carried tucked inside their boots. Still the incident had served as a warning! On the third lap Walter tore passed the pits just 27 seconds behind Porter, who was struggling with a leaking oil tank. Walter was now comfortably in the lead. He was the first at Ballacraine and was leading on the roads. Wal knew that all he had to do was to take things steadily. In blustery conditions, he won the 4-lap, 150-mile race at an average speed of 53·45 mph.

The spotlight now turned on Walter for the Lightweight event. Would he be able to win three in a row? For the 250cc class there was an entry of nineteen and Walter must have been pleased to be again near the back of the line-up at number 17. He was a small inconspicuous figure in his black leathers, wearing as usual the cloth cap and only donning his gloves and helmet at the very last moment. He was barely noticed by spectators as he calmly proceeded to inflate the front tyre while waiting for the starter; an action bearing some significance in

After winning the 1925 Junior TT, Wal Handley stands behind the trophy.
On his left is Fred Povey, the Velocette rider, in the centre is the Douglas rider, Gus Kuhn.
Front row second from left: Len Bramley, the son of one of the Rex Acme directors,
far right: Sam James and, behind Henry Thistleton, Wal's mechanics.

the light of subsequent events. Did he become the victim of a slow puncture?

Right from the start he led off with a record lap at 60·22 mph the first time a 250cc machine had lapped the course at over 60 mph. He had gained a lead of over 24 seconds on Porter – who retired on his second lap. As Walter began his third lap he held a lead of over two minutes from Paddy Johnston (Cotton-Blackburne) and a TT hat-trick for the Rex Acme star looked to be on, if only his new found luck would hold.

Tom Handley was watching the race from a vantage point at Brandish Corner. He recalled that although Eddie Twemlow, the eventual winner, was in sixth position and over five minutes behind Walter at the end of the second lap, Eddie was leading the race on the roads. By virtue of his win in the previous year he had been given the number one start position setting off at 9 AM – but by now Walter was closing in. The crowd at Brandish, sensing this, were getting more and more excited. As Walter swept down the mountain, passing Stanley Woods (New Imperial), only the Twemlow brothers, Eddie and Kenneth, stood before him and open roads. Tom wrote:

> On the third lap, I recall that the Twemlows had just disappeared up the road when the crowd jumped to their feet with excitement as Walter streaked through in hot pursuit, having almost made up the difference in their starting times. We all shouted that Wal will catch them before the grandstand, but it was not to be as a burst tyre threw him just before Governor's Bridge.

Although the front tyre had not come off, the tube was badly torn and there was damage to the clutch so Walter had no option but to pull the bike off the course so as to avoid causing danger to other riders. The spectators watched in silence as he remounts and coasts slowly up to the grandstand where cries of 'Hard luck Wal,' await him. Despite what had happened he was, at this point, still over two minutes ahead of Johnston, who now became the new race leader. So ended the brave attempt at what would have been the first TT hat-trick. Instead for the fourth successive year he had been leading the Lightweight TT only to strike trouble and retire.

Amazingly there were only five finishers out of the nineteen starters. Eddie Twemlow riding a New Imperial went on to win his second TT race at 57·74 mph after several faster men had retired or struck trouble including Porter, Johnston, Horton and Stanley Woods. The faith of the JAP people in their push rod operated overhead valve twin-port engine had proved fully justified.

If the New Imperial and HRD people had good cause to celebrate the 1925 results, this was nothing compared with the jubilation of the Rex Acme company. Wal Handley had won not only two TT races, he had also made record laps in all three

The City of Coventry salutes the first man to win two TT races in a week: riding local Rex Acme bikes. Walter Handley is at the Council House, the Lord Mayor is Alderman Snape.

races in which he had competed. As a result of this performance applications poured in from dealers throughout the country for the agency. The following week there were celebrations in the new home of Rex Acme – the Mills Fulford Works near the canal bridge on the Stoney Stanton Road, culminating in a Civic Reception on the evening of 23 June in Coventry's Town Hall. This was something of an ordeal for Walter Handley who preferred to keep in the background and avoid the limelight. Dense crowds not only greeted Walter's arrival at the railway

Walter leaving the Council House in Coventry amidst
packed crowds after his two TT victories in 1925.

station, but also awaited him in the city centre before the reception and the speeches had even begun! It was an eloquent testimony to the tremendous interest in this Midland town brought by the double victory of the local Rex Acme Company and to the popularity of the handsome, somewhat abashed, twenty-three-year-old at the centre of the civic recognition.

Walter's star was now clearly in the ascendancy. Life was becoming easier for him financially. His fame ensured that bonuses from tyre, fuel, oil, electrical and accessory manufacturers were becoming more generous. In October he indulged his passion for sports cars by buying the elegant Vauxhall 30/98. Yet his character was quite unaffected by this rapid rise to fame and fortune. Despite the hardship of his youth it did not make him value money, in fact he could be absurdly generous. On one occasion he declined a three figure sum offered him for a series of articles he had agreed to write for *Motor Cycling*. So it is perhaps not surprising that he was reported saying on one occasion that, 'it's not earning money that worries me, it's hanging on to it!' He also remained sensitive to the hardships of others. Headed for home through the streets of Birmingham late on a winter's night, it was not unknown for Walter to stop and relieve some aged newspaper vendor of his remaining stock of papers paying twice or thrice their value, reasoning as he once told his brother, 'now the poor fellow will have to go home.'

CHAPTER 9
WHEN THE LUCK IS VARIED

There were mixed fortunes for Wal Handley in 1925 and some strange happenings. In the Irish Republic on 18 July, he won the 350 class of the Leinster Hundred in Co. Meath on his Rex Acme. In this event Wal received the compliment of being placed next to the scratch man, Stanley Woods, so that his Rex Acme Blackburne conceded starts to all but one of the other sixty-two riders, many of whom had much larger machines.

Walter then made his way to the small Ardennes health resort of Spa for the Belgian Grand Prix. He duly notched up his second win in this event, this time in the 350 class at over 63 mph. He had won the 222-mile race by the comfortable margin of 11 minutes after, at one stage, having suffered a deficit of 13 minutes due to an oiled up plug. The margin of the win was the only thing that was comfortable for he had crashed, as he admitted, for the third successive year at the notorious Francorchamps hairpin on the first lap and had his right footrest broken clean off. For the rest of the race he had to hold his balance by placing his foot first on the gearbox, then on the magneto timing cover, and so on until the race ended. This Belgian meeting underlined British racing supremacy with a triple win. Alec Bennett (Norton) won the Senior Race for the second successive year, while Jock Porter (New Gerrard) won the Lightweight class. Unfortunately the meeting had been saddened by the tragic death of the popular twenty-two-year-old Billy Hollowell (AJS) who was engaged to be married. He was fatally injured when he had shot off the road near the Stavelot hairpin while still leading the 350 class in the early stages.

Due to a dispute between the FMB – Federation Motor-cycliste Belgique and the FN Company, the Belgian Grand Prix had been subjected to delay. So Walter had to hurry back to England for the following Saturday and was just in time to demonstrate his versatility by swapping the twists and turns of the beautiful Spa circuit for the Brooklands track at Weybridge. Here he scored his first victory in one of the 200-mile races he enjoyed so much. Not only did he win the *News of the World* Gold Cup, including a cheque for £25, but also captured the world record for 200 miles in Class B (350cc solo) at 78·33 mph. Quite an achievement when you bear in mind that he managed to do this despite a fuel blockage at 90 miles. Walter wrote:

> I was going well when the engine suddenly spluttered and stopped, in order to carry enough fuel I had twin two-gallon petrol tanks fixed side by side on the frame with an interconnecting pipe between them.

Walter's intention had been for the level in the two tanks to remain constant, but he now discovered that the flow had been restricted and so he had used up all the fuel in the one tank while the other remained full. After he discovered the trouble he proceeded to fill up the one tank and used it alone, 'all the stops for fuel not being quite sufficient,' wrote Walter, 'to prevent me from winning.'

It can be said that Walter's quiet determination to press on and finish had overcome various packets of trouble, but in the last two big events of the season he was forced to retire when in each case his chances of winning had been excellent. In the 350 class of the Ulster Grand Prix he had snapped into the lead 'gobbling up' over twenty-one competitors on a really fast opening lap but had been forced to retire before the half distance of the 205-mile race. His friend Alec Bennett was even more unfortunate in that he suffered a flat tyre when almost in sight of the finish and victory in the 600 class.

The final episode of 1925 was the Italian Grand Prix. It was designated the 'Grand Prix des Nations.' This was the beginning of the pre-war custom of conferring the title 'European Championship' annually in rotation on certain major meetings on the continent. It was not until after the 1939–1945 war that the FIM decided that in future there was to be a points scoring system for both riders and manufacturers in a World Championship series of International Classes.

So in 1925 the more adventurous spirits amongst the British riders and manufacturers made their way to Monza, near

Handley

Il vincitore del Tourist Trouphy 1925, — Categ. 350 - 175
e del Giro più veloce, Categ. 250.

Milan 1925 before the Italian Grand Prix at Monza. Wal Handley had to retire on the last lap when in the lead ahead of Tazio Nuvolari (Bianchi), the winner.

Milan, where the biggest track in Europe had been built in one hundred days and opened in a blaze of publicity just a few weeks before Mussolini and the Fascists entered Rome in 1922. The illustrious history of the Autodromo Nazionale di Monza was to span a little over fifty years until the double tragedies of May and October 1973 closed the track to two wheel racing forever. The original Monza circuit combined a 3·4 mile road course and a 2·8 mile banked circuit to give a lap length of just over 6·2 miles. Monza was always fast and early on proved to be a stiff test for man and machine.

In the 350 class Walter Handley was to meet the 'champion of Italy', the man known to his compatriots as the 'flying Mantuan', none other than Tazio Nuvolari. This small but wiry man was already thirty-three years old and by this time trying his utmost to break into the more costly world of car racing. He was finding it a frustrating business. Just a week earlier he had suffered a serious accident in an Alfa Romeo at Monza and so he had been advised against taking part in the motorcycle race. However, like his English adversary, Tazio had great personal courage and was the last person to take such advice. So it was no surprise to see him in the line up seated on his 'Blue Arrow' Bianchi – a single cylinder, twin-port, overhead camshaft model that had already proved itself on Italian circuits.

An equally determined Englishman, Wal Handley, was mounted on the identical Rex Acme that had brought him victory in the Junior TT. The specification included an auxiliary pump operated by pedal on the near side of the bike. Extremely useful for Walter's entry into the Monza arena must have been the two rear brakes fitted so that he could use either his right or left foot.

In Italy it is customary for the riders to wear the racing colours of their country. So as the field surged away in a mass of colour, mainly the red of Italy and the green of England, it was seen that Handley and Nuvolari completed the first lap jointly in the lead of their class. It was a thrilling contest, virtually wheel to wheel, as they roared round on and off the banking with the capacity crowd estimated at 50,000 urging on the Italian ace. However, it was Walter who gained the advantage and continued to hold off Nuvolari who was making the most desperate efforts to get back on terms. Towards the end the rain started, but it made no difference to the speed these two kept up. Walter still held the lead as they went into the 30th and final lap; surely he had won the Italian Grand Prix on his first visit to that country. Yet it was on this last rain soaked lap that English hearts must surely have missed a beat as the red-shirted Nuvolari roared into victory having averaged 76 mph. He was followed by the figure of Walter pushing in his Rex Acme across the line for what he presumed to be the consolation of second place. Once again appalling luck had struck the Englishman for within half a mile of victory a valve rocker had broken. It was thus left to the Scot, Jock Porter, riding his New Gerrard to cheer up the British contingent by carrying off the 250cc trophy.

Naturally Walter, having run in pushing the machine, fully expected to claim second place to the Italian. Initially he was placed second but later was informed that he had only completed 29 laps. 'I am quite confident that I had done the 30 laps,' wrote Walter shortly afterwards, 'and the men in my pit confirm this.' However, it was no use arguing and Walter came away believing that he was recorded as disqualified for not finishing the race. Due to language difficulties it was not made clear that he was the victim of a technical rule that required competitors to complete the race 'under their own power' – apparently this did not include pushing in!

A certain similarity between Tazio Nuvolari and Walter Handley has been remarked upon. They were both tremendous competitors always seeking victory. Their difficulties stemmed from the vagaries of their machines rather than from any other cause. Both men were capable of overcoming any lack of power and speed with daring skill. Many years later when it was announced that Walter Handley was going to join the ranks of the car racing fraternity, Nuvolari, by then a world famous star on four wheels, must have recalled their Monza scrap, for he told reporters that he saw no reason why Handley shouldn't become a force to be reckoned with in the car racing game. High praise indeed but we are getting ahead of ourselves. So far we have made passing reference to Brooklands, it is not always appreciated that it held an important position with motorcycles as well as cars.

CHAPTER 10
FURIOUS AND BRILLIANT

We owe a great deal to that band of enthusiastic volunteers of the Brooklands Society who over the years have worked hard to give us a very clear idea of how Brooklands must have looked in the pre-war era. Not an inconsiderable amount of banking and track remains of the famous old 'concrete saucer'. From the top of the old test hill you can look across the sprawling sheds and workshops to the distant Byfleet banking and let the imagination roam. It is not all that difficult to visualise in the mind's eye the sweeping angled views of the track which would have confronted the car and motorcycle stars as they circled the 'Surrey Bowl' all those years ago.

Walter's first acquaintance with Brooklands occurred when he was eighteen years old. At the end of the ACU Six Days Trial, which in 1920 had begun at Darlington, he rode his 248cc OK Junior bike into the Weybridge arena to gain his first gold medal – a happy augury of what was to follow. However, his real involvement from a high speed angle began two years later when Ernie Humphries had entered him in the first international Lightweight TT race to ride the new OK Junior Blackburne. The OK chief immediately decided to send his young protégé to meet Dougal Marchant who was in charge of Blackburne interests at Brooklands.

Invalided out of the Royal Marines after Gallipoli, Marchant had, when peace came, begun his association with Blackburne engines designing, building and racing a Blackburne powered Bleriot Whippet Cyclecar. Between 1922 and 1924 Dougal

Marchant was the man responsible for fixing Blackburne engines into whatever frames were sent to him, usually Chater Lea, but in Walter's case OK and later Rex Acme models. Marchant, a former Zenith apprentice and one time market gardener, proved to be one of the shrewdest and most determined of the Brooklands exponents. In 1924 he caused great excitement by covering the flying kilometre at 100·81 mph on a 350cc Chater Lea – it was the first time that a bike of that capacity had exceeded the 'ton'. When in 1926 Dougal left Brooklands to take charge of racing design at Motosacoche in Geneva, he did so on a high note. The World's Flying Kilometre records for the 350 and 500 classes were taken at 102·99 mph on his 350 Chater Lea. No one had a clearer idea of the business of taking world records than Dougal. He would show his resourcefulness by such devices as wearing plimsolls and ballet tights for lightness and minimal wind resistance. It was not unknown for him to also fit the tiniest brakes that would comply with the regulations!

Walter could hardly have had a better introduction to Brooklands than this early partnership with Dougal Marchant, who early on had encouraged him to develop his natural ability in the direction of track and road racing. It was Dougal who probably had the greatest influence on Walter's racing technique, encouraging Walter to favour the richer running of his engine, possibly enlarging the engine sprocket to compensate. The two men soon got on very well together, both having a keen sense of humour. Often they would delight in telling sarcastic stories against each other that would send the attendant company into fits of laughter.

Marchant was something of a 'character' and many stories are told of him. On one occasion Walter was waiting with some friends to meet Dougal in a Midland hotel. In walked Dougal looking rather like a sinister Chicago gangster with his overcoat collar turned up against a wintry wind and his trilby brim low down over his eyes. With the hat and coat removed, Dougal remained completely deadpan as a gale of laughter greeted the revelation of a hot water bottle suspended from his neck.

Oblivious of appearances, Dougal had 'nipped' off the train en-route to acquire what he called his 'bit of comfort'.

With Dougal's tuning skills and Walter's brilliance as a rider, it is fair to say that the two men complemented one another. Nor is it so surprising that Dougal Marchant became the nearest person Walter ever had to what could be described as a racing manager. That is insofar as Walter ever allowed anyone to manage him! Dougal, it was, who accompanied Walter on the continent in those early years when the 'Continental Circus' of British riders and manufacturers was beginning to take shape.

It was not long before the newly forged partnership began to 'deliver'. In September 1922, Wal and Dougal rode in turn a 250cc OK machine round the outer Brooklands track for just over seven hours; the small side valve Blackburne engine covering 400 miles at 56·60 mph. In doing this they smashed all the existing records in the 250 solo class up to that time and distance. They had started with the idea of carrying on as long as possible, but the attempt was brought to an abrupt end when the saddle pillar snapped causing Walter to complete his ride sitting on the tank!

For the short distance records the Brooklands track would be closed while you were timed in both directions. You had to pay for the track closure and meet the timekeeper's fees, this was expensive for the small manufacturers. Perhaps this helps explain why enthusiasts on holiday in August 1923 read that Wal Handley had hurried to complete the flying kilometre and world records up to 10 miles in the 250 class at almost 80 mph. He had done this on his overhead valve Rex Acme Blackburne model, having left the OK Company earlier that year. At the end of his career it was claimed that Walter Handley had broken over one hundred world records, most of this had been achieved at Brooklands but later, as speeds increased, the 'old saucer' became unsuitable for records and Walter was obliged to continue the record breaking in France. It was typical of the man that many of these successes came as a by-product of his racing instinct rather than as calculated set pieces.

An outstanding example of this was Walter's exploit in the 350 class of the 200-mile solo race held at Brooklands on 24 July 1926. There is general agreement amongst commentators that this race was made forever memorable by Walter's incomparable performance. Arguably this race turned out to be one of the greatest, if not the greatest, bike race in Brooklands history. As might be expected from his remarkable record it was a race Walter did not win. He had won this event in the previous year and there is no reason to doubt that the Rex Acme flyer was confident that he could win again.

As he wheeled his Rex Acme Blackburne to the line his confidence turned to dismay. The front tyre had suddenly deflated. While the hapless Walter and his mechanic Sammy James carried out a hurried examination, the other twenty-nine riders came under starter's orders and roared away down the railway straight towards the distant Byfleet banking. 'It didn't look right,' recalled Sammy, 'there seemed to be a smudge of oil on the tyre.' A quick scrutiny of the tyre revealed a long clean cut hidden by the groove of the outer cover. The cut had been impossible to see until the tube had punctured. In one respect it was fortunate that it had done so, for it could have meant disaster for Walter if the tyre had burst at top speed. Sammy James, Wal's loyal mechanic, took the wheel out, slung it into the sidecar and hurried to David MacDonald, better known as 'Dunlop Mac', a chunky cockney who could fit a tube and cover to a wheel rim in the proverbial 'jiffy'. A few thumps, a clatter of levers and the job was done. Even so by the time Sammy had returned, Walter had had the frustrating experience of watching helplessly while the leading competitors steadily reeled off lap after lap. When at last he could go he was about 14 minutes behind the race leader Bill Lacey on his Grindlay Peerless-JAP bike.

By this time every nerve in Walter's tense alert figure was concentrated upon attacking the race leaders. He was already across the starting line and ready for the push start. To his eternal credit, the chief timekeeper A. V. Ebblewhite, or 'Ebby' as he was affectionately known, noticed this and sensing that Wal was in the mood to really motor, told him to get back across the line so that they could time him for world records. Sammy told me that 'Walter seemed quite calm but he rode superbly.' Walter commenced lapping at speeds in excess of 90 mph – he firmly leaned the bike over to the left as he nipped in close to the grass verges on the banking runs and using those strong wrists of his he 'whanged' the bike down the straights inside the fifty foot line. In ignoring the apparent hopelessness of his position, Walter was at this moment inspired, fearless, untouchable. After 40 laps Walter had almost overtaken the whole field and was already third. Beyond half distance he was only three laps behind Lacey. At the end of 62 laps in this 73 lap race, Walter was three minutes behind the leader and eventually finished just one lap short of Bill Lacey, having lapped his highly polished Grindlay Peerless machine six times during the race. Lacey's winning speed was 81·20 mph while Walter, in second place, had covered the 200 miles at 88·22 mph although his official speed for the race was 80·26 mph.

Ebby's presence of mind had been fully justified, for it meant that a 350cc machine had covered the distance in less time than any other motorcycle up to and including those of 1000cc engine size. No such performance had previously been accomplished in the history of Brooklands bike racing and now that the track is permanently closed, following World War Two, this 1926 ride of Walter's will remain forever unique in the annals of Brooklands. It meant that for a short while the highly prized classic hour record was held by the rider of a 350 single, to my knowledge the only time that this has ever happened.

Graham Walker may well have had this kind of race in mind when he commented that Walter, riding under the goad of an injustice, was a 'dynamic whirlwind of almost superhuman brilliance'. There were certainly some suspicions voiced in the Press at the time, that the cut tyre might not have been an accident. Walter and his mechanic Sammy James did not believe it was a 'dirty trick', and Walter stated that he did not like to consider that anyone would do such a thing. In any case he was temperamentally averse to making a fuss and no protest was lodged. Even so he would have been less than human if, in the heat of the race, he had not felt anger at this staggering stroke of misfortune after so much careful preparation. Strange to relate his riding, always fast and stylish, would become positively breath taking in its audacity when his 'dander' was really up. I do not believe that world records were uppermost in his mind when he eventually got going. He just got down to it and rode as even he had never ridden before in a furious attempt to win the race.

In this gallant failure Walter had the splendid consolation of gaining the following fourteen world records, while at the same time steering a course to thread his way through the field of twenty-nine competitors. These were literally golden days at Brooklands, when records brought considerable prestige and bonus payments particularly from the suppliers of accessories, tyres, fuel and oil.

During the mid 1920s Walter's Brooklands rides were usually made on 250 or 350 Rex Acme Blackburne overhead valve pushrod operated models. There were exceptions to this and in 1926 he surprised everyone by appearing in the British Motor Cycle Racing Club, better known as the 'Bemsee' Championship meeting on 18 September mounted on a formidable looking

Records set 24 July 1926 by W. L. Handley	Speed in mph	Class
50 kilometres	91·22	350
50 miles	91·42	350
100 kilometres	91·39	350
100 miles	91·12	350, 500
200 miles	88·22	350, 500, 750, 1000
1 hour	91·20	350, 500
2 hours	88·31	350, 500, 750

745cc Rex Acme V-twin. The precursor of this had come earlier that year when he would surely have won his first Isle of Man Senior TT race on a 500cc version of the V-twin but for a long delay on his second lap. Those Brooklands enthusiasts, who were aware of what had happened in the Isle of Man and who had witnessed his performance on the track in July, must have nodded sagely at the big Rex Acme twin and settled back for the 'fireworks'.

The 750 class turned out to be one of the finest motorcycle races seen at Brooklands up to that time. It was the sheer speed and the competitiveness of the race which catches the imagination. Walter led off from the start, I almost catch myself writing 'as usual', and kept his lead for the first three laps of this outer circuit race. Close behind him came Horsman (595 Triumph), Walters (730 Zenith) and Staniland (588 Norton). Yet despite some really quick motoring inside the ten foot line, Walter eventually had to be content with second place to Staniland, who apparently had been biding his time on a very fast Norton. The three heroes of this race were Wal Handley, Chris Staniland and H. M. Walters, who had now all joined that select band of men who had lapped Brooklands at over 100 mph in a motorcycle race. There were only seven other riders who had achieved this distinction up to that time. They were, Owen Baldwin with one of his big 996cc Zeniths, doubtless entered as usual by HRH the Duke of York, later King George VI, Roy Charman (976 Zenith), E. W. Guyler (976 Brough Superior), Victor Horsman (600 Triumph), H. J. Knight (976 Zenith), George Patchett (976 McEvoy), and Joe Wright (996 Zenith).

By now the reader will appreciate that Wal Handley was not only a road racing star, he was also a track star. His remarkable versatility was displayed to good effect at Brooklands in the years between 1923 and 1927. A fine example of Walter's versatility comes with sidecar racing on his Rex Acme Blackburne machines with the Coventry firm's own Mills Fulford sidecar attached. Sammy James was very useful to Walter when going for sidecar records since he turned the scales at only 9 stone and 10 lbs and fitted bravely feet first into the sidecar – 'near to the accident,' as Walter would say. Race-goers must have wondered whether the addition of the third wheel would reduce Walter's effectiveness – they need not have worried. A reminder of this ability on three-wheels is that throughout the 1950s and 1960s it was decided to award the Walter Handley Trophy for the fastest lap in the Isle of Man Sidecar TT race.

As so often happened with Walter, success with sidecar racing did not come immediately. In 1925 and again in 1926 he had no luck at all. He had been obliged to retire with either mechanical or tyre troubles in the 200-mile events. Indeed apart from beating the world records set up by Marchant in 1925 on his Chater Lea outfit, Walter had very little to show for his enterprise. In the end it proved to be a case of third time lucky when on 14 May 1927 Walter's efforts were rewarded with a win in the 350 class of the 'Bemsee' 200-mile sidecar race.

He did so after a terrific scrap with 'Woolly' Worters (Excelsior-JAP). Sammy, who was in the sidecar, recalled: 'I twisted round to see Worters dropping out with some kind of trouble, I shouted to Wal gleefully, "He's gone, he's gone," Wal just nodded.' This happened to Woolly at about the three quarter distance with the consolation of some class records. Walter won this race at the record speed of 68·96 mph in a time of 2 hrs, 54 mins, 0·55 secs. In doing so Walter had set up a new class world record for the 200-mile. This was achieved despite picking up a nail in the rear wheel tyre. This was the day when the tyre trouble of the previous year paid off, as Sammy had wisely had a wheel ready for just such an emergency. Then, as was so often the case at Brooklands, came the amusing postscript as related by Walter:

I stopped to light a cigarette and meditated long enough to qualify for the three-hour world record. Had I driven straight off the track on finishing the 200 miles I would not have got this as I would have left too soon!

At his third attempt Wal Handley wins the 350 class of the two-hundred-mile
Sidecar Race at Brooklands on 14 May 1927. In the sidecar is Sam James.
Behind the pair is Reuben Harveyson.

Cartoonist Leslie Grimes, who lived near Brooklands, sees humour
in Walter having to 'meditate long enough,' to qualify for the three-hour
world record in the 1927 200m BMCRC Sidecar Race.

Walter's last sidecar race at Brooklands was in the 200-mile event in 1929. On this occasion Walter rode a 350cc AJS outfit. The preparation had been watched over by Nigel Spring, an old friend of Walter's, who had recently entered into a professional engagement with the Wolverhampton concern. Not surprisingly the 'cammy' Ajay proved a real 'goer'. Walter immediately surged into the lead from a massed start and succeeded in holding off the challenge of those superb track exponents, Freddie Hicks (Velocette) and Chris Staniland (Excelsior), for lap after lap. Yet by the half distance he had slowed perceptibly, he fell back and eventually retired. Hicks went on to win that rare thing, a 200-miler with an astonishingly close finish – when just two-fifths of a second separated Hicks from Staniland at 70·70 mph. By a sad coincidence the three riders who had featured so prominently in this race all died in tragic circumstances. Hicks was killed just two years later when, by that time riding AJS, he crashed in the Senior TT at Union Mills in an all out endeavour to catch the faster Nortons. While in similar circumstances to Walter, the cheery, modest Chris Staniland, who later became chief test pilot with Fairey Aviation, was killed in a wartime flying accident, aged only thirty-six years.

CHAPTER 11
BROOKLANDS AND THE TT STARS

Despite its importance, Brooklands seldom attracted vast crowds at its motorcycle race meetings. There were complaints that for the spectators the races were often dull affairs. This was probably due to you losing sight of competitors down the long railway straight before they swung onto the distant Byfleet banking. It was also often heard that it was difficult for the spectators to have any idea of what was happening in a typical outer circuit race. It was also apparent that with few exceptions the TT stars stayed away. One of the exceptions was Walter Handley who had joined Rex Acme in 1923 and rented one of the sheds adjacent to the club house for the next four years. His neighbours in the sheds alongside reads like a 'Who's Who' of Brooklands bike history, there was George Patchett, Victor Horsman, Dougal Marchant, Freddie Dixon another famous TT star, and that man of few words – Joe Wright. Altogether it was a very colourful and distinguished company.

By now Walter spent at least a third of his time at Brooklands, his mechanic, Sammy James rather less so. Many of Walter's friends regarded him as having left home. This was not surprising as his home life was not a happy one. For most of the time he would stay at the Queen's Head, near Weybridge. He mixed well with the other riders and tuners and was popular, but it was noticeable that he would not join them in drinking on the eve of a race – afterwards it was a different matter.

It was while he was at Weybridge in March 1924 that he got caught up in the Blue Anchor murder enquiry. Friends met a very agitated Walter; apparently on the previous night he had been with a party of riders who had been drinking at the Blue Anchor public house in Byfleet, when upstairs the landlord, Mr Alfred Jones had died after taking a drink of health salts. The Police regarded the death as suspicious and started murder enquiries. Everyone was a suspect including all the riders who had been there. One of the riders joked saying he was okay 'I couldn't have done it because I was drunk under the table,' he thought it was a splendid joke and it raised a good laugh, but Walter's friends recalled that Walter was very upset by what had happened to the poor man. It subsequently transpired that strychnine had been put in the man's drink causing him to die in agony. A certain Pierre Vaquier, who had been having an affair with the landlord's wife, was later convicted and executed.

The reason why Walter spent so much time at Weybridge cannot be entirely explained by either his difficulties at home or his racing. Many companies engaged Brooklands specialists for their development and tuning expertise and their handiwork was later seen in the Isle of Man or the continent in the hands of the road racers. In Walter's case Rex Acme was too small a company to indulge in the customary separation of these activities, and so if the Coventry firm was to compete with a chance of success Walter had to not only race in every conceivable type of event, he also had to do most of the testing and development work himself.

Walter took the preparation of his bikes very seriously. Sammy James recalled the careful attention given to the fitting of the Blackburne engines into the Rex Acme frames. Steel plates were always made by hand and had to be just right. No countenance was given to bent fittings or castings of any kind. 'Lots of things went wrong for Wal, but at least we didn't have things falling off the bikes,' – commented Sammy with a wry smile. Although not a professional engineer, Walter had that marvellous gift, a natural feel for an engine. He could quickly and accurately diagnose what was wrong with an engine just by listening to it. Unlike many of his fellow riders, he not only knew what was what on a racing machine, he also understood design problems such as the implications of altering fork angles. An interesting comment along these lines came from Harold Willis of Velocette's famous 'Hall Green Din House'. Harold had commented to the journalist, Peter Chamberlain, that he had received most valuable suggestions from Walter even when he was not riding a Velocette.

Writing in 1928, Walter neatly described the role of Brooklands:

> As a TT machine is in advance of a production model, so is a Brooklands machine in advance of the TT model. There is only one TT race week, but Brooklands is open all the summer. It is at the track, therefore, that new designs are first tested. If they prove satisfactory they are incorporated in the TT machine, just in the same way as the good points of the TT machine are incorporated later in the production model.

This was the theory and for those who carried it out the result should have been increased sales and profitability; alas it was not always so. We British, it seems have never been particularly outstanding as sales people, and so we have often lacked the ability to exploit the brilliance of our designers and our racing men. This must surely be one of the reasons why our motorcycle industry is littered with failures, some of whom deserved a better fate. It is a strange irony that the Rex Acme Company which could, with justification, proudly call itself 'the motorcycle which is making history', should be swept away in the slump of the 1930s. They were reckoned to be very pleasant motorcycles to ride. Tyrell Smith remembered with affection the Rex Acme he acquired which was reputed to be one of Wal's TT mounts. 'It was the nicest bike I've ever ridden, I wish I'd still got it,' he told me.

As already indicated it was not easy for Brooklands to attract the top TT riders. Crowds were often sparse even when the races were excitingly close. A 5-lap scratch race on the

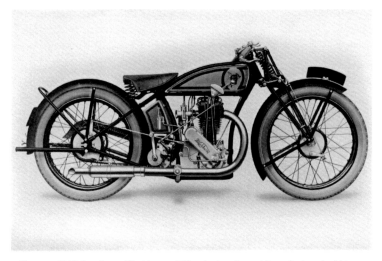

The new 1928 Rex Acme Blackburne 348cc featured a weldless duplex steel frame and newly designed cylinder head, 'produced under the personal supervision of our Mr W. L. Handley.' The price was £63 or £70 with a Motosacoche engine.

'Bemsee' Cup Day on 15 July 1926 was billed by the Press as a JAP versus Blackburne battle. In the 350 class a tremendous struggle developed between the respective champions, Worters (Excelsior-JAP) and Handley (Rex Acme-Blackburne). Walter led off in TT style clipping the grass verges and easing away from Worters, whose JAP engine was proving slightly quicker along the straights. Woolly told how he quickly decided that he had to try and emulate Wal's riding technique and heel his bike over and firmly hold it close in on the banking if he was to have any chance of victory. His chance came at the very last gasp, Woolly managed to squeeze past Wal and win by about two yards at 91·89 mph. The two men ended arm in arm laughing with the sheer exhilaration of the scrap. Even so a cartoon appeared, doubtless with some pardonable exaggeration, showing just two spectators in the grandstand on their feet to the Worters–Handley duel!

Later that year on 9 October, 'Bemsee' decided it was time to innovate and follow the example of the Junior Car Club. They organised the first Grand Prix meeting over what was to become known as the short 'mountain circuit'. It was an ingenious 1·17 mile route, 43 laps of which offered the prospect of an exciting 50-mile race where overall flat out speed counted for little, thereby placing a premium on riding skill. Furthermore from a spectator's viewpoint the riders were never far away and so the race was much easier to follow. The course began on the finishing straight by the club house paddock and shortly afterwards the riders had to negotiate a sharp 'S' turn between the sandbanks and thence into the home banking travelling in an unusual, for Brooklands, clockwise direction. They then rounded the Timing Box at the fork to re-enter the finishing straight.

At that first mountain meeting Wal Handley, Freddie Dixon, Frank Longman and Tommy Bullus were the only TT riders competing. The conditions of this tricky little course, with its two 'S' bends and a hairpin at every mile, were tailor made for a rider of Walter's quality and sure enough he led the 350 class from the start. So meteoric was his effort that with lap speeds of over 60 mph he held a half minute lead at the end of only 10 laps. On his 34th lap Walter's clutch failed and then Hicks (Velocette) went on to win fairly easily. One commentator wrote, '... what a beautifully finished rider Handley is! It struck me however, that he would have won his race comfortably had he curbed himself at half distance ...' It was not Walter's style to curb himself, when by lapping his rivals he could make certain of victory! In a race, Walter believed you could not afford to 'hang around' unless you had built up a good lead and you were near to the finish. In any case there were no complaints from the spectators that day who had witnessed the excitement of TT style cornering with scarcely any breaks in the continual flow of action. The *Motor Cycle* reporter commented:

> I have seen all the car races in which corners were employed, but I have never been quite so amused and thrilled as I was to see Freddie Dixon, Wal Handley, Hicks, and others fighting it out among the sand hills.

It was obvious after this success that the mountain course had come to stay.

Up till this point there had always been a clear divergence between the road and track racing stars. After the 500-mile race for bikes in 1921 had led to protests at ten hours of incessant noise by the long suffering residents of Weybridge. It was decided to abandon this event and produce a compromise. This led directly to the very successful and prestigious 200-mile solo and sidecar events on the outer circuit. These races soon became acknowledged as the most important in the Brooklands Calendar. Yet it was never certain in those early days that the TT stars would turn up. It so happened that in 1924 the 200-mile races were scheduled for the first Saturday in September; this clashed directly with the Ulster Grand Prix. In the previous year, Walter had taken part in the first 200-miler at Brooklands and had also won the Ulster race, but now he was placed in a position where he had to choose. For the up and coming young racing star there could only be one choice and Walter Handley crossed the Irish Sea to compete on the Clady circuit. He was not alone.

In Ulster on that Saturday you would also have seen Alec Bennett, Joe Craig, Paddy Johnston, Jock Porter, Jim Whalley and Stanley Woods, to name but a few. On the same day at Brooklands you would have seen, Victor Horsman, Bert Le Vack, Dougal Marchant, Woolly Worters and also two road racers, Frank Longman and that brilliant rider-tuner, Freddie Dixon. That such a clash could occur illustrates the point that the road and track devotees, with a few exceptions, tended to go their own way.

With the advent of the mountain circuit this was about to change. In the following year, 1927, it became apparent that the good news about this new kind of race at Brooklands was going to attract the motorcycle racing stars. So the second Grand Prix meeting was graced with the presence of Alec Bennett, Wal Handley and Jimmy Simpson – what a trio! The TT stars proceeded to show their enthusiasm by each getting a result, the

250, 350 and 500 classes going to Handley (Rex Acme), Simpson (AJS), and Bennett (Norton) respectively.

In the 350 class solo race, Walter sustained what was to prove a rather troublesome injury. He was battling with Jimmy Simpson for the lead when he came down from a great height at the fork bend, injuring his right hand. Woolly Worters, who on this occasion was not a competitor, was asked by an official if he would take Walter in his car to the Cottage Hospital. Woolly thoughtfully acquired a bottle of whisky from the club house before setting off. However, when they had to remove Walter's thumb nail, it was poor Woolly who passed out despite the 'hard

Massed start at Brooklands for the second BMCRC Grand Prix, 8 October 1927. Wal Handley is number 21, he goes on to win the 250 class at 50·38mph.

Wal Handley (Rex Acme) winning the 1925 *News of the World* Gold Cup
covering the two-hundred-mile race at an average speed of 78·33mph.

stuff'.All that has been written about Brooklands confirms that
the atmosphere between the riders was very friendly. Despite
the serious intent, there was an air of carefree informality.
Often the riders would meet, swap stories get the latest news
and betting odds in the club house or the famous old café. As
someone once recalled the spirit was a bit like, 'Okay, I'm down
to my last plug, but if you're stuck help yourself.'

These 'Bemsee' Grand Prix meetings can be said to have begun
a new kind of bike racing at Brooklands. The outer circuit races
steadily lost their pre-eminence as more events were held on the
increasingly popular 'mountain' circuit. Eventually, just prior
to 1939, the outer circuit races over the full 2·75 mile perimeter
took up only about a third of the race calendar.

The shorter races over the smaller circuit were not only
welcome to the spectators, the competitors also loved it. The
trouble with the longer races was that it required you to hold the

same riding position for lap after lap on machines with limited springing. The 200-mile races were held over 73 laps of the outer circuit and were physically punishing.

In 1925, Wal Handley won the 350 solo class at 78.33 mph, it was a race that lasted for just over 2 hrs, 30 mins. The riders also had to contend with the poor track surface. In the aforementioned 200-mile meeting, in which the riders were required to wear coloured jerseys for the first time in motorcycle racing history, Marchant (Chater Lea) was knocked out after striking his chin on the bike's handlebars in going over one of the bumps.

The *Motor Cycle* in reviewing 1927 at Brooklands commented that the condition of the track had hindered record breaking and made individual achievement difficult. When I asked Tyrell Smith, the famous member of the Rudge team, who had experienced the Brooklands surface a little after Walter, what he thought of it, he replied 'murderous,' and went on, 'as you came off the Home Banking you just hung on and really did not know what was happening.' For some perverse reason, which no-one ever understood, the authorities always spent a great deal of time and money improving areas like the Railway Straight, which were comparatively innocuous, while ignoring stretches like the infamous Home or Members Banking. All of this goes some way to explaining why the more traditional type of Brooklands racing was not popular with the TT riders. It seems all the more creditable that almost alone of the recognised TT stars in this period, Walter Handley should regularly race at Brooklands in addition to his other commitments in the Isle of Man, Ulster and the continent. It meant that his natural ability was now augmented by a wealth of experience and know-how that few of his contemporaries could match.

Gradually the big money went out of bike racing at Brooklands. By the early 1930s the manufacturers no longer built special machines for outer circuit events. The onset of the trade depression of 1929–1930 had another effect; it caused the bonuses given to the successful stars to be cut down. Many of the professional riders departed or turned to four wheels. After

1927 Walter's appearances at Brooklands became infrequent. The main reason for this was his decision to leave the Rex Acme Company in 1928 and to join Dougal Marchant in Geneva where, by this time, Dougal was in charge of racing design and team management for Motosacoche. When Walter did return to Brooklands in the thirties, it was car racing that provided the spur and hence another chance to demonstrate his wonderful versatility.

CHAPTER 12
NEVER DESPAIR, KEEP GOING

> People sometimes think that it is the winners of big
> races who put up the finest rides, but I'm inclined to
> believe that in most cases it is those who finish second
> and third or even further back, who have the hardest
> work.
>
> Walter Handley

Walter was certainly in a position to know the truth of this. In
1925 he had won two TT races with no trouble runs bar a little
misfiring. In the following year it was a very different story.

The decision of Rex Acme to enter for the first time their
star rider in all three of the classic races, Junior, Lightweight
and Senior, coincided with the new ACU regulations requiring
seven laps over the mountain course and the use of only petrol
benzole mixture. With the pessimists predicting calamitous
consequences from these changes and the general strike
looking likely to stop the TT races altogether, the outlook
appeared bleak. These forebodings proved unfounded. The
programme went ahead as planned and produced a race week
full of excitement.

The opening race of the week was the Junior TT. On the
strength of his win in the previous year, Walter was accorded
the honour of the number one position. He disliked it, for
while it gave him the advantage of open roads in his front, it
denied him the full exploitation of his racing flair to overtake
riders who had started earlier. He knew that his two closest

rivals in this race would be his friends, Alec Bennett at number 5 and Jimmy Simpson at number 35.

Alec, like Walter, had two TT wins to his credit at this time. Many people believed Alec to be a Canadian, but he had been born at Craigantlet, Belfast, and had gone to British Colombia at a very early age. Upon the outbreak of hostilities in 1914, the sixteen year old Bennett returned to Britain, and before the end of the conflict he had distinguished himself on the Western Front as a fighter pilot in the Royal Flying Corps. Upon demobilisation he decided to stay and taking advantage of his motorcycling experience on the dirt tracks of western Canada, he joined John Marston Ltd – the manufacturers of the Sunbeam motorcycle. They provided him with his first TT ride in 1921. From then on he had gone from strength to strength and was cannily selective about which events to enter and what to ride. For this race he had approached Veloce Ltd in order to ride their overhead camshaft Velocette. Bennett was outstanding at calculating the speed at which a race could be won, adhering to his judgement and refusing to be drawn. He had the deserved reputation of keeping a cool head and steady nerves even in the tightest of situations. Being a family man he was fond of quipping that he could not afford to take risks. Undoubtedly he must be considered one of the star riders of the 1920s.

Birmingham born Jimmy Simpson was a sharp contrast to Alec in style and temperament. Since 1923 he had been mounted on AJS machines and was still looking for his first TT win. Simpson liked to set a fast pace, take an early lead and consolidate. He was very fast at cornering but it was said that he treated his gears unmercifully. Some took the view that this win or bust policy, that had usually ended in 'bust', was due to the hard treatment of his engines while others felt that Simpson had even worse luck than Walter Handley and was now due for a win.

With this formidable pair riding behind him, Walter just knew that he could not afford to 'hang about'. He never was a great believer in stories about carefully organised lap times. He once said, 'This is journalistic nonsense – everyone is going as fast as they and their machine can go, you can't afford to play around.' Plenty of TT riders, past and present, not blessed with outstandingly potent machinery will echo these sentiments. It was only on the last lap, with a good lead signalled that Walter believed you could afford to ease up. He was to do exactly this in the 1930 Senior TT.

Walter set off on his 260-mile race on the stroke of 10 AM and 34 mins, 19 secs later flashed passed the grandstand having clipped four seconds off his 1925 record lap from a standing start. In the process he had taken a 22 seconds lead over Simpson on the AJS. The calm precision of that opening lap was the only thing destined to go smoothly for Walter that day. Soon it was apparent to the most casual observer that number one was in some kind of trouble, for he was perceptibly slower and Simpson had gained a five seconds lead at the end of the second lap. By lap three it was Alec Bennett who, riding a carefully judged race, had come to the front and stayed there. He steadily increased his lead on each of the remaining laps to win by nearly 10.5 minutes from Simpson, whose 'big port Ajay' simply had not got the 'horses'.

The ultimate winner of the 1926 Junior TT, Alec Bennett (Velocette 348cc) at Ramsey Hairpin on the second lap, follows Wal Handley (Rex Acme 348cc) who came in third having suffered mechanical troubles.

Meanwhile what had happened to Wal Handley? He had been riding under the most trying conditions, for this race was to demand another of those fights against adversity for which he was becoming famous. Later he explained what had happened after that opening lap:

> First of all the wear on the brakes was more than I had anticipated. When the rear brake was applied the pedals came very near to the ground. This meant that I had to do all my braking on the straight and get it finished before I banked over for a bend. Then the front brake wore too, with the result that the lever fouled the twist grip, so that I was altogether slowed considerably. The next thing that happened was that the jet got bunged up good and hearty, and as I couldn't blow it clear, I tried to borrow a pin! Whilst I waited I fitted a one size smaller jet which I had with me. Then the pin came along, so I shoved it in my pocket and carried on. Later the jet choked again so that pin came in very handy. Then, while on the third lap, a more serious problem arose when my bottom gear packed up. I was now losing speed on the mountain section up which I was having to climb in second gear. In order to keep the revs going, I had no other option but to slip the clutch on occasions. Even so my progress up the mountain seemed painfully slow; this was proved when Alec Bennett came alongside, and with a cheery grin streaked off and away as though I had been standing still. The strain to which my gearbox, clutch and engine were being subjected told even further on the fifth lap, when a screw came out of the gear control quadrant and made it impossible to change gear. I tried changing by means of the rod; this however proved to be rather dangerous, so I decided that it was better to stay in top gear.
>
> I commenced the sixth lap determined in spite of all these troubles to do my best, although I was now

feeling worn out with the strain of urging my lagging machine along. You might realise that when I did get a bit of straight and level ground where I could get going in top gear, I had to bang the throttle right open and leave shutting off until the last moment in order to get the last possible ounce of speed from the model. This in turn, wore my brakes down rather badly and I had to make a further stop to effect adjustments to these. As I started my last lap my pit attendant told me that I was losing places and was now in fifth position. I determined at all costs to try to put up a good lap in spite of my difficulties. On this last lap I managed to get past Gus Kuhn (Velocette), and Freddie Dixon (Douglas) again, whilst I also pulled a minute back on Jimmy Simpson who had finished second. So that I found, after a most hectic ride, that I had scrambled into third place.

Ixion in the *Motor Cycle* commented: 'Handley rode splendidly under great difficulty. To lap the island at nearly 66 mph when a lost pivot pin leaves you with a single gear is amazing.' His average speed was 63·37 mph.

This 1926 Junior TT race brought Alec Bennett his third and perhaps most famous victory at the record speed of 66·70 mph. It was also a triumph for Birmingham's Velocette factory; the result being notable for bringing the first success by an overhead camshaft model on the Manx course. The bike had produced over 20 bhp and was simply years ahead of its rivals. Alec said that he had only used three-quarter throttle and had plenty in reserve if it had been needed. Significantly the first of the legendary KTT racers was just three years away. Soon after Bennett's win this family business made the final move to the factory at York Road in Hall Green, previously occupied by Humphries and Dawes, and where Walter had begun his career in 1920.

The Lightweight race came next and unlike the Junior event, it proved a real cliff hanger, full of excitement and ending with a sensational decision following a steward's enquiry. As early as 1925 there had been rumours in the island concerning the imminent arrival of the red Italian Guzzis. In 1926 these rumours became fact with the main threat to British supremacy posed by the impressive single overhead camshaft Guzzi in the 250 class. Thus Wednesday's race, given the international flavour, had more interest than usual. The Guzzi entry was to be ridden by Pietro Ghersi, a twenty-six-year-old Genoan who was to prove one of the most capable of the Italian stars on the Island circuit – but he had no luck at all. The Italian was certainly painstaking in his efforts to learn the course: it was reported that he had completed 36 laps before the official start of practising! Pre-race speculation went along the lines of whether the Guzzi rider would be able to contend with Handley's 'brilliant riding'. Ghersi started as favourite since it was generally conceded that the Guzzi had the heels of the Rex Acme.

Once again Walter was scheduled to start the race at number one because last year's winner, Twemlow, was not entered. As before, Walter hurried to beat his own lap record of the year before from the standing start. Yet it was not enough to prevent the Italian taking the lead with an even faster lap at 63·12 mph. Walter was doing his best to coax the last ounce of speed from his Rex Acme, knowing that the crowds were relying on him to stave off this foreign challenge.

Both men were getting a tremendous reception from the spectators lining the course who were looking forward to an exciting duel. However, it was not until Walter reached his pit at the end of the second lap that he learned of Ghersi's performance on the opening lap. He had guessed that something exciting was happening from the frantic yells and signals of 'faster' that he was receiving from the crowds at the various vantage points. Walter wrote:

> I was doing my utmost to satisfy their wishes, but already trouble had started to assert itself, my petrol pipe was leaking badly and my front brake had given up the ghost. I learned that Ghersi had increased his

lead and was now 2 mins, 25 secs in front. The crowds in the stands, as I was refuelling, shouted calls of encouragement to me to catch Ghersi, and as my pit attendant told me the position I meant to do my best, but as I pushed off I felt disappointed at the knowledge that circumstances would prevent me from satisfying the crowd's wishes. The third lap was a troublesome one, but I managed to keep going, although my speed was dropping, and it was at this point that Paddy Johnston on the Cotton managed to get into second place, and take up the challenge which I had so unfortunately been unable to keep up. The fourth lap saw the end of my ride, as I had to retire near Ramsey with a broken valve spring.

Walter was not at all insensitive to the strain a TT race placed upon his machinery, and it was the realisation that this last piece of trouble would result in unnecessary damage to his engine that brought this effort to a sudden end.

The race had an exciting finish as Ghersi slowed with troubles of his own. Johnston closed on him in an effort to keep intact Britain's long line of racing successes. In the end what proved decisive was the small size of petrol tank fitted to Ghersi's Guzzi. At the start of his last lap Ghersi pulled in to refuel while Johnston was able to go straight through and win by 20 seconds at 60·20 mph. There was an unfortunate postscript to this thrilling race. Great was the consternation in the Italian camp when it was learned that Ghersi was excluded from the race awards on a technical disqualification. Although at the time it was an unpopular decision, the stewards quite rightly stood their ground by the race rules. Upon examining the Guzzi after the race it had been discovered that the Italian had used a sparking plug not mentioned in his specification. This is no small matter since the type of plug can make a tremendous difference to the performance of a racing engine. Had the stewards not stood by their own rules they would have opened up the races to all kinds of abuse. However, as a special concession they allowed Ghersi to keep the credit for his record lap. The seven laps must have taken their inevitable toll for out of twenty-one starters only nine finished.

The record shows that time and again it was not so much the races that Walter Handley won, as those he lost, which were often his finest, representing as they did the pure drama of a furious struggle against overwhelming odds. There can hardly be a more striking example of this than the next race on the Friday of the 1926 TT week. After Walter's TT wins in the previous year there were those who said, 'Ah, wait until he gets onto a 500cc Senior mount, you will see, he'll fall off!' How wrong they were going to be proved.

This was his first Senior TT and it was a race to remember for those fortunate enough to be there. The fifty-seven starters represented sixteen different manufacturers, a sharp contrast to the position today. The two chief protagonists in the line up were Norton and AJS, while other less fancied makes included Sunbeam, Rudge-Whitworth, HRD with JAP engines, P&M, the Horsman tuned Triumphs, the Douglas entry and the Le Vack tuned New Hudsons.

Pietro Ghersi was again able to supply an international flavour to the event with his four-valve overhead camshaft Guzzi, that is, until he wiped off the brake controls with an early crash. Before having to retire Jimmy Simpson (AJS) made history with the first 70 mph lap of the TT course. His team mate, Charlie Hough, was also unlucky when his tenacious ride ended on the last lap just as he had the race leader, Stanley Woods (Norton) in his sights. Yet with all this excitement, the really outstanding memory, shining across the years, is that of 'Wal – the Wizard' popping up from nowhere to gain second place on the last lap.

To place this achievement in perspective one has to remember that the chances of Handley's Rex Acme-Twin were not taken all that seriously. For one thing Rex Acme's commercial preoccupation was with the 250 and 350cc engine sizes and so for TT race-goers this was the first time they had seen Walter on a big bike. What must the sceptics have thought as they saw the slight youthful figure of Wal Handley preparing to handle the 'fire-eating' Rex Acme-Twin?

Many years later Sammy James, Walter's mechanic, could still vividly recall the awful struggle they had in fitting the unusually wide angled 60 degrees Blackburne twin engine into the frame, 50 degrees was more usual. It consisted of a 998cc crankcase to which had been fitted two sets of 250cc overhead valve engine ports. The Rex Acme had awesome acceleration and fine flat out speed, but it was a brute to steer, and knowledgeable onlookers had noted that the Rex Acme had not shown any real form in practice. Despite working round the clock, Sammy knew that with the three machines to prepare for the race week, there had just not been enough time to put the V-Twin through its paces. Anything could happen and it probably would.

Howard Davies (HRD) had the honour of setting the race in motion by virtue of his victory the year before. Half a minute later Wal Handley heaved the Rex Acme into the fray. In a remarkable piece of riding he had caught Howard Davies by Glen Helen on the opening lap. Now Walter had open roads ahead and was the first to roar past the grandstand to start his second lap. When the times were posted up, it was observed that Simpson (AJS) led the field, followed 37 seconds later by Woods having his first season with Norton, and then came the surprise packet of Wal Handley, only 13 seconds down on Stanley Woods.

It was too good to last and it was while Walter was on his second lap that things began to go wrong. In the grandstand, 'Handley watchers' soon spotted that his pointer was obstinately stuck at 'K' on the new scoreboard. What had happened was that on the approach into Ballaugh the back wheel of his Rex Acme had suddenly locked solid. With those lightening reflexes of his, Walter had got the clutch out just in time and brought the machine under control. It requires great coolness to work steadily at the roadside while rider after rider roars past. This was the quality he needed as he calmly proceeded to extract the plugs.

Wal Handley pushes off his Rex Acme 498cc V-twin
at the start of the 1926 Senior TT, he finished second after a long delay.

He discovered that the rear plug was too hot, it was of the semi-touring pattern which someone had advised him to use in order to avoid over oiling the rear cylinder! Unfortunately the use of this plug had permitted the back piston to overheat and a temporary seizure of that rear cylinder had occurred. Walter wrote:

> It was the very dickens of a job to get the back plug out of the cylinder, this was due to the fact that there were two petrol pipes, a foot operated oil pump and an oil tank, all in the way of that back sparking plug. I could only just get a spanner on to it and move it a sixth of a turn at a time, and all the time minutes were passing. I then had to free the cylinder by getting bits of sticks and straw from the roadside and with these coax drops of oil through the plug hole. I had two 'hot stuff' plugs in my pouch, so I fitted these in and at last got going again, but that little trouble had delayed me over 7 mins.

The delay meant that at the end of the second lap Walter had fallen back to about twenty-second place. He had lost the race but he was not the man to admit defeat and he now proceeded to race, as even he had never done before, over the remaining 200 or so miles of the Isle of Man course. Many of those present never forgot the sight of the slight figure tucked down on the big twin. Geoff Davison was spectating at Bray Hill when Wal arrived at the start of his third lap, several minutes after he was due. Geoff wrote:

> I have seen many riders going down Bray Hill, but never have I seen anything like Walter on that occasion. He was absolutely full bore, flat on the tank, and using every inch of the road.

Graham Walker had also witnessed Wal's effort from a rider's angle, having raced a Sunbeam that day. He wrote:

> It took the genius of Walter to handle that flying man-killer, but the sight of his slight boyish figure struggling with the writhing snarling projectile was worth going many a mile to see.

By the end of the third lap Walter had moved up in truly meteoric style to tenth position. It was on this lap that Jimmy Simpson, while still in the lead, had been forced to retire when the con-rod popped out through the bottom of the AJS crankcase. By now the Rex Acme was the fastest machine in the race. The crowds lining the hedgerows, clustered wherever a vantage point afforded some shelter from the blistering heat, had picked up the Rex Acme's startling challenge. Could Handley do the impossible and come from behind to secure a place in the first three? It would be the first time since 1914 that a V-twin design would have been placed. On that occasion Oliver Godfrey piloted his Indian into a second place tie with Howard Davies on his Sunbeam.

The answer was not long in coming. At the start of the seventh and final lap, it was discovered that Walter had moved up through the field to fourth place and was just one second behind Longman (AJS). Then to add to the suspense Charlie Hough (AJS), who had been second to Woods since the third lap, crashed near Sulby when momentarily blinded by a wasp getting into his goggles. Hough's misfortune, though spoiling the main finish, had the spectators on their toes regarding second place, would it be Handley or Longman – the rider agent from Ealing?

In just under four hours racing, Walter came up the Glencrutchery Road to receive the chequered flag. Since Longman had started 14.5 minutes after Wal, a seemingly intolerable wait followed before the AJS roared in. Walter must have wondered if that further stop to adjust his brakes was going to deprive him of second place. His rear brake had worn so much that the pedal had raised sparks off the road when banking over for the corners. It was so close that amateur timekeepers gave up and waited for the official verdict. A great cheer went up when it was announced that Wal Handley was in second place having gone four seconds up on Frank Longman, who very sportingly was among the first to congratulate Walter.

The first 7-lap Senior TT had given Stanley Woods, riding a well judged race, his second Tourist Trophy at an average speed of 67.54 mph. That it had been a testing race was borne out by the fact that only twenty-two out of the fifty-seven starters had managed to finish. Perhaps even more telling was the fact that only thirteen riders were quick enough to qualify for replicas of the trophy.

Walter's achievement was typical of the man, adversity always brought out his fighting spirit. Many good judges of the sport consider this to be one of his finest performances. Walter wrote:

> Never despair, keep going. Many times I have been delayed in races with troubles, and the position has seemed absolutely hopeless. I have kept the foregoing in mind and have started off again many times to eventually finish in the first three.

After one of his greatest rides, Wal Handley is congratulated on
coming in second in the 1926 Senior TT on the 498cc Rex Acme V-twin.

Had it not been for those stops Walter would easily have won
his first Senior Tourist Trophy. As it was he had finished 4 mins,
21 secs behind Stanley Woods; deduct Walter's time delays and
you get the measure of what he achieved – this lad of whom it
had been thought, could only handle the 'small stuff'!

It was much the same story for the rest of 1926. Walter arrived
at Spa for the Belgian Grand Prix, designated the Grand Prix of
Europe. This was a race he had won in style just twelve months
ago but now such races kept slipping away from him. On a hot
sunny day in the Ardennes he had to face the disappointment
of being forced to retire with engine trouble when in the lead.
By a strange irony the 350 class winner turned out to be Frank
Longman (AJS). Consoling himself with the thought that he
had at least escaped the bearded kisses that were the lot of a
continental race winner, Wal hurried back to Brooklands.

He was just in time, six days later on 24 July, to lose that epic

Two great riders together.
Left: the winner of the 1926 Senior TT, Stanley Woods (490 Norton).
Right: the runner-up, Wal Handley (498 Rex Acme).
Note the Irish emblem on Stanley's helmet.

'200-miler' in which, as already related, he suffered an inexplicable cut tyre right on the start line. Despite this setback some inspired riding still saw a 'jackpot' of world records fall to the Rex Acme ace. In August he was out record breaking again. This time with a sidecar attached to capture the records set up by Marchant's Chater Lea a year earlier. Most notable was the hour record going at nearly 80 mph. All this was some consolation for the 200-mile sidecar race, run earlier in the year, when a puncture far from home, added to a sequence of other troubles, proved to be the last straw and finally persuaded the intrepid Wal to allow himself to be towed in – a sad end to a brave show.

Despite the various misfortunes that befell him at this time, there was no doubt about his form and a victory was clearly on the cards given a clear run. Just when it must have seemed that fortune would never favour him, his luck changed. Walter crossed over to Belfast, as was his custom, right on the eve of the Ulster Grand Prix – the last classic of the season. He was as determined as ever and his perseverance got its due reward – his third victory on the Clady Circuit at record speed. He won the 350 class by a whopping 13 minutes at 68·89 mph. Only Graham Walker (Sunbeam), the winner of the 500cc race had a faster time at 70·53 mph. In his race Walter had set such a pace that only three out of ten finishers gained gold medals for being within 20 minutes of the winning Rex Acme! All those hard struggles of the summer must have become a distant memory. As Graham Walker commented; 'Believe me, when Walter really tried he could break the heart of any other competitor!'

Wal Handley, after having just won the 1926 Ulster Grand Prix 350cc Race, is surrounded by youthful admirers.

CHAPTER 13
'THE VALENTINO OF THE ISLAND'

The talkies were a year away; Charlie Chaplin and Mary Pickford were still the big stars of the day. Charles Lindberg was to cause a sensation by flying the Atlantic solo. Hits of the day were, 'Ain't She Sweet', 'Only a Rose', and 'Blue Skies'. People were trying to forget the awesome tragedy of 1914–1918. It was the age of Noel Coward, of champagne parties, of dole queues and of hope.

Consumer goods were coming down in price, thanks to ever improving mass production techniques, and this was bringing them within the reach of many more people. Motorcycles were a lot cheaper than cars and their sales were booming. In 1927 registration figures rose to 690,000, the figure for cars being only just over 100,000 more. Britain's motorcycle manufacturers led the world, and the prestige and design know-how gained from racing was of profound importance. In those far off days the Isle of Man TT races always had the greatest influence, especially in this country, and in 1927 the TT winners, both men and machines, were all British.

Two years earlier the Rex Acme Company had scored a spectacular TT 'double' and very nearly a triple. A repeat performance from their star rider, Wal Handley, would certainly help to stave off their looming financial difficulties. It so nearly came about, but fate can indeed be cruel. Throughout 1926 and 1927 Rex Acme had avoided expensive racing commitments in Europe. Their annual entry in the Belgian Grand Prix at Spa was the only exception to this 'stay at home' policy. So with Rex Acme preferring to support events here, it's hardly surprising to find that Walter's name rarely appears in the European Grand Prix events during this period.

Walter's race schedule was largely a preparation for the TT races in June. It was not lost upon him that it was his 250cc and 350cc Rex Acme Blackburne singles that had swept all before them in the Doncaster Speed Trials at the close of the 1926 season. At the same event his, 500cc and 750cc Rex Acme-twins had shown no form at all. On Easter Monday it was again the 350cc Blackburne overhead valve engine that had produced the second fastest time of the day at the Gopsall Park Speed Trials in Derbyshire. Then on 14 May at Brooklands he had that great morale boost of a win in the 350cc class of the 200-mile sidecar race.

In view of all this, it was not so surprising that during the practice period for the 1927 TT races, Walter finally decided to remain faithful to the well-tried formula of the push rod operated overhead valve Blackburne engine fitted into the Rex Acme. After a test run, Walter, who was generally reckoned to exercise a shrewd judgement in these matters, said no to the Blackburne alternative, a skew gear camshaft machine, this type of engine being developed after Velocette had shown the way in the previous year.

During the practice period the Velocettes were generally fancied to win with Alec Bennett their star rider. This was confirmed in a totally unexpected fashion. One morning, Walter's Rex Acme being out of action, he borrowed a Velocette, and during practice, proceeded to demonstrate the born rider he was by clocking the fastest Junior time of anyone in 34 mins, 8 secs.

In Monday's Junior TT Walter seized the lead from the start and on his second lap created a new lap record for the race of 69·18 mph in 32 mins, 44 secs. It was his sixth lap record on the TT course in the space of five years, a record without equal in this period. To Walter's surprise his closest rival in this race turned out to be, not his friend Alec Bennett, but an experienced rider who had first raced in the island in 1912. This was Freddie Dixon of Middlesbrough, nine years older than Walter and recognised as a 'character'. Dixon had won the sidecar TT of 1923, but in his mind that hardly counted and so he was desperate to win his first solo TT race. He was mounted on a JAP powered HRD that had received one or two typical Dixonian touches. The HRD had footboards, a home made foot operated clutch and gear change for second to top position, a backrest to the saddle and a windscreen, for Freddie loathed goggles! Another innovation was the left hand twist

This was an unlucky day for Wal Handley (Rex Acme); he led the 1927 Junior TT until the last lap when he retired with engine trouble. Here he is at Ramsey.

grip throttle control which had a cunning lever interposed between the cable and the slide, permitting variations of throttle opening for a given amount of 'twist'.

Despite taking a nasty toss on an oil patch at Quarter Bridge on his third lap Walter was, as usual, unhurt and carried on with no sign of any slowing. With the race less than half completed, Graham Walker's Sunbeam ran out of oil and promptly seized up. The disaster had at least one consolation for Graham who wrote:

For the first time in my life I was able to see a TT race. Hitherto I had either managed to finish or else had broken down in the last few miles. Armed with a large glass of beer, I sat on Kirk Michael Corner and learned just what could be done by a real rider every time Handley came round. I'll never forget watching him on the fourth lap, he was miles an hour faster than anyone else, all that Dixon could do was to carry on and hope for the best.

At the end of that fourth lap Walter's only words spoken to his pit attendant were, 'Where's Alec?' and 'Goggles.' As the band struck up the popular American standard, 'Bye, Bye, Blackbird', Walter pulled away knowing he had a lead of nearly three minutes over Dixon and was nearly four minutes ahead of Alec Bennett. This was a clear winning margin as he began his seventh and final circuit, but no matter how comfortable the lead, the suspense of the race leader on his last lap is no less.

Imagine how taut Wal Handley must have felt as he dived down Bray Hill for the last time. Then sweeping past the lamp post that used to be allowed to stand at Quarter Bridge and on to the 'S' bend at Braddan. Almost immediately this is followed by the fast but tricky section leading to Ballacraine. The finger on Wal's Grandstand Clock number 32 jerked to 'B' signifying his onward march to victory. The scoreboard was the only guide to what was happening behind the Manx Hills etched clear cut against the blue sky of a warm summer's day. The leap into the air at the old Ballig Bridge was followed by the darting run through Glen Helen. After this came the rise over Creg Willey's Hill, and on to the fast winding downhill run into Kirk Michael. The clock of number 32 registered 'K' and alas stays there. It was on the approach into Ballaugh that Walter experienced that sinking feeling in the pit of the stomach as the crackle of the Rex Acme died away.

Two miles down the road, Graham Walker had watched Handley go through to win, as he thought, the Trophy and the 'bags of gold'. Little did he know that Wal's piston had failed. Just a year later, poor Graham was to suffer the same anguish. He was leading the Senior TT by three minutes on the last lap when the big end of his Rudge failed near the twenty-eighth milestone.

Meanwhile Dixon knew as he started his final lap that he had but the remotest chance of catching the Rex Acme star. Imagine Freddie's surprise when just outside Ballaugh he saw the despondent figure of Handley standing beside his bike. Only then did he know that victory was his for the taking. Freddie roared up the mountain crouched behind his windscreen in that familiar sitting up style of his going on to win at 67·19 mph, in doing so he had at last achieved his ambition of winning a solo TT race. Dixon's win also meant that the HRD was able to go out in a blaze of glory. Later that year Howard Davies sold his interest in the marque he had founded to Ernie Humphries of OK motorcycles, who after selling off the spares and machine tools, eventually disposed of the HRD interest to a young man named Philip Vincent who continued production at Stevenage to develop yet another motorcycling story.

For Walter, what had happened was a bitter blow and it was scant comfort to learn that his average for the six completed laps was 68·1 mph. However, the Burney & Blackburne Engine Company headlined the fact in their adverts that summer. By now the Press were becoming accustomed to the Handley 'proverbial bad luck', as one Press report headlined it. Such was Walter's popularity that it was reported some of the ladies in the crowd were moved to tears by this cruel stroke of fate handed out to the handsome, rather shy, twenty-five year old from Birmingham. His personality seemed to attract and in the Press he was being called 'The Valentino of the Island'. After the race, Walter pushed his stricken Rex Acme into Ballaugh but declined to say anything until he had had a drink! Later, when he had recovered his composure, there was no word of complaint about what had happened, he just commented, 'Never mind, I can win the Lightweight.'

CHAPTER 14
THE ITALIAN CHALLENGE

Before World War Two the Tourist Trophy races in the Isle of Man were seen as the laboratory of the motorcycle industry. Just think of the improvements almost always associated with manufacturers that have supported the TT races. One only has to think of braking, carburation, magnetos, better gearbox design coupled with the introduction of the foot change, and not least better steering and road-holding induced by improvements in frame design, forks, wheels and tyres. The British motorcycle industry was 'top dog' throughout the world. It dominated the classic races at home and on the continent, so much so that attracting foreign entries in the TT was seen as a difficulty, and the Manx Government felt the need to offer financial incentives to help attract foreign entries.

Long before the post-war foreign invasions of the TT races, which culminated in the fatal Japanese onslaught of the 1960s, there had been ominous warnings of what was to come. The success of the British 'single', in particular – the Nortons – discouraged innovation here but had no such inhibiting effect abroad. The warning signs were soon apparent, and smooth, powerful multi's meant gains in terms of speed, acceleration, comfort and reliability. In 1935 and 1937 the Italian Guzzis had broken the British monopoly of the TT, which had lasted since the celebrated 1-2-3 places of the American Indian bikes in the Senior TT of 1911. Then just before World War Two along came Germany's supercharged BMWs, and the DKW two-strokes to exploit the breakthrough before the outbreak of hostilities put a temporary end to racing.

It is often overlooked that a foreign invasion of the TT had been threatening over a much longer period. In the early 1920s the Italian Guzzis and Bianchis had been doing well on the continent in their respective classes. Rumours of their imminent arrival in the Isle of Man were put about as early as 1925. In 1926 the arrival of a Garelli, two Guzzis and three Bianchis ended the rumours – they were here! In the 350cc race the two-stroke Garelli failed to finish, and the Bianchi threat was seriously blunted when it was learned that the great Tazio Nuvolari had been injured in practice and would not be allowed to compete by the stewards. As for the Guzzi entries it was generally agreed that Pietro Ghersi in the Lightweight race posed the greatest threat. As we have seen he would have won had his Guzzi had a larger tank. So in view of the fright Ghersi had given everyone, there was considerable excitement when it became known that Moto Guzzi were sending a three man team in 1927 to contest the 250cc Tourist Trophy.

Chief defenders of Britain's supremacy were Alec Bennett on an OK and Wal Handley riding, as usual, his Rex Acme. Walter was in great form during the practising and he was as confident about the outcome of this race as he ever allowed himself to be. His friend, Geoff Davison, was entered to ride a Rex Acme, very similar to Walter's machine. In between the hectic business of producing his new *TT Special* race journal, Geoff was out practising, but he felt very disappointed with the model's speed. In his book, *Racing Through the Century*, he wrote:

> I felt that my bike must be miles an hour slower than Wal's and plucking up my courage, I told him so. He gave me the customary Handley glower. 'There's nothing in them, Geoff,' he said, 'but if you like I'll take yours out tomorrow.' I was delighted, that'll show him what a dud I've got, I thought. Wal didn't offer me his own bike in exchange, so next morning I had a lie-in. As it happened it was a beastly morning, with thick fog from the Gooseneck to Hillberry, but in spite of that, Wal did

a faster lap than I had ever done under ideal conditions. Further he made third fastest lap of the morning – on a 250cc – and was only a few seconds behind the best Senior! When I looked at my machine after Wal's lap on it, I found the under part of the exhaust pipe and both footrests well chamfered off from contact with the road, and I had never touched either in a week of practising. After that I didn't talk any more about slow machines; I knew that the trouble was the slowness of the conductor.

It should be remembered that in those days a foreign challenge was exceptional and it was thought desirable to provide every encouragement. Apart, therefore, from the usual hospitable welcome, a special gesture was made to the Italian party when it was learned that they were to be given the privilege of being able to choose their own race numbers. This in itself added an extra spice to the situation for it led to much speculation as to the tactical use the Italians would make of their advantage.

They decided to position the experienced Achille Varzi, who had first raced in the Island in 1924, to ride number 10 to Alec Bennett's number 9. Luigi Arcangeli, the holder of the 500cc 200-mile world record on a Senior Guzzi, was positioned at number 21 to start one minute before Wal Handley at number 22. This left Mario Ghersi, the younger brother of Pietro, who was in an Italian hospital with both legs in splints, to ride at number 4 behind Paddy Johnston, who as the previous year's winner would be number one and the first away. It was surmised that the task for Varzi and Arcangeli would be to lead Alec and Walter on to 'blow-up', thus leaving the way clear for Mario to go forward and avenge his brother's defeat.

Like most pre-race theories it foundered completely. Walter was determined to put behind him the disappointment of Monday's Junior Race when he had come so close to victory. He was quietly confident that his push rod operated 250cc Rex Acme Blackburne was capable of winning. Walter attacked the

The 1927 Lightweight TT and Walter is in the lead: he pulls into the pits for replenishment and encouragement from Nigel Spring.

The Lightweight TT of 1927 saw Wal Handley defeat the Italian challenge. He has just overtaken Achille Varsi, Guzzi 248cc, at Governor's Bridge.

Italians from the start, he passed Arcangeli on the mountain descent and created a new lap record from the standing start. It was found that he had beaten Ghersi's 1926 record by a whopping 38 seconds at 64·23 mph. This was a great performance bearing in mind that Monday's idyllic weather had given way to blustery conditions. On Snaefell a gale was blowing and the telephone operator on the mountain section complained that he was in danger of being blown over in his hut!

Despite a tumble at Governor's Bridge on the second lap, in which he had scraped his face and shoulder, Walter continued to press home his advantage. He was pursued by Alec Bennett (OK) and Arcangeli, who had also dropped his bike at the same place. On the sixth lap, Alec was forced to retire when trailing Walter by only 1 min, 47 secs – his oil pump had failed early in the race and he had been operating a hand pump ever since. Bennett's retirement left Walter with a comfortable lead for his third TT victory at 63·30 mph over eight minutes ahead of Arcangeli in 4 hrs, 10 mins, 22 secs. As usual when Walter had a clear run he always won in style. The Works Director of Rex Acme crossed the line to receive a tremendous ovation from a crowd, not only grateful for his thwarting of the Guzzi challenge, but also mindful of his desperately bad luck on Monday. 'Good old Wally', they called as he was carried shoulder high round the paddock.

The Italian challenge had in the event proved less formidable than expected, Mario Ghersi had retired, while the best that Varzi could manage was fifth position; he came in covered in oil having lost the oil filler cap early in the race. However, the genial Luigi Arcangeli, in his second year in the Island, had shown his mettle since his speed, despite some ignition trouble, would have been enough to have given him victory in 1926. Sadly the twenty-five-year-old Arcangeli, who went on to drive Maserati and Alfa Romeo cars with the same verve he had shown in the TT races, was killed at Monza in 1931 when his new twelve-cylinder Alfa left the track during practising for the Italian Grand Prix.

Wal Handley (Rex Acme), the winner of the 1927 Lightweight TT,
and the runner-up, Luigi Arcangeli (Guzzi), congratulate each other.

Despite Walter's clear cut win, he did not on this occasion
take the lap record, the honour went to Alec Bennett, who on
his fourth lap clipped two seconds off the Rex Acme rider's best
time. Walter had bet Alec that he would get the fastest lap – 'I
had to pay up,' said Walter with a laugh. His riding consistency
took him into first place and had kept him there.

There were no Guzzis on the Island in the following year, but the former Italian champion, Pietro Ghersi, had won the 1928 350cc German Grand Prix on a Norton, and he must have been hoping to repeat this form on his 250cc Guzzi when he returned to the TT races in 1929. His was the lone Italian entry in the Lightweight TT. Wal Handley was the favourite to win this race, and once again was looked upon as England's hope against the red Guzzi challenge. By this time Walter had left Rex Acme and was to oppose Ghersi with an OK Supreme, the stable with which he had begun his road racing career. However, as the practising progressed Walter was not satisfied with the performance of the machine. He dropped the JAP engine and fitted a Blackburne – his old favourite, but still the machine lacked pace. He even tried to get another OK over to the Island for the race. All this frenetic activity behind the scenes made no difference to the public fancy. Walter Handley was still the eye catching favourite. It did not escape notice that Frank Longman had won last years Lightweight Race on the OK Supreme-JAP, at a slightly slower speed than Walter's Rex Acme win over Arcangeli in the previous year. So it is easy to see that it was not entirely wishful thinking that caused the enthusiasts to expect Wal Handley to put up another strong showing against the Guzzi.

Unfortunately, Walter was obviously in trouble right from the start. Reports from around the course paid tribute to his daring cornering, and at the grandstand he was seen going through absolutely flat out with his back horizontal, but despite this he never got above fourth place. The bike had simply not got the urge. At the end of the fourth lap Walter toured into the pits and retired, his engine having suffered a broken valve spring. So with Syd Gleave, SGS-JAP (Syd Gleave Special) walking in from the Nook, only Syd Crabtree (Excelsior) was left with any chance of catching Pietro Ghersi, the race leader, who now appeared to have the race 'in his pocket'. Yet it is often the unexpected that happens in a TT race. The Italian, who had already taken the lap record, was destined to remain unlucky in

This picture portrays the romance of the TT course. It is the 1929 Lightweight TT
and Wal Handley (OK Supreme) leads Bernard Hieatt (Cotton) at Hillberry.

the Island, for his bike failed him on the seventh and final lap
when he had no-one to beat. This enabled that young veteran,
Syd Crabtree from Warrington to win at 63·87 mph. It was well
deserved, for Syd had first competed in the 1921 TT races when
just seventeen years old.

It was the first TT victory achieved by Birmingham's
Excelsior Company, which on this occasion had fitted a JAP
engine. It was not the last challenge made by Moto Guzzi, their
persistence finally bore fruit in 1935 with the experienced piloting
of Stanley Woods in one of the greatest and most exciting races
of TT history. However, 1929 proved to be Pietro Ghersi's high
water mark in TT racing. In the following year his chances
ended when he was injured during the practice period, while
in 1931 his Guzzi was never in the picture before he retired in
the Lightweight race. In the meantime he had acquired an Alfa
Romeo and joined those of his compatriots who had decided to
move over from two wheels to four.

CHAPTER 15
GOING 'FOREIGN'

Today, the fact that nearly every British road racing star is mounted on a Japanese motorcycle is taken for granted. When in such circumstances a British rider becomes World Champion we do not like to consider it 'half a triumph'. Yet in the heyday of the British motorcycle industry there was no such ambiguity. If a British rider so much as used a foreign make, he had 'gone foreign' and his victory did not count in the list of British successes. Our superstars have long been the target of foreign manufacturers who have always been well aware of the commercial value of racing success. Seeking impact they have gone for big names in the sport, Stanley Woods, Geoff Duke and Mike Hailwood are names that spring to mind. It was however Wal Handley who became the first of our aces to 'go foreign', when he signed for Motosacoche of Geneva in 1928.

Although what happened is not now accurately known, it seems probable that Walter's departure from Rex Acme of Coventry was foreshadowed in the 1927 TT races. It will be recalled that in those races, he had won the Lightweight and had almost won the Junior TT for Rex Acme, by employing the overhead valve Blackburne engines. Initially it was expected that in the Senior Race Walter would ride the Rex Acme V-twin upon which, a year earlier, he had managed that wonderful ride into second place. Despite a new frame which had helped him to reach 102 mph – eight miles per hour faster than before, the truth was that the machine would not steer straight.

Walter tried everything, including sending Sammy James

to Liverpool on the midnight boat to have the frame reset. Results were disappointing, and on one high speed practice descent of Bray Hill, Walter had such an awesome speed wobble that watching journalists gave him the sobriquet, 'Hell Diver Handley'. So when it was announced that Walter was a non-starter, there was a note of relief amongst reporters who felt that he had done enough to satisfy honour and that the Blackburne twin represented an unnecessary risk.

The alternative bike was powered by the new MAG (Motosacoche-Acacias-Geneva) engine designed by Dougal Marchant but it was hardly ready. The machine looked massive, the frame was not of the usual Rex Acme pattern and had much thicker tubing. The upright engine gear unit was surmounted by a huge pistol grip shaped fuel tank. Its appearance was certainly eye catching but it looked unwieldy. It was rumoured that the bike lacked speed and Walter was reported to have said that it was unrideable, and if he said so it probably was.

Why Rex Acme were prepared to risk so much, when their star rider and competitions manager had achieved so many brilliant successes with the conventional Blackburne engines, is a mystery. There seem to be two possible explanations. One is commercial in that it enabled them, with minimal capital outlay, to offer the public a much wider choice of Blackburne, JAP or MAG engines for the 1928 season. The second reason was that the push-rod Blackburne engines were being overtaken by the overhead camshaft Velocettes and Nortons. The camshaft MAG engine can be seen as a response to this threat. It was billed as the only proprietary engine with the overhead valve gear unit totally enclosed and mechanically lubricated. It was the forerunner of a similar design used on Marchant's Belgian FN a few years later. It was the latest in a long line of quality engines which the Swiss company had been producing, since 1913, for the top end of the market.

The 350cc TT Sports Model had been redesigned by Wal Handley; it had a new duplex cradle frame and with the MAG option it was priced at £70 in standard form. The *Motor Cycling* test report described it as 'a very nice motorcycle'. It should be remembered that in those days the racing motorcycle was much closer to the production model than it is today. The racer of one year often became the sports model of the next season. Walter was one of those rare racing stars who understood engines and design features that would influence performance. He was already getting recognition abroad, and not just as a rider, the Italian newspaper *Il Paese Sportivo* said at this time that 'Handley is the most able motorcyclist in the world today he has no rivals, either as a rider or a technical man.'

Armed with an ambitious Rex Acme sales catalogue listing a range of four-strokes from 175cc to 750cc Walter sailed in November 1927 for South Africa, where it had become apparent that there was a great deal of interest. As he headed south with Jimmy Simpson aboard the SS Dunluce Castle, they were both looking forward to the South African TT to be held at Port Elizabeth. Motorcyclists from across the Union were excited at the prospect of seeing Handley and Simpson perform. Unfortunately it was not to be, Walter found that the injury to his hand, sustained three months earlier at Brooklands, was still proving extremely painful when he began practising on the rugged Kragga Kama circuit. So it was with the greatest reluctance that he found he had to withdraw from the race. Walter's non-appearance and the early race retirement of Jimmy Simpson came as a great disappointment to their many South African admirers.

Not long after his return, Walter paid a surprise visit to Geneva where he made the final arrangements for MAG engines to be fitted to the Rex Acme machines in the Isle of Man. The MAG engines had quality and were known to be fast. Wal Handley, the meteoric star of the TT, had decided to add some 'pep' to the 1928 TT programme. In the Isle of Man there was considerable interest shown in these new Rex Acme engine units – the twin port bevel driven overhead camshaft MAG engines with the valves controlled by hairpin springs. Crowds would gather as soon as the covers were removed to reveal the bikes, easily distinguished by their blue enamelled pistol grip shaped tanks. Unfortunately, it soon became apparent that Walter had taken on more than he anticipated. These machines had never been on the road till they reached the Island. This was not the usual Rex Acme policy which was to assemble the machines in Coventry. It was almost miraculous that Walter and his small band of helpers had got as far as they had. They found themselves working day and night in a locked garage as they attempted to 'unearth the knots' and cram twelve months experimenting into two weeks. Their problem was that the bikes had simply no 'urge' at all.

This soon became apparent as Walter had, for him, the strange experience of finding himself virtually an outsider in the popular reckoning. This is not so surprising when you consider that the Motosacoche engines had arrived from Geneva unassembled. According to Walter, people used to reach the Island with most of the 'bits and pieces' in their pockets ready to finish the job. It is difficult for us today to conceive of those early hectic and improvising days. In the modern era racing camps travel to the Grand Prix circuits with the bikes fully prepared with a team of mechanics on hand to make any adjustments or alterations well before the race. In the 1920s it was a very different matter. Then you had to be a mechanic as well as a rider. No wonder that the almost inevitable late arrival of a rider in Walter's position at the weigh-in was greeted by good humoured banter. Walter joked that he must have paid for a new wing at Nobles – the fines of the TT riders late at the weigh-in being customarily paid to the Douglas hospital.

Walter Handley, being the individualist that he was, preferred the independence he gained by riding for a small firm and probably would not have liked it any other way, but he often paid a high price for this independence. This happened in 1928 when for the first time in four years of TT racing he would be unable to achieve a fastest lap or gain a podium place. Always in the news, Walter created a sensation right at the start of the meeting by announcing that he was a non-starter in the Junior Race. He had decided that his Rex Acme was too slow for him to be able to put up a 'decent show'. The MAG people were terribly disappointed, but his decision was probably a wise one. Knowledgeable spectators seeing a first class rider way down the lists are apt to draw unflattering conclusions about the machinery. The race itself was notable for giving Alec Bennett his fifth and final TT win. It came on a Velocette fitted with the Willis designed positive stop foot operated gear change. Although none of the Norton team managed to finish, it was their first venture in the Junior TT and it marked a new challenge.

Walter was often late at the weighing-in, due mainly
to the pressure of a small manufacturer getting bikes ready.
Here Walter is taking his 1927 Junior Rex Acme to the weigh-in.

Walter started in the Senior Race just after Stanley Woods (Norton), and a lively contest was in prospect, but the Rex Acme-MAG only got as far as Glen Helen on the opening lap. It was a wet day and water had got into the magneto. It was a further disappointment for all concerned, including Marchant, who had arrived from Geneva and Sammy James who had re-joined Walter after a spell with BSA. The 1928 Senior Race turned out to be the wettest and most miserable since Tom Sheard's win in 1923. Not surprisingly, in view of the awful conditions, the competitors were convinced it was the wettest TT of all time! So Walter's early retirement was a merciful release from what was generally agreed to be a thoroughly unpleasant experience. The conditions probably helped to produce an unexpected result. The diminutive Mancunian, Charlie Dodson, rode his Sunbeam steadily to victory with an average speed of 62·98 mph; this made it the slowest Senior since 1924.

For the Lightweight TT held in midweek, Walter had no option but to use the push rod Blackburne engine since the 250cc version of the new MAG design was still a year away. It must have been with a sense of relief that he returned to the engine unit he knew so well. Early in the race Walter powered his Rex Acme into second place and held on to the OK Supreme-JAP ridden by veteran, Frank Longman. The OKs were sporting a new cylinder head design which was reputed to produce an extra five miles per hour. Despite not having the speed to match the OK, Walter fought every inch of the way, producing what was described as some exceptionally lurid cornering, and proved that he had lost none of his racing verve. Then on the sixth lap with several minutes in hand over the rest of the field and a good result in prospect, he had to retire and coast in off the mountain road. Once again the Coventry rider was out of luck and when his retirement was announced it was greeted with what sounded like a sigh. According to the *Motor Cycle,* Handley cornered like 'an inebriated panther', in trying to make up for the lack of all out speed. It was the only chance that week for the crowds to see Walter swerve the curves with another memorable 'ten-tenths' effort.

It was from about this time that the fortunes of the Rex Acme company went into a slow decline from which they never recovered. Sadly the firm proved to be an exception to the general axiom that racing success brings its commercial reward. The company had scored many notable successes; in the five year period between 1924 and 1928 that Walter had ridden for them in the TT, he had scored three firsts, one second, one third and four record laps. With no other rider did the Coventry firm have comparable success. His racing ability had meant that the bikes were pushed to near capacity limits. To win at an average speed of say 64 mph the actual top speed might be no more than about 75 mph. Today the difference between the average speed for a race and the top speed could be twice as much. Pre-war the bikes were being pushed close to their capacity and could not always last the distance.

Wal Handley had retired with various troubles in eight of his thirteen Rex Acme TT starts. Yet it would be wrong to assume that he was 'hard' on his engines. This charge has been refuted by all who knew him, and especially by those who examined his bikes after a race. Of course, in the 1920s our metallurgical knowledge was still in a relatively primitive state, and riders capable of pushing against the limits often exposed these deficiencies.

Having made his name with a small manufacturer, it would have surprised no-one if, at this stage of his career, Handley had been snapped up by one of the better known British manufacturers. 'If I were a manufacturer of modest means limited to a single jockey,' said the *Motor Cycle,* 'I would choose Handley today, because he is brilliant, safe and younger than Bennett.' In fact Walter's friend, Alec Bennett, was of similar mind, and in 1927 he was reported as saying, 'I consider Handley to be the prettiest rider in the island, a brilliant career lies before him.'

So it came as a surprise to most observers when, in the late summer, it was announced that the brilliant young road racer had signed for Motosacoche of Geneva. It had been a long and arduous road that had taken the lad from the back streets of Small Heath to the shores of Lake Geneva. He had got there in the end because of a talent amounting to genius and a mental attitude that refused to give up no matter how hopeless his position seemed. The offer from abroad had proved irresistible. According to Walter it meant that his rivals had to win their races in order to equal his earnings. There can surely be no better tribute to his growing reputation.

It was at this point in his career that there was an unexpected twist that caught most people by surprise. On the morning of 16

June the *Daily Mail* commenting on that great test of endurance and speed – the twenty-four hour Le Mans race that was due to start later that day – stated that:

> An interesting newcomer to a big event is Mr Walter Handley, one of the greatest of Tourist Trophy motorcycle racers … If he drives a car as brilliantly as he rides a motorcycle he will shine among the many stars of all the nations who are competing.

It was indeed a colourful international gathering at the Sarthe Circuit, 140 miles southwest of Paris. Included were the British Bentleys, the American Stutz and a team of Chryslers. In 1928 this was very much the marathon for standard production cars which could be bought by anyone in the market place.

The *Daily Mail* had picked up that Wal Handley had been nominated to drive in the Lagonda team for whom racing was a new venture. They had entered three 2 litre cars that had been well prepared and had been timed at over 95 mph on the 5-mile stretch leading to Mulsanne Corner. Two drivers were allowed to each car, each driver taking turns of three hours at the wheel. Walter was due to join Captain Clive Gallop in car number 43.

Unfortunately, what the *Daily Mail,* hadn't picked up in their report was that Walter hadn't reached Le Mans until the evening of Thursday, 14 June, just 48 hours before the start. On reaching his hotel Walter learned that the Lagonda people, fearing that he was unable to get there in time had nominated in his place a reserve driver who had done the necessary practice. Why had it taken Walter six days after the Senior TT had ended in the Isle of Man on 8 June to reach the Sarthe Circuit? We do not know, but his friend Harry Perrey told me that Walter could be too casual in such matters.

Whatever the cause it was a great pity because later on the day of his arrival he went up to the course for practice with the other members of the team. The excitement and glamour of a big international contest was now upon him and he immediately responded. On his third lap of the 10·7-mile course, which in those days extended from Pontlieue Corner to Mulsanne, Walter flashed his car through the dust and smoke of Le Mans 20 seconds faster than any other Lagonda driver. Whereupon that most genial of men, 'Bertie' Kensington-Moir, the Lagonda team manager, used his powers of persuasion to try and reinstate the famous racing motorcyclist in the team, but not even he could alter the decision of the Managing Director, General Metcalfe.

So Walter had the frustrating experience of being left out of one of the great races which saw an epic struggle between the black American Stutz and the green British Bentleys. After a race of changing fortunes, the final victory went to Woolf (Babe) Barnato and his co-driver Rubin. It was to be the first of the future Bentley Chairman's three successive Le Mans triumphs. At this distance in time we do not know why Walter had arrived so late, but his friend Bert Perrigo felt that in most instances, Walter would have had a good reason. Unfortunately, Walter was left to reflect on a missed opportunity.

CHAPTER 16
FROM THE BALTIC TO ALGIERS

In the previous six years of professional road racing Wal Handley had limited opportunities to make his mark in what was becoming known as the 'Continental Circus'; this was the group of British riders and machines that made their way from circuit to circuit on mainland Europe. The TT had been seen as the vitally important race meeting for the sale of British machines, the continental races much less so. In any case in those days there were only three races that really counted; the TT, the French and Belgian Grand Prix. Walter's comparatively rare appearances in Europe had hitherto been chiefly limited to the latter event in which he had already gained two class wins, the 250cc at Dinant in 1923 and the 350cc at Spa two years later.

By 1927 the number of races gaining support from British riders and manufacturers increased as the more enterprising spirits ventured further afield. In 1928 Walter began spending most of his time in Geneva. There, in company with Dougal Marchant, he was about to embark on a spectacularly successful schedule with AJS and Motosacoche. In the space of eighteen months their travels ranged from the shores of the Baltic to Algiers, taking in Vienna, Rome, Monza, Le Mans, Monterey, Barcelona, the Benelux countries and the famous Nürburgring.

Here was a life of high adventure at a time when travel was expensive and enjoyed by very few. Walter was aware that people tended to over glamorise. Walter wrote:

Some people think that the life of a racing man is just

one long holiday moving from country to country –
fêted everywhere. Believe me it is nothing of the kind.
[But he added] I shall never tire of travelling among
foreigners and seeing strange sights and places.

What a pity those two raconteurs, Handley and Marchant, are
not here to enliven the story in their own inimitable style.

They were soon making their presence felt on the race circuits
of Europe. Ted Mellors wrote:

> The combination of Walter and Dougal Marchant
> was indeed a formidable one, and rival camps had
> many sleepless nights when their entry was in the
> programme.

Fortunately, Walter's first ride after leaving Rex Acme was
not typical of what was to follow. He entered the 1928 Belgian
Grand Prix on his new camshaft AJS 350cc model and led the
race only to retire with engine trouble. The lead was then taken
up by Jimmy Guthrie (Norton) for a short while before he too
was obliged to retire. It was the first time these two famous
racing men had met, but it would not be the last.

What was especially noteworthy over the race programme
with AJS and Motosacoche was the number of times Handley
was to win races on what were for him strange new courses.
Harry Perrey, who knew Walter well, summarised his attitude
as follows: 'Right, these people know this course – I've never
been here before, so I've got to show them what I can do.'
Walter could memorise a course quickly, one ride round and
he would quickly take it all in. He was to win his next six races
in this fashion.

Marchant's new overhead camshaft Motosacoche machines
were not ready for the Dutch TT, the French or the German
Grand Prix, but very appropriately they were ready for the
Swiss Grand Prix. That year it was run on the flat 5.5-mile,
triangular Meyrin circuit, near Geneva. It was here that Wal

Handley made his first appearance for the Swiss company. Since 1924, when the Swiss Grand Prix had entered the racing calendar, it had grown steadily in importance and in 1928 it gained the honour of being designated the 'Grand Prix des Nations'. It was the most international motorcycle race up to that time with not only British and Swiss entries, but also Italian, French, German and Belgian riders and machines. The total entry of one hundred and nine included forty-nine British riders in the three races, 250cc, 350cc and 500cc. Since

This is the Motosacoche designed by Dougal Marchant.
A fast and powerful bike but heavy, note the thick frame housing it.

the latter two events were not run concurrently, Walter took the opportunity to enter both races and he proceeded to win them amidst considerable Swiss enthusiasm.

Each race showed up a different aspect of Walter's character. At the start of the 350cc event there was thunder over the Jura and heavy rain fell. After taking an early lead Walter took a fall on a patch of oil and bent things pretty badly. Ever strong in adversity he was next seen at his pit straightening things with a hammer,

In 1928 the Swiss Grand Prix in Geneva was designated the Grand Prix of Europe.
Here is Walter Handley (Motosacoche), number 8,
the eventual winner, leading Stanley Woods (Norton) in the 500 class.

before setting off in 12th position to fight his way back through the field to win by over two minutes from second placed Guthrie (Norton) at 68·35 mph. On the following day in the 500cc race Walter found his Motosacoche being slipstreamed by riders keen to get a tow. Stanley Woods, being the great speed exponent that he was, succeeded in hanging on to Walter and, try as he might, the Motosacoche rider found Stanley still tucked in almost wheel to wheel – the famous pair travelling together at around 100 mph along the straights. Walter coolly calculated that he might lose Stanley at a particular bend where there was a slip road, and leaving braking to the last possible moment he sent Stanley into the slip road, no mean achievement. It was a perilous manoeuvre, but it had worked and Walter went on to win the 250-mile race after 3 hrs, 19 mins, 2 secs at 74·8 mph, Ernie Nott and Graham Walker, both riding Rudge-Whitworth, taking the second and third places. The Handley–Marchant partnership had triumphed at the first outing, they were 'Champions of Europe'.

Walter was now twenty-six years old and a bachelor. Like most young men he liked to travel unfettered by family responsibilities. Road racing made this possible, it was thrilling, exciting and dangerous. It was because of the danger that Walter felt that the time for him to think seriously about marriage would be after he had hung up his helmet and racing leathers. Any other decision would be unfair to all concerned. Although no flirt, Walter certainly enjoyed female company, and once when asked which courses he preferred, he replied with that quiet drawl of his, 'Those with the best social amenities!' It was only after the races were over that he would join in the social life. Before a race he took his preparation seriously.

After the Swiss Grand Prix there was scarcely any time to relax. Almost immediately he travelled to the shores of the Baltic for the German Kolberg races. Prior to the Hitler war Kolberg was in Germany, but today it is inside Poland and has been renamed Kolobrzeg. True to his form Walter covered the 206·5 miles on his 350cc AJS at 62 mph for another decisive victory. The winner of the 500cc class was C. T. 'Count' Ashby who had also won the 250cc class of the Swiss Grand Prix, sadly these were poor Ashby's last triumphs for he lost his life during the TT races the following year.

Less than three weeks later Walter was in Vienna for the Austrian Grand Prix. The circuit was of the triangular type situated just three miles south of the Austrian capital. It was an unusual race in that it was scheduled to run against the clock, lasting for six hours exactly. Within this time limit Walter's 350cc AJS covered 355 miles at 59·2 mph to finish 22 miles ahead of the next man and three miles ahead of the 500cc class winner. Six hours in the saddle at racing speed is a tremendous test of physical and mental endurance by any standard, especially on the motorcycle frames of 1928. It was the longest race that Handley ever took part in.

Walter's run of success continued into 1929 as the Motosacoche programme got into top gear. He began in April with a 500cc victory in the Grand Prix of Algiers on the Staoueli course. He was the only British competitor and made a great impression. In just under an hour he covered the 69 miles at a record speed of 73 mph – his nearest rival finishing two laps behind. Amazingly, just after the Algiers Grand Prix, he found time to return to Birmingham, to open the new Perry Barr Speedway for his old friend Jack Parker.

Just under a month later at the Tre Fontane, near Rome, Walter first raced Dougal's new creation, a 248cc single overhead camshaft Motosacoche producing a formidable 27 hp

Algiers, April 1929: Wal Handley, standing, (Motosacoche) wins the 500cc Algerian Grand Prix at 73mph. In the background is Dougal Marchant.

running on alcohol. The 250cc class of the Royal Italian Grand Prix went to Wal Handley at the record speed of 63·8 mph. The race was memorable for being the first occasion in which the Italian Guzzis had suffered defeat on their home territory at the hands of a 'foreign invader'. The cries of 'Bravo Ahndelaye' had scarcely died down when Walter's run of success was broken in the 500cc race when, while leading, a burst tyre put him out, but not before gaining another lap record at 70·2 mph.

In due course arrangements were made for the victorious motorcyclists to receive the blessing of his Holiness, the Pope. To the horror of the Italians, Walter, fiercely independent and jealous of his dignity, refused, and so he was escorted out of Italy by his indignant hosts! Walter was a person who was afraid of no-one, no matter how powerful or influential, and although in one sense we can admire this sturdy attitude, he might have been even more successful in life had he been able to curb it.

Generally one could consider 1929 to have been a very successful year for Walter on the continent where his Motosacoche machines gained five wins and 10 record laps. The models were very fast and it was the first year in which Walter had competed in all the major European race meetings. Unfortunately various packets of trouble prevented his tally of successes from being a 'razzle-dazzler'.

The first in a series of disappointments came in the French Grand Prix, the one important road racing classic that was to continually elude him. At the Circuit de la Sarthe he had been well in contention with the leaders up to the half way stage, when the frame of his 500cc Motosacoche snapped. They were heavy bikes and a broken frame inevitably led to retirement. The eventual winners replicated the Isle of Man TT result – 500cc Charlie Dodson (Sunbeam); 350cc Freddie Hicks (Velocette); and 250cc Syd Crabtree (Excelsior). Nor was Walter able to repeat his triumph of the previous year in the six hour Austrian Grand Prix. With the race nearly five hours old and leading comfortably, the 500cc Motosacoche died on him. There was nothing for it but to push this heavy machine the three miles from the Laxenburg Chaussee through the pouring rain to the pits. Dougal diagnosed lubrication trouble and so there was nothing for it but to wait patiently on the course. At 4 PM the race was due to end, and right on cue Walter pushed across the line for his fifth place. Up to 2·45 PM when he stopped, the Motosacoche had covered nearly 300 miles at 62·6 mph. The overall winner, Simcock (Sunbeam) had covered 360 miles at 60 mph. Walter's appearance in this race with his head bandaged drew some comment at the time, and the explanation is worth relating for the interesting light it throws upon the problems of racing men long before the days of world wide air travel schedules.

On most of their journeys Handley and Marchant used a fast 30 cwt Chevrolet Truck and took turns at driving. The rear of the van was converted into a 'drawing room' with deck chairs and a table. It was their mobile headquarters. On this particular occasion they were nearing Vienna at the end of a long journey and they were both feeling tired. Walter had found himself almost dozing at the wheel and had narrowly missed some telegraph poles. He and Dougal decided that they could not drive any further and reluctantly handed the wheel to their French mechanic, of whose driving they had already had a foretaste! They threw themselves into the deck chairs and were immediately asleep, only to be awakened by the feeling you get when, to use Walter's own phrase, 'you make a bad loop through the air.' The Frenchman had gone to sleep whilst driving and the heavy truck had plunged down the banked side of the road into a field turning right over in the process. No-one was badly hurt despite being shot out of the back of the truck with accompanying chairs and tables. It was the sort of story that Walter would love to tell, leaving his listeners amused at the dry way he would relate it, his slight lisp adding to it.

There were two other major race meetings in 1929 where the Handley–Marchant partnership came away empty handed. That year the Grand Prix des Nations was held at Monza, and in an event thoroughly dominated by the Italians, Walter's 250cc Motosacoche failed him early in the race. Then right at the end of the season in October, the Spanish Grand Prix was designated the Grand Prix of Europe for the first time. Although again foiled by engine trouble when leading both the 250cc and 500cc races, Walter did leave Spain with the respective lap records. He had produced some thunderous riding on a course that, judged even by the standard of the time, was not easy. The race was held on the 10-mile Circuit de la Ametlla, situated about

20 miles inland from Barcelona near the town of Granollers. It consisted of the four sides of a square and was made up of narrow local roads, full of twists and turns, with steep drops on either side of tree lined gradients! Despite or because of these difficulties the races were a triumph for not only the skill of the British riders, but also for the reliability of their machines. The respective winners of the 500cc, 350cc and 250cc classes were Tim Hunt (Norton), Leo Davenport (AJS) and Frank Longman (OK Supreme).

Graham Walker would surely have won a prize, had there been one, for the most mascot conscious rider of all time. Graham was reputed to wear not only a bronze tortoise sewn on his jacket, but also suspended from his neck a shilling piece rubbed smooth on one side, a pair of Alec Bennett braces, one of Alec's pullovers several sizes too small for him, and a pair of stockings under his boots! Compared to Graham, Walter was an 'also ran' in the mascot department, but like many riders he was not without superstition. Perhaps his notorious bad luck encouraged him to take counter measures! He sported a little stuffed monkey which, with its little thumb to its nose, was fitted onto his back mudguard.

Half jokingly, Walter attributed the success he was having to this powerful talisman. When, at about this time, he eventually lost his little monkey he was really upset and wrote letters to the motorcycling journals imploring the finder, if any, to return it. It says a lot for the affection in which he was held that, while the mascot remained on the missing monkeys' list, sympathisers in many countries sent him gift replicas before, to his delight, the original arrived, having been found on the Isle of Man TT Course. Whether the little stuffed monkey was powerful 'medicine' or not, its return coincided with wins at Assen, Spa and Nürburgring.

The Dutch TT in 1929 was memorable for one of those wins on first acquaintance of the course and also for a flash of the well-known Wal Handley temperament. It was run on the Drente Circuit, near Assen, a course noted for its narrowness being flanked on either side with deep dykes for the unwary! Walter arrived late the previous evening and had only time to put in a touring lap before the race. Yet, from the massed start his 250cc Motosacoche streaked away to such good purpose that, after 10 laps he had caught five riders on 350cc machines who had started two minutes earlier. The win was completed in just under two hours at 68·39 mph. The other classes run concurrently produced all British triumphs, the 175cc and 350cc trophies going to Syd Crabtree (Excelsior) and Freddie Hicks (Velocette) respectively.

However, the real drama so far as Wal Handley was concerned came in the 500cc race which was held after lunch. There had been a thunderstorm just before the start, but despite wet roads Walter's first lap beat 75 mph from a standing start. This gave him a lead of a few hundred yards from Charlie Dodson (Sunbeam) and Stanley Woods (Norton). His third lap created a new lap record at nearly 80 mph – Walter's sheer speed and pressed down riding position making him easily recognisable to commentators and Press reporters alike. His troubles began when he pulled in to refuel. The 500cc engine running on alcohol on a wet day proved difficult to restart. When Walter finally got going he made up ground to the extent that he had caught the leader, Dodson, on the 9th lap. This was commented on at the time since Charlie Dodson had, after his two Senior TT wins of 1928 and 1929, gained the reputation of being something of an expert in wet race conditions.

The final Wal Handley sensation took place near the pits at the end of the next lap. The Motosacoche would not be tempted back to life after the second refuelling. Again and again Walter made his run and vaulted into the saddle – but it was no use. Then in a sudden surge of fury, Walter picked up the bike and threw it bodily into the ditch. Tyrell Smith (Rudge) had pulled into the pits behind Walter and remembered the incident forty years later when we met. Walter's temper was well known and it showed up vividly on this occasion, but Tyrell felt that it was very understandable: 'You are not in this world when you are racing, your nervous system is keyed up – I can quite understand how poor Walter felt.'

The Rudge team, of which Tyrell Smith was an important part, was beginning the most successful period in its history and this race was one of its early successes being won by Tyrell's team mate, Ernie Nott, with Graham Walker (Rudge) pipping Dodson for second place.

On the following Sunday the Belgian Grand Prix was due to be held at Spa. So the British contingent lost no time in getting across the frontier to the Hotel de Portugal. The Francorchamps Circuit is by any standard an exacting course, especially so in the pre-war period. Its many hairpins and bends, keep on bending, to make it very challenging. Its difficult nature meant that it was tailor made for corner artists like Wal Handley. Marchant decided to enter Walter in the 350cc class, it proved a wise decision. It was a remarkable victory, for despite a collision, Walter managed to retain control and sweep on to secure his third Belgian Grand Prix in seemingly effortless style.

In most continental races at this time all classes were run together. Walter wrote:

> I was negotiating a bend which I knew I could just squeeze round at about 95 mph, Imagine my horror at finding a foreign competitor on a 175cc motorcycle cutting right across in front of me, just touring and taking all the road. Well I hit him! There was nothing else possible. The impact bent my handlebars at least three inches backwards and downwards, but although I had some really nasty moments I did not come off.

It was the likelihood of incidents like this that made continental events infinitely more dangerous at the start than the Isle of Man TT. Many of the continental competitors were less skilled and consequently could not be relied upon to do the right thing at the right time. Furthermore, unlike the TT races where competitors start at timed intervals with the same size of machine, the typical continental race had a massed start of all classes. It was for reasons such as these that, based upon his own

Wal Handley (Motosacoche) after winning the 1929 350cc Belgian Grand Prix despite a collision; note the bent handlebar. Marchant has the open necked shirt.

experience, Walter always opposed the introduction of massed starts in our own Isle of Man TT races.

Very few people watching the 1929 Belgian Grand Prix knew that Handley had had such a close shave. Ted Mellors wrote:

> The outstanding thing about this race, to me, was the terrific speed at which Wal Handley twice passed me on a 350cc Motosacoche. In fact he made the fastest lap of the day on this machine; it was a joy to see.

It was again the 350cc Motosacoche which, in the hands of Walter, mastered that most challenging of road circuits, the Nürburgring, set near where the little town of Adenau nestles in the Eifel Hills some 43 or so miles south of Cologne. This specially constructed course was set in delightful mountain scenery with pine clad slopes on all sides, the Nürburg Castle set on its hilltop added a touch of romance. To say that the course is like a figure of eight is somewhat misleading. True, it had two loops one just over 14 miles, the other nearly five miles or so in circumference, but both seen from above appeared as irregular rings with innumerable loops and curves. In the 1920s a total of one hundred and seventy-two such sudden twists, curves and switchbacks were reported, with at least one of the hills offering a gradient of 1:4. At the centre of this irregular figure of eight, two parallel lines ran in front of the flag bedecked grandstands, pits and garages. It was an impressive sight.

It was an impossible course for a newcomer to learn and so it was a pure test of riding ability, quick reflexes and courage. Wal Handley led his 350cc class throughout to win the German Grand Prix at his first attempt in his usual irrepressible style. Another British rider, Tyrell Smith (Rudge) won the 500cc class on his first visit to the circuit with the terrifying reputation. The Nürburgring has never lost its awesome power. By the 1970s it was felt, in the opinion of many racing men, to be too dangerous and in 1984 a new circuit was opened, but it has never gained the acceptance that the old road circuit had in the minds of race enthusiasts.

Nothing in Wal Handley's experience could have prepared him for his next challenge, one of the longest and most sinuous of the European hill climbs. Linking the Swiss towns of Altdorf and Linthal is the Klausen Pass which, according to George Eyston in his book, *Motor Racing and Record Breaking,* was probably the most important hill climb in Europe. Walter arrived at the Hotel William Tell and Post at Urnerboden, too late to gain any detailed knowledge of the course. It seems doubtful whether he would have been greatly assisted by an earlier arrival since the Pass is reckoned to have over one hundred bends and corners plus a score of hairpin turns. In short an impossible course for any racing man to memorise; it was another event that would test the rider's skill, judgement and courage.

In hill climbing a man is racing against the clock. Time pressure brings its own problems. If a rider misjudges a turn he comes out badly placed for the next bend, while skids can be potentially lethal as the rider can find himself overlooking

Walter roars up the 1929 Klausen Pass Hill Climb to win the 350 class at record speed on his Motosacoche.

sheer drops of several thousand feet. Into the narrow and dusty mountain road of the Klausen Pass Walter hurled his 350cc Motosacoche. He did so to such good effect that his time of 17 mins, 52 secs was not just a new record, it had beaten the previous best performance by a whopping 31 seconds. This was simply amazing since it usually took several years to chip away as much as a full half minute from the Klausen.

Although Walter's average speed of just over 45 mph may sound slow, this is to take no account of the physical and mental strain of climbing to a maximum height of over 6,300 feet in just over 13 miles of constant unremitting concentration. With hardly a pause to admire the snowy crests of the Clariden, Chammliberg and Sheerhorn peaks, Walter climbed again this time in the 500cc class. It seems likely that his earlier ride had inevitably taken its great toll. This is the most likely explanation of the crash on one of the hairpin bends which ended his fine effort. Even so there can be no doubt that his success in the Klausen Hill Climb, still described in a modern travel guide as an 'alarming' pass, was another example of Walter's amazing versatility. In his first full season in Europe Wal Handley's efforts had met with some disappointment but also considerable success.

CHAPTER 17
SELF-SACRIFICE

It has been remarked upon before that it was the races Wal Handley lost which produced the purest drama. This was certainly true of the 1929 TT meeting which produced one of the classic struggles in TT history and also the fastest race the Island had seen up to that time. Sadly the races were also marred by tragedy.

For the demanding Isle of Man course Walter had chosen to ride AJS rather than the heavier Motosacoche machines. In the 1920s it was the exception rather than the rule for European manufacturers to compete in the Isle of Man so Walter's decision was not so surprising. This was the first time Walter had ridden on the Island circuit using machines with their own power units. The AJS bikes had overhead camshaft engines with heavily webbed crankcases, dry sump lubrication, a new four-speed gearbox with cam operating striking gear, and also for extra safety twin sets of upper link forks.

Although they were reputed to be fast and reliable, Walter said that the 'Ajays, tended to dispute who was in charge on some corners,' and put the wind up himself as well as the spectators! Nevertheless Walter was confident of putting up a good show with the help of his friend Nigel Spring, the Norton track expert, who had been engaged by the Wolverhampton firm. Pre-race speculation for the Junior TT tended to favour the Velocette camp. A year earlier they had made history by being the first 350cc machines to lap the island at over 70 mph, taking the first two places in the process, moreover they were known to be faster in 1929. Even so there were those prepared to favour Handley's AJS, and there was Dodson's Sunbeam or the Nortons of Woods and Simpson to consider.

Right from the word go, the Junior Race proved to be a real scrap. On a bright sunny day, with a stiff southwesterly breeze blowing, the crowds were kept on their toes with an opening lap which left only 38 seconds separating the first six riders. Simpson, making his island debut on a Norton, led off with a record lap in 31 mins, 59 secs closely followed by his new team mate Stanley Woods: but the day of the Nortons had not yet arrived, they were soon in trouble and dropped off the Leader Board.

The lead was now taken by Birmingham's Freddie Hicks (Velocette) riding in only his second TT, pursued by last year's winner and his team mate, Alec Bennett, in third position was Wal Handley. Hicks proceeded to give a jolt to the popular view that Brooklands' exponents were of little use in the Isle of Man. By the end of the third lap Walter had slipped into second place by gaining a one second advantage over his friend and rival, Alec Bennett. On his fourth lap Walter captured the lap record at 31 mins, 58 secs, just beating Simpson's earlier effort. Hicks replied with 31 mins, 55 secs at 70.95 mph to keep the crowd agog. By the end of the fourth lap Hicks was just 13 seconds ahead of Handley who was only five seconds ahead of Bennett.

At the end of the sixth lap Walter was only 17 seconds behind the leader, and as he passed the grandstand he was seen to give a low sweeping thumbs-up to the AJS camp – surely he was going to catch Hicks in what would be one of the great finishes of all time. He might well have done so but for his old enemy, mechanical trouble. It seems almost incredible to relate, but on his 7th and last lap Walter's AJS was slowed by a brake 'seized on'. The springs attached to the brake shoes had snapped and the fragments had become embedded in the linings and fouled the brake drum. Yet, Walter still managed to come in second, thus getting in between the Velocettes of Hicks and Bennett. Typical of the period there were only sixteen finishers out of forty-three who started.

It was a popular and well earned win for the twenty-eight-year-old Hicks at the record speed of 69·71 mph. In the paddock afterwards, Walter, who had finished at 69·29 mph, smiled and simply said, 'I did my best, but I could not catch Hicks.' After paying tribute to the winner, Ixion wrote:

> Walter Handley, to the best of my belief, was on a motorcycle 10 mph slower and only got as close as he did because he is the world's finest road racer. My Adam's apple absolutely jammed up tight when I saw some of his 80 mph kerb shaving.

Later Ixion described Walter's riding style in these terms:

> He welded his body into a miraculous unity with his machines, steel merging into muscle and muscle into steel. He never seemed to be fighting his mount.

Certainly this race provided some of the finest action pictures of Wal Handley, the stylish crouch, the very attitude of his body willing his machine to go faster.

In the Lightweight race, held in mid-week, Walter was racing on an OK Supreme – with the familiar Blackburne type engine and was one of the favourites. He had been holding a strong fifth place when, at the end of the fourth lap, a broken valve spring prevented him leaving his pit. It was a race that had seen a good tussle between Syd Crabtree (Excelsior), the eventual winner, and the unfortunate Pietro Ghersi (Guzzi), whose machine had also broken down. Out of thirty-four starters only thirteen managed to finish. This race left Walter hoping for better consolation in the Senior Race.

After the wet Senior TT of 1928 had given everyone the 'slows', the official record for the course was a lap in 31 mins, 52 secs put up by 'Tim' Hunt in the Amateur Races. Wal Handley proceeded to cause a sensation by demolishing this time with an unofficial practice lap of 30 mins, 50 secs at 73·4 mph. Had he

Wal Handley (AJS 348cc) in the 1929 Junior TT: he came in second to
Freddie Hicks (Velocette 348cc). Here is Handley banked over at Creg-ny-Baa.
'No-one rode so resolutely or in lovelier style,' wrote Ixion.

In the Junior TT 1929 Wal Handley (AJS 348cc) banked over on the turn at Quarter
Bridge. The lamp post occupied its dangerous position for many years.

done it by using alcohol? No, it was true enough. After Birkin had been killed during a TT practice session in 1927, legislation had been enacted to close the roads during practice. Walter had taken full advantage of this fact. Down Bray Hill at 90–95 mph his progress had been likened to a 'mountain goat leaping from crag to crag.' At Creg-ny-Baa, spectators gasped as he used all the road. By the end of this meteoric practice ride he had grazed knuckles so close had been his cornering. Despite the presence of the fancied Norton and Rudge teams, with the Sunbeams of Bennett and Dodson also very much in the reckoning, it was no surprise to find Handley tipped as the dark horse choice of many after his very quick practice sensation.

Apparently Walter had decided to fit his 350cc AJS engine into the Senior frame, a surprising decision for which he must have had good reason. His main worry remained the trailing link forks. He had found these to be satisfactory on dry roads but treacherous in damp conditions. In Monday's ideal conditions the trailing forks had behaved admirably allowing him to go really fast; it was to be a very different story on Friday. Heavy overnight rain rattled noisily against the windows of the Douglas hotels and boarding houses where the riders must have stirred uneasily. The wild night had left the course wet and the surface treacherous.

Matters were not helped by the rain coming down heavily again just as the riders wheeled their machines to the start positions. Just as the old hands were muttering darkly about it being like 1928 all over again, the rain ceased as suddenly as it had begun and the sun came out to dry the course. Yet the damage had been done and no fewer than fourteen riders had crashes during this race, many occurring when the race was barely under way at a place called Greeba Bridge. It is situated just over six miles from the grandstand and, in the days of which we write, would be considered a medium left hand bend which would normally be taken fairly fast and safely. On this occasion the leaves from the overhead trees and the rain had rendered Greeba very treacherous. The second rider of the day was the Manchester speedway star, Arthur Franklyn (Scott), who was the first to find himself sliding round the bend on his back. Another rider, Tyrell Smith (Rudge), who led the race in the early stages, remembered how the roads were drying fast, so that it was dry at the point where you normally shut off the throttle, but wet as you neared the bend under the trees. The result was that Tyrell had a hundred-yard skid, 'I took my hand off the front brake as I felt the slide and lack of wheel response, and just reached a dry patch in time.'

Walter Handley, number 15, was not so fortunate. He told what happened:

> I distinctly remember executing a terrific slide at Braddan where there was water on the road. I approached the bridge as near backwards as I've ever been and very nearly killed a Pressman who usually takes up a most dangerous stand at that point. Even the race marshals leaped clear as I squeezed round. Everything was all right at Union Mills and we were going grand through Crosby. Then the Greeba road began to look not too good. I shut off and braked very gently, the machine went into a real dirt track slide from which I divorced myself on the crown of the bridge and spent a few hectic moments rolling away from the AJS which was still chasing me. As I gathered myself together I could hear followers approaching. I remember thinking that someone was bound to get badly hurt.

There is a stone parapet on the right hand side of the bend around the side of which Walter pulled his AJS. He was here working to straighten the footrests, when young Douglas Lamb (Norton) skidded, hit the kerb and was thrown over the handlebars through some bushes against a cottage wall. Walter downed tools and rushed to Lamb's assistance. He lifted the Norton, which had fallen on top of the unconscious rider, and was busy attending to the injured man when further disaster struck. Suddenly the road was blocked with roaring machines and sprawling riders. Jack Amott (Rudge) number 42 and Jimmy Simpson (Norton) number 48 had arrived together, but not in the manner they would have chosen. Jack suffered a broken collar bone and was never able to completely straighten the one arm. Jimmy was also injured and could recall nothing of what had happened. Walter worked frantically to clear the road of injured riders and machines, and did so just before other riders came through at about 60 mph.

All the injured were taken to a nearby cottage. Walter remounted his AJS and went to Ballacraine for assistance. Lamb, the Coventry youngster, was just twenty-two years old and had a broken jaw and had fractured the base of his skull amongst other injuries. He died later that night. So tragedy had marred what had otherwise been a fine race. Charlie Dodson (Sunbeam) had won the fastest TT race of the 1920s at 72·05 mph with a new lap record of 73·55 mph clipping just three seconds off Wal's unofficial practice time.

Amidst the turmoil on the Greeba road Walter had given up his own chances in a race he might conceivably have won. Nigel Spring, who was in charge of the AJS pit told me, 'It was just like Walter to sacrifice his own chances.' An old family friend, who knew Walter well, said, 'this was the moment when we saw the real Wal Handley.' Sportsmen and women, the world over, will always value such action more than any trophy. Tom Loughborough, Secretary of the Auto Cycle Union, wrote to Walter expressing deep appreciation of his conduct:

> The committee realises that your action not only definitely deprived you of any chance of obtaining an award in the race, but also probably prevented other serious accidents to riders who might have come to grief because of machines belonging to fallen riders lying on the course.

Motorcycle road racing is acknowledged to be dangerous, and especially the Isle of Man TT mountain course. The 1929

Walter Handley, a portrait taken in 1929.
He is twenty-seven years old, note the AJS badge in the lapel of his jacket.

series had served to underline this, for in addition to the loss of Lamb, Monday's Junior Race had seen the experienced rider agent, Cecil Ashby, from Kingston-on-Thames, die after receiving head injuries when he crashed at Ballacraine. Despite the obvious dangers, it is a sport that continues to attract young men who are willing to come forward and pit their skill, daring and judgement, especially the latter, against the most challenging road race in the world.

Walter was well aware of the dangers, but he emphasised that he was unwilling to take unnecessary risks. He felt that he had an inner pilot, whom he strove to encourage, which guided him on just how fast he could take a particular corner. He never claimed any credit for this; he saw it as a gift that had been granted him. By now his whole life breathed action, it was the very fibre of his being. At about this time Walter started to learn to fly, his tutor, Flight Lieutenant Tommy Rose, recalled:

> After a while, Walter confided in me that he thought flying rather dull. I saw him race in a TT shortly afterwards, and understood why: of all the dangerous, thrilling lives in the world that must be it.

CHAPTER 18
THE RIDER WITHOUT A MOUNT

In November 1929 came the announcement that the Handley–Marchant partnership had signed up with the FN Company of Liège. The full name, La Fabrique-Nationale d'Armes de Guerre, pointed to the company's origins, but Wal and Dougal were wanted for their motorcycle racing and design skills. After the conclusion of the Englishman's very successful season with the Motosacoche Company such a development was not unexpected, although no-one had tipped the Belgian company to make this coup. Only a month earlier, Walter had taken the 498cc Motosacoche to Montlhéry and captured a number of world records including the 100-kilometre and 50-mile categories at over 108 mph. It was a triumphant note on which to wind up the season, and evidently it had not gone unnoticed.

By now the onset of the depression and the high cost of racing were raising the question of whether British support for road racing would continue. The news that FN had acquired the services of Handley and Marchant was seen as a serious foreign challenge and added to the sense of foreboding. In the event these fears proved premature, there were one hundred and nineteen entries for the 1930 TT races, only slightly down on the year before. Then in late May, the news trickled through that Walter's FN machines, on which he had been entered for the Junior and Senior Races, would not be ready in time. The real drama was about to begin for suddenly it looked as though the TT had lost one of its chief personalities and the rider who had, up to this time, broken more record laps than anyone.

The FN Company obligingly offered to transfer the entries to Handley so that he might ride any other machine he chose. Unfortunately this proved impossible because, since the previous year, the ACU had introduced a new rule in the TT regulations which forbade the change of entrant or machine after the closing date. Too late, by just a few hours, Walter learned that the FN bikes would not be ready. He tried hard to persuade Tom Loughborough, the ACU Secretary, to make an exception in his case so that he could transfer his entry. Remembering Walter's chivalrous action at Greeba in the previous year, the ACU was anxious to help and called a meeting to discuss the situation, but in the end they found themselves bound by their own rules. One journalist summed up the situation:

> Poor Wal Handley, here we have almost every manufacturer in the country only too anxious for him to ride one of their models and yet he cannot get an entry in.

Hopes were expressed that someone would drop out and offer to nominate Handley – but who? The answer came unexpectedly on the first morning of practising. It transpired that Jim Whalley, the rider agent from Bristol, was willing to nominate Handley to ride his privately entered Rudge. Learning of this development George Hack, the Rudge development engineer and team manager disappeared after breakfast to hold discussions with that eccentric genius John Pugh, the Rudge Managing Director. It seems probable that in reviewing Handley's availability the two men were mindful that the 1928 and 1929 Senior TTs had unluckily slipped away from the company's grasp.

In that miserably wet TT race of 1928, Graham Walker's machine had broken down on the last lap when within a few miles of victory. Just a year later Tyrell Smith had been winning, only to have the misfortune of grounding his exhaust when banking over for the turn at Glen Helen. The resultant spill had meant three broken ribs and a lot of pain, but 'the

Irishman without a temperament,' as his team mate, Graham Walker, had once described him, courageously carried on to still come in third. This time there was the chance of making victory certain, so ran the argument, by offering works support to a rider of Handley's class. John Pugh was in something of a dilemma, on the one hand he wanted to secure victory, but he felt it was unfair to his own riders. He finally decided, in a typically sporting gesture, to leave it to the team to decide whether their personal ambitions or the firm's chances should come first.

To understand the full import of the decision the Rudge team was asked to make, one has to remember that Graham Walker, the thirty-five-year-old 'Daddy of the team', Tyrell Smith, and the former works tester, Ernie Nott, had gained notable successes in Ireland, Europe, South Africa and at Brooklands, where Nott on his 500cc model had become the first man regardless of engine capacity to cover 200 miles in two hours. Two weeks earlier, Nott had won the North West 200 at record speed. When later that morning it emerged that Tyrell Smith had turned in an unofficial record time of 31 mins, 29 secs – 72 mph on the new radial four-valve Junior Rudge, the confidence of the works riders was immeasurably strengthened. Clearly the Rudge team had every reason to feel that their chances of TT success were very good.

After the practising was finished, Hack returned with Wal Handley and Jim Whalley to put the 'bombshell' question separately to each member of the team. In essence it came down to this, 'Shall we make certain of victory by having Wal on our side?' Graham Walker described their understandable mixture of emotions:

> Here we were with the intuitive feeling that our bikes were good enough to win and being asked to decide if a far better rider should join the team with the inevitable result that we should say goodbye to our own individual chances of the trophy. I am glad to say

that there was scarcely a moment's hesitation. We all liked Walter immensely and above all we thought the world of John Pugh.

This unanimous decision to give works support to Walter was confirmed by Tyrell Smith to the author.

With the decision taken, Hack called Walter and Jim into the room and gave them the news. Walter's delight was obvious although he only responded with one word, 'good!' Then as they walked out to the garage, Graham heard Hack deliver one of the bluntest speeches he could ever recall. He had heard that Wal Handley was 'difficult,' and he wanted to make it quite clear that, although everything would be done to enhance his chances, he George Hack, was in charge of the camp and would be responsible for everything that was done to Wal's bike. In other words, if Walter would fetch his model each morning, return it after practising with a list of items needing attention and then disappear until the following morning, he Hack, would be pleased. He certainly made it very clear. To everyone's amazement Walter took all this without any adverse reaction.

Hack was a man who commanded respect, not only did his engineering and metallurgical experience with Rudge-Whitworth date back to 1919 he was above all a very strong personality. It turned out that Hack had shown good judgement and done just the right thing. During the whole of the practising period Walter was the perfect team man. To quote Graham again, there was:

> no temperament, no temper – always wisecracking and completely giving the lie to the theory that he was the uncontrolled rocket in a bottle that we had been led to believe.

Walter had responded well to the atmosphere in the Rudge camp which was a particularly happy one – everyone, team manager, riders and mechanics alike being genuine pals.

On the second morning of practice, Walter set out on Whalley's hastily prepared Rudge only to have the gearbox seize up, yet he returned quietly and never said a word. In the Rudge camp they had a fourth motorcycle, Graham Walker's reserve Senior mount, it was known to be in good order and from then on until the day of the race this was the machine that Walter used.

There was little to choose between the 499cc overhead-valve Rudge bikes which were fitted with the latest version of their well tried pushrod, four-valve dry-sump engine design with pent roof combustion. The 1930 version was hardly changed, it had slightly longer connecting rods to reduce side thrust on the piston, and longer induction pipes. Accordingly the frame had been slightly raised and lengthened. The weight was no more than about 300 lbs, this, Sammy James believed, was about half that of the cumbersome looking Motosacoches that Walter had been riding on the continent. Test bed performances revealed that the power units developed a handy 29 bhp at 5600 rpm. The only difference of any note being a slightly lower compression ratio of 7:1 on Walter's machine compared to the 7.25:1 employed on the other Rudge entries. They all had a top speed of about 100 mph.

The next morning Walter went out again and Graham Walker was able to study Walter's brilliance at close quarters:

> He overtook me just up the brow of Creg Willeys, when I did my utmost to hang on to him along the flat plateau before the drop to the eleventh milestone. I knew that the maximum speed of the two models was dead level, but he just crept away from me in an effortless manner, ultimately to disappear into the mist ahead.

As the practising progressed the usual war of nerves between the rival camps gained momentum as the lap times crept nearer to Dodson's 1929 record of 30 mins, 47 secs. The Norton Company had introduced for this year the square bevel box vertical shaft drive that was to become one of their design hallmarks down the years, but Woods, Simpson and Hunt still seemed a little short of speed. Were the Sunbeam riders 'foxing'? Certainly, the Raleighs, prepared by Dan O'Donovan of Brooklands fame, were fast but did their riders have the experience? So ran the arguments but the Rudge camp remained cheerful.

As Walter went about the business of steadily notching up his seven Senior practice laps, he knew that notwithstanding the generous decision of the Rudge team, he could still end up a non-starter. In the belief that he would ride his FNs throughout the 1930 season, he had signed agreements with several firms to use their products. Equally, Jim Whalley had signed similar agreements but with other concerns. Since Whalley was the entrant his list of accessories had been handed in to the ACU, and so Walter had the problem of making his accessories tally with those stipulated by Whalley. As the week wore on a worried Walter found that his backers were persistent in their refusal to release him from his commitments.

As a result of this wearisome dispute, and the time consuming search for a Junior mount, he had left doing the minimum four qualifying laps on his Lightweight machine rather late. For the Lightweight race Walter had been nominated to ride his old love, a Rex Acme Blackburne. It was to have been ridden by Bernard Hieatt, who had tragically lost his life after crashing in the Hutchinson '100' sidecar race run a few weeks earlier at Brooklands. On two successive mornings of the last week of practice Walter had reeled off the necessary laps, the last one at an unofficial record speed to set the cafés buzzing.

On Thursday evening there a new development. With only two practice periods left, Gilbert Emery agreed to nominate Handley to ride his Blackburne-engined Cotton in the Junior TT. On the same evening Walter's spirits rose when he learned that his dispute with the accessory people had been amicably settled. With the clouds lifting at the eleventh hour, Walter set off the following morning determined to do at least two practice laps on the Cotton, in order to stand a reasonable chance of qualifying. Walter must have wanted an early breakfast for the *TT Special* reporters timed him through the two Braddan Bridge bends at 8·6 seconds – the same time attributed to the Junior Nortons of Jimmy Simpson and Stanley Woods. Then at the Highlander, the Cotton said, 'No' – it was after all Friday the thirteenth, and Walter had no choice but to walk to Crosby and get a lift back to the start. From what followed we can guess at his mood! He managed to wheel out his Senior Rudge before the 6 AM deadline and from a standing start and in the face of a blinding sunrise he proceeded to knock 40 seconds off Dodson's record with a time of 30 mins, 7 secs. The next morning Walter dashed off a couple of laps on Emery's Cotton in the vain hope that the ACU would relax their rules and permit him to race in the Junior TT. Meanwhile, Charlie Dodson, showed his hand by rushing his Sunbeam round the course to equal Walter's unofficial record. With that climactic end to the nine day practice period a great week's racing stood in prospect.

Monday's Junior race gave the Rudge Company the most convincing victory since AJS had scored 1-2-3 in 1921. An entirely new and relatively untried radial cylinder head design had proved its reliability by sweeping the board. Tyrell Smith, Ernie Nott and Graham Walker had taken the chequered flag 1-2-3 within 58 seconds of each other. The night before the race Hack had calculated the winning speed on the back of a cigarette packet. His forecast had been within seconds of the actual lap speeds. George Hack had masterminded one of the proudest moments in the history of the Coventry firm.

For Wednesday's Lightweight race Walter was able to discard the pit attendant armband he had worn on Monday, and get back into the racing business. Having put down the fastest lap in practice he was the favourite to repeat his 1927 win on the Rex Acme Blackburne. This feeling had been strengthened since injuries had put out two strong rivals. The unfortunate Pietro Ghersi (Guzzi) had crashed in practice, while in Monday's Junior Race Freddie Hicks had taken a spectacular toss at Quarter

Bridge, providing one of the most dramatic action pictures in motorcycle road racing history.

So imagine the general astonishment when at the end of the first lap it was the South African rider, Joe Sarkis, on the new overhead camshaft OK Supreme who led the race. Sarkis, known to his compatriots as the 'Handley of South Africa', was 36 seconds ahead of Walter and that meant that he was a great deal ahead of everybody else. As Walter flashed past the pits he cast one incredulous glance at Jack Bayley's pit signal and set off to peg back the flying South African. Sure enough at the end of the second lap Walter was only six seconds in arrears after putting up the lap record for the race – 33 mins, 52 secs at 66·86 mph. With Sarkis pulling into the pits to replenish, Wal Handley, riding under the number 13, was now the new race leader, but not for long.

He was about to experience the most frightening thing that can happen to a racing motorcyclist; an unexpected and uncontrollable skid that was to call upon all his years of

Walter on his Rex Acme Blackburne 248cc takes the jump at Ballaugh in the 1930 Lightweight TT. He puts up another record lap before having to retire with a broken oil pipe.

experience. He was streaking down to Braddan Bridge, his compact figure flattened out in the customary style. Those steely wrists of his pinning the bike down to the desired racing line as he called on the engine for more revs. Then suddenly he felt the back tyre slide as though he were riding on ice. Walter slammed the throttle shut, and hung on for dear life with the bike in complete charge. The terrified spectators saw the race leader fighting for his life in one long sickening, decelerating wobble. The machine was behaving like some terrified animal with Walter clinging to it, and keeping it now out of this hedge, now missing that wall, and the speed dropping all the time.

Just when Walter was wondering how it would all end, the machine mounted the pavement and he was able to put his feet down, even he looked rather astonished. Drawing a deep breath of relief, he looked down and then saw his rear tyre drenched in oil. The oil pipe leading from the tank to the crankcase had come apart a few miles back and a steady stream of the black liquid had been running over the back wheel. Walter was bitterly disappointed. Before the race it had been pointed out to Walter that the rider due to hold number 13 in last year's race had lost his life in the Junior TT, but Walter only smiled. Although obliged to retire, Walter came to see this hair-raising episode in a humorous light:

> Unable to take the corner my only alternative was the Pressman, who despite his life of ease, showed a fair turn of speed! [In typical vein he went on] Meanwhile I bounced off the wall, and being still unable to get round the right hand bend, I had to make for the crowd who were blocking the slip road. From a standing start that crowd was commendably quick off the mark!

Unknown to Walter his mother had arrived in the Island for the first time. She became so anxious when her son did not come round on a third lap that she declared she did not want to see him race again, but she did just two days later!

After lying sixth in the early stages of the Lightweight

race, Jimmy Guthrie, the quiet modest garage proprietor from Hawick, riding a great race had gone on to win decisively the first of his six TT victories at 64·71 mph in 4 hrs, 4 mins, 56 secs. He did this on the AJS vacated by his injured team mate, Hicks. Out of thirty starters, only thirteen managed to finish demonstrating once again the demanding nature of the greatest road race in the world.

Despite his setback in the Lightweight race, Walter remained supremely confident for Friday's Senior TT. No one had yet achieved the 30 minute lap, so Walter's decision to back himself to the tune of £20 to lap the course in 29 mins, 40 secs took some beating in the war of nerves. On the Thursday afternoon, before the bikes were handed in, Hack relented and allowed Walter's mechanic, Sammy James, to give the Senior Rudge a final once over. Apart from a few minor riding adjustments, there was very little left for Sammy to do after the Works Rudge mechanics, Jim Dalton and 'Goldflake' Wills had completed their work.

By the late afternoon heavy clouds gathered overhead and in the evening the storm burst. Torrential rain lashing against the windows was hardly conducive to sleep on the eve of a motorcycle race. Throughout the morning of Friday, 20 June, tremendous crowds were reported to be gathering at all the vantage points. The pulling power of the Senior TT was much in evidence in the overnight arrival of six boats from Ardrossan, Fleetwood and Liverpool. They brought in an estimated extra 16,000 visitors. Although they were greeted by a glorious sunrise, the clouds remained low over Snaefell and as the race time drew near the sun disappeared. This circumstance, coupled with the overnight rain, had left damp patches under the trees, and had reduced the general expectation of record speeds, since many felt the conditions bore too ominous a resemblance to the Senior TT of the previous year and the tragic pile up at Greeba.

Some might say that Wal Handley was fortunate to know the lash of misfortune in many years of defeat. It is in the fire of failure that great souls are made, not along the rose red path of victory. It was now his turn and his race, he was ready physically and mentally and no-one ever travelled to glory in as steady a march. In this race he was like steel that had gone through the furnace. At the conclusion of the opening lap, the crowd gasped as Wal roared past the stands 29 mins, 47 secs after he had left the grid to average 76·03 mph. He had become the first rider to lap the course in under 30 minutes. He had taken a 34 seconds lead from Tyrell Smith, but only another 34 seconds separated the next five riders. Despite reports of mist rolling down the mountain, Walter went round again in 29 mins, 45 secs to further increase his lead and incidentally give another fright to his bookie. No rider had previously lapped in under 30 minutes; now Handley had made another piece of TT history by completing two laps in under the hour.

By the end of lap three Walter's first pit stop was scheduled. Despite the need for changing down and braking well back on the Glencrutchery road, he completed the lap in 29 mins, 41 secs at a speed of 76·28 mph. This broke the lap record for the

Wal Handley (Rudge 499cc) in the 1930 Senior TT
gaining speed out of the bend at Ballacraine.

In the 1930 Senior TT Wal Handley stops to take on fuel at the start of the fourth lap. His pit stop of 28 secs is watched by Captain A. W. Phillips of the ACU.

third time and this one turned out to be the fastest lap. It was lucky for Walter's bookie that the Rudge plans required that pit stop, otherwise Walter would have broken through his 29 mins, 40 seconds target. After three laps, the Rudges were running 1-2-3 after Graham Walker had gained third place by completing the only other 'under thirty' circuit in 29 mins, 59 secs. John Pugh, delighted by the Rudge 1-2-3 in the Junior Race, had now

Wal Handley (Rudge 499cc) picking up speed out of the bend at Quarter Bridge.
Ixion wrote, 'He welded his body into a miraculous unity with his machines, steel
merging into muscle and muscle into steel, he never seemed to be fighting his mount.'

backed his men to finish 1-2-3-4 in the Senior, and it looked as
though he might get his wish.

Despite the pit stop and the start of rain being reported from
the mountain box, Walter's fourth lap was only 30 mins, 38 secs
enabling him to make another piece of history, the first rider to
do four laps in under two hours. As the clouds darkened and
rain began to fall on the fifth lap, he now had a nice cushion
lead of 1 min, 43 secs over second-placed Tyrell Smith. The
rain now became general. Even though the conditions were
worsening, Walter continued to take the mountain descent at
speeds approaching 100 mph to maintain an average of 75 mph.
Another 'under thirty' in 29 mins, 44 secs must have sent
Walter's bookie in search of a double scotch! Meanwhile Tyrell
Smith was forced to drop back with a mysterious loss of power.
Later it was discovered that one of the fingers of his exhaust
rocker had broken off, and so for three laps he had only one
exhaust valve in action.

The last two laps were run in dreadful conditions. Visitors to
the beautiful Isle of Man know that no rain is more pervading

or persistent once it sets in on the Island. From a grey murky sky torrential rain fell pitilessly in an unending downpour. The mist had become a solid pall from Waterworks Corner right over the mountain and down to Hillberry. The riders' leathers were completely soaked. Graham Walker described how it was:

> Every movement of our feet was accompanied by the squelching of displaced water and gloves had become like shiny sponges with bubbles oozing from between the fingers every time the brake or clutch lever was gripped. Goggles were also a problem and had to be lifted to let out the rainwater.

With just one lap to go Walter had a lead of just over five minutes, and decided to ease up. However the man by now in second place, Graham Walker, had to hurry after receiving a 'Go like Hell' signal from Hack, who knew that only 12 seconds separated his man from Jimmy Simpson's third-placed Norton.

Taking the slowest turn on the course at Governor's Bridge in the 1930 Senior TT,
a corner that commands respect from even the star riders.
Wal Handley is close to victory as the rain sets in.

Winning in the rain, Wal Handley (Rudge) takes the
chequered flag to win at the record speed of 74·24 mph.

The conditions on that last lap were memorable. Graham nearly
had heart failure as his engine proceeded to cut out on the
descent to Creg-ny-Baa. Then as his speed dropped the engine
cut in again. Mystified he looked down and discovered the
reason, the inch of water covering the road produced a bow
wave from the front wheel at anything over 80 mph and this
washed right over the cylinder head shorting the central plug!

Tom Handley had taken up a position at Hillberry with their
mother. He was feeling understandably anxious as he watched
and waited for his brother to emerge out of the mists. On the
last lap Walter was third on the roads, only Simpson, number
4, and Dodson, number 13, were ahead of number 28. Tom
remembered it as though it were yesterday:

> You could not see more than a few yards up the road,
> then suddenly to our immense relief we saw number
> 28. How Walter could see where he was going at that
> speed I do not know, he had his goggles down over the

white neck bandage, that he alone always wore, and was riding with his head tucked to one side, and then he was gone.

Wal Handley's winning speed of 74·24 mph had left him over three minutes ahead of Graham Walker, who had successfully fought off the determined challenge from third placed Jimmy Simpson. In a race remarkable for the speed of the leaders and the ever worsening conditions, a high proportion of crashes and retirements were to be expected, and sure enough only thirteen of the thirty-nine starters managed to finish. Of these brave thirteen only nine were fast enough to receive replicas, despite Walter's leisurely last lap through, as he termed it, 'the long fog.' If one compares Walter's 74·24 mph with the speed of the winning Senior race a mere eleven years earlier in 1920 at 51·79 mph, one is struck by the fact that in the pre-war era, the period 1920–1930, saw the most marked speed increase in TT history. As Mac McDiarmid has pointed out, over time you come to diminishing returns, with continual improvements in the technology and the course, incremental race speed increases inevitably lessen.

In a race meeting remarkable for the number of landmarks it produced, the BBC had broadcast the TT live for the first time. They covered the last hour of the Senior Race on the 'long wave' and commentaries from the grandstand and Creg-ny-Baa were picked up even in parts of Western Europe. After the race, the BBC tried to fill-in while a broadcaster tramped off in the pouring rain in a vain attempt to find the elusive Handley, to say a few words.

The devastating pace set by Handley, had led some critics to suppose that he was hard on his engines. Yet incredible as it may seem he had not used more than three quarter throttle throughout, to make the 1930 Senior Race the landmark it was. On 23 June at the Civic Reception given by Coventry to the victorious riders and machines, George Hack refuted the idea that Handley was hard on engines. He stated that Walter's

Rudge had ended the race in perfect condition, and that he was told that not since the end of the World War One had an engine finished in such good shape. Walter was the kindest rider with an engine that he had ever experienced.

So how had Handley managed to draw away from the field so effortlessly? According to an article Walter published in *Motor Cycling*, shortly after the race, his success was not, as some people thought, due to years of experience, but as he

It's all smiles after winning the 1930 Senior TT. With Wal Handley is the entrant Jim Whalley. Note the microphone, it was the first year that the BBC had broadcast the TT live.

termed it an 'inner pilot' or instinct that enabled him to bank the machine on the right line and angle when cornering. Every rider has this mental pilot but in the racing man it is very finely developed. So, according to Walter, motorcycle road racing is not a sport in which the proverb, 'practice makes perfect' is wholly appropriate. Foremost is the natural ability which can then be developed through practice.

Tyrell Smith was able to confirm another interesting fact that mystified the Rudge team. Walter used a larger jet, size 62, in the Amal carburettor than the members of the Works team who fitted the more usual size 59. Only Walter could do this without 'eight stroking', and as a consequence he was able to run his engine cooler than anyone else. No-one ever understood then or since how he alone was able to do this. Sammy James told me that it was his technique that accounted for him running his engines so cool. Yet as Walter once said with some feeling, 'You may be the best rider the world has ever seen, but your name's mud without a good machine.' He was quick to acknowledge that in the Rudge, he had ridden 'a marvellous motor,' and the most comfortable machine on which he had ever raced.

For Rudge-Whitworth the 1930 meeting was a total triumph. After Monday's 1-2-3 and the team prize, they had now added 1-2-6-7 and another team prize. Yet although the Coventry firm went on to complete a fine season, we can now see that this was the high tide of their achievements. It is notable that Handley's win was the last occasion that an overhead valve pushrod machine was to win the Senior TT. It was also the last time we saw a near standard road machine, that the public could buy, win the Tourist Trophy.

Walter was undoubtedly the man of the hour. Ixion wrote, 'Wal Handley is definitely the finest road racing genius whom motorcycling has yet produced.' Walter had now won all four of the pre-war solo classes, the 175, 250, 350 and 500 Trophies. He was the only rider ever to do this. There is no precise modern equivalent, the nearest might be the 125, 250, 350 and 500 TT races, in which case only two riders, Mike Hailwood and Phil Read have won all four. Read gained his fourth category on a Suzuki in the 1977 Senior TT, a remarkable seventeen years after his first TT win in 1961.

One might have expected a rider of Handley's natural ability to win more than one Senior TT, the 'Blue Riband' of motorcycle road racing. It is a remarkable fact that during one of the most arduous careers in the history of the sport, spanning some fourteen years in the Island, Walter had only six Senior TT starts, and of these three did not permit him to finish the first lap. Yet out of the remainder he finished twice, and when he did so he was terrific, second in 1926 after that long delay and first in 1930. The position in 1930 was that in nine years of TT racing Walter had not only four TT wins to his credit, but also eight record laps. Only Alec Bennett could surpass this with five TT wins but even he could only lay claim to four record laps, while Jimmy Simpson, a name forever associated with TT record breaking had notched up five record laps in the same period.

It was to prove the peak of Walter's fortune in the TT; for in the world of motorcycle road racing it is the machine that has the final say. Up to 1930 Wal Handley had become famous competing against the world's greatest riders, mostly on his OK and Rex Acme machines. All this was about to change with the emergence of what became known as the 'Norton Supremacy'.

Perhaps Walter had some sense of what was to come. After all, as the man without a mount he had been fortunate to be riding a Rudge with works support. Would 'Dame Fortune smile so readily again?' Over the years Walter brought home many cups, medals and replicas. Yet he never did attach any great importance to the 'loot' of victory, rather the reverse for he gave away more TT replicas than he kept. He was equally generous with his collection of gold cigarette cases that P. J. Evans, a veteran of pre-1914 TTs, used to bestow on lap record breakers. He had more of these, he used to say, than the most suicidal smoker could use, so why not scatter them among his friends. It was the Senior Trophy, the premier award, which meant a lot more to Walter. It was not long in his possession since it is entrusted to the winning entrant for the ensuing year, which in this extraordinary race of records, meant the first successful agent entrant in the Senior TT, Jim Whalley. Walter decided on a sudden whim, that before the magnificent Trophy took its place of honour in Whalley's Bristol showrooms, he would have made, at his own expense, a full size reproduction statuette about 3 feet high. The only detectable difference being that the winged wheel, on which the Mercury, the Roman equivalent of Hermes the Greek messenger of the gods stands, was a solid disc instead of the spoked original. Gazing at it, Walter remarked, 'You never know I may never win another.'

CHAPTER 19
FLYING AND BUSINESS

In the late 1920s aviation was in the news and changing the world. It was also making a strong appeal through the private flying clubs as a fashionable sport. Yet it was still regarded as something very unusual. Walter Handley's greatest relaxation was to come from flying. When did Walter's essential air mindedness begin to take root?

Although Walter's interest in aviation may have been first awakened at Brooklands; he had joined the Midland Aero Club at Castle Bromwich in 1928 and shortly afterwards he began learning to fly in one of their Tiger Moths. This was how the majority of enthusiasts learned to fly. They were sturdy, practical light aeroplanes which Geoffrey de Havilland had designed at exactly the right time.

Flying was a natural extension of Walter's genius for handling mechanical transport. He had the necessary co-ordination and sensitivity of touch that distinguishes the born pilot. People tended to notice Walter's immaculate hands with their long sensitive fingers. They enabled him to handle the controls of his aircraft with extreme delicacy. Even the lightest pull on the control column of a Moth and she is climbing; a finger push forward and she is diving; only a touch on stick and rudder and she is banking.

Walter's progress was astonishingly rapid, and his tutor, the future holder of the London to Cape Town record flight in 1936, Flight Lieutenant Tommy Rose, had no doubt that he had met his best pupil. Tommy mused:

I've taught scores of people to fly, but none of them as good as he. His judgement was never at fault, his hands were beautiful, light as a feather on the controls, but dead sure all the time – and he possessed just the right amount of confidence.

The tests soon came for the 'A' Licence – these included the altitude test and the 'figure of eights test'. In the first he had to show that he knew how to lose height and make a sound approach, and in the second that he could make steep turns with reasonable accuracy, but in both tests landings were of supreme importance. He had to satisfy the Royal Aero Club's observer and give satisfactory oral replies to questions on the rules and regulations of the air before the Air Ministry would have issued the coveted private pilot's licence, which they did on his twenty-seventh birthday. Having the ability to make a good landing is the key to being a sound aviator and Walter's mechanic, Sammy James, who flew with him from Speke after the Isle of Man races, told me that his abiding memory was the smoothness of the landings. 'He was a beautiful flyer,' Sammy told me.

It was reported in January 1929 that Wal Handley had bought from the comedian, Will Hay, one of the finest and most successful fighter aircraft used by twenty-four squadrons of the RFC and RAF in the Kaiser's War – the SE5A. It had a 200 hp Wolseley Viper eight-cylinder engine capable of about 135 mph at 15,000 feet. Four years of war had given the SE5A an interesting cockpit and Walter could read off an altimeter, tachometer, air speed indicator, clinometer, compass, air pressure and oil gauges and a thermometer. Shortly after the TT races, Walter proudly entered his SE5A–GEBTO in the 1929 Kings Cup Air Race with Tommy Rose as pilot. Unfortunately engine trouble forced Tommy to land somewhere in Kent. Despite this disappointment Walter had great faith in GEBTO, he wrote:

> My plane is a good steady flier with a fair turn of speed
> … and it is not so sluggish that I cannot perform

one or two little tricks in it for the amusement of my passengers.

Later Walter acquired a Puss Moth and asked his friend, Bert Perrigo, the BSA expert, to go up with him. Bert recalled what happened:

> He shouted something to me, I couldn't quite hear. Walter shouted again, I still couldn't quite catch it; he obviously wanted an answer so I shouted, 'Yes!' I've never been so frightened in my life. One moment we were level and I could see the horizon. The next moment I didn't know what was happening as it was just all sky! Apparently Wal had asked me if I wanted to loop the loop!

Not surprisingly, Walter enjoyed injecting a bit of excitement into his flying. At Castle Bromwich the Midland Aero Club was in receipt of a request from the RAF to ask, 'a certain pilot to please give more air space when flying over the RAF hangars!'

Walter found it convenient to use the commercial airlines to get to the continental races. By so doing he could take part in the event and return to Birmingham the same evening. His comments sound extraordinarily nostalgic in the days before flying became associated with the delays caused by security worries:

> I can strongly recommend anybody, who wants to go abroad quickly and comfortably, to fly. For the extra expense – and after all it is only £7.50 return to Paris (1930) it is not so much in the long run when one takes into account meals, tips, taxis and time saved.

It was on one of these return flights from Paris when Walter's intuitive understanding of things mechanical suddenly alerted him that all was not well. The plane had left the French coast and was about a third of the way over the channel when, almost subconsciously, Walter felt himself aroused from the book he was reading. One of the two old Farman engines was beginning to miss. Walter was the first passenger to realise what was happening, he glanced up at the two engine rev counters, mounted at the forward end of the cabin, and noted that the needle registering the revs of the port engine was dropping. The pilot made a sharp turn and headed back for France on one engine. As he did so, Walter quickly undid the two cross bracing wires which were laced across the door when all was set for flying. Walter knew that if they came down in the sea there would have been some difficulty in getting out through the door with the wires restricting the exit. Walter's precaution proved unnecessary, but only just, so close was the margin that the pilot had to land on the beach at Le Touquet. An hour later they were off again in another plane from St Inglevert, this time all was well.

It was not long before Walter was elected a member of the Council of the Midland Aero Club and was reputed to be the

Walter with his newly acquired DH60 Gipsy Moth G-ABJJ. The picture was probably taken in 1931 at the Midland Aero Club in Castle Bromwich. Amazingly this aircraft is reported to be still active in air shows across North America.

best pilot on the 'Drome'. In his book, *Racing Through the Century,* Geoff Davison recalled that his first long cross country flight was with Wal Handley. They flew from Castle Bromwich to Hooton in Cheshire on the last day of 1932. Geoff wrote:

> As I flew with him, I realised that he was as fine a pilot as he was a racing motorcyclist. Wilfred Sutcliffe and 'Buster' Heaton taught me my text book flying and got me through my 'A' Licence tests, but it was Wal Handley who put me through my finishing school.

This cross country flight took place not long after Geoff had begun to learn to fly with the help of the club's instructors. Geoff had hoped to reach a reasonable level of proficiency before his efforts were spotted by either Wal Handley or Harold Willis whom he knew were active and experienced members. One day in November his luck ran out. Geoff recalled:

> The wind was tricky, I had been holding off too early, coming in cross wind, doing wheel landings and behaving like a perfect mutt. Buster Heaton nearly despaired of me and we taxied back to the club house.

There on the veranda waiting for Geoff was Walter, 'Er, hello, Wal, I'm, er, trying to learn to fly.'

He gave Geoff the well-known Handley glower, 'So I see, you'll have to keep on trying for quite a bit yet!'

Walter had known Geoff ever since their first meeting back at the OK Works in 1922, but it was their mutual interest in flying and membership of the Midland Aero Club that finally brought them together again and established their friendship. It was also the mutual interest in flying that cemented Walter's friendship with another famous name in the motorcycling world, Harold Willis, the former RN Midshipman and trained engineer, who joined Velocette in 1926 and thereafter took charge of the Hall Green firm's racing programme.

The year 1929 was significant in Walter's life for his career took another new direction. Plans were laid for the launching of the business that was to proudly bear his name in Birmingham for over thirty years – W. L. Handley Ltd – 'The Obvious Firm for Motor Cycles.' Walter had the backing of two men who had played a formative part in his career, Dougal Marchant and Ernie Humphries joined him as directors. The manager was Bert Kershaw, the competitions expert and a man of fine upstanding character, but with virtually no commercial experience.

With hindsight we can see that it was fortunate that Walter and his associates had earlier set aside the issued share capital and sufficient working capital to get the new venture launched. Otherwise, Walter might have lost considerably more than he did in the great financial blizzard of '29. Insofar as Walter's racing career in the 1930s was hindered by a lack of finance, the stock market crash undoubtedly was a damaging factor. It was against this worrying background that Walter's new business began trading on Christmas Eve 1929. There is a picture of Walter and Kershaw standing proudly in the doorway of 14–16 Holloway Head, otherwise known as 'Economy House', both wearing the fashionable plus-fours of the period. Peter Chamberlain of *Motor Cycling* saw the showrooms just after the opening and described the effect:

> … all round the walls are flags and banners won in various continental races and hill climbs, intermingled with numerous photographs of Handley flashing round corners or filling up at the pits. Complete with a good display of the current models the general effect was colourful and pleasing.

Despite these efforts, results were not good. The business made substantial losses in the first two years of its existence and might well have foundered but for Walter's wise decision to bring into the business his brother, Tom Handley, early in 1930. Tom, may not have known much about the motorcycle business but, having worked for many years in the coal industry, he had gained valuable experience in office administration and financial management. It was his brother who, by dint of perseverance and working long hours, almost certainly saved the fledgling company. There were many adverse factors facing the firm at this time, not only the frequent absences through racing commitments of the man the enthusiasts wanted above all to meet – Wal Handley; but also the location in Holloway Head was not ideal, having a rather dubious reputation. As if this were not enough, there were two other factors, the commercial inexperience of the staff, and the fact that most of the popular motorcycle agencies were under the control of the established distributors.

It was, however, the onset of that great economic disaster – the trade depression of the 1930s that really made life difficult. To put this in perspective, after World War One there had been a boom in motorcycle sales. The figures show that the total number of motorcycles in use in Britain had risen in every post-war year up to a peak of 731,298 in of all years – 1929. From 1930 onwards the total number fell each year until 1940 when the figure stood at only 278,300. It's a fact that the 1929 figure wasn't finally overtaken until 1950. One can see that 1929–1930 was not a good time to start a new retail business selling and servicing motorcycles. Could the warning signs have been detected at the time? The increase in the number of motorcycles in use had been steadily dropping year by year since 1926, but it is easy to be wise with hindsight, it was clearly not apparent at the time.

What had happened was that the young men who should have been earning enough to buy a motorcycle were either on short time or were unemployed. Almost overnight there were more motorcycles in dealer's showrooms than customers to buy them. Most of Britain's forty or so manufacturers entered 1931 with half their 1930 motorcycle production still unsold. These symptoms of over production and poor sales were evident in the big price reductions of brand new unsold models of the previous year, this phenomenon persisted right into the second half of the decade. It was not until 1933, when the world slump was lifting, that W. L. Handley Ltd first returned a significant profit.

One of the bright spots amidst the gloom was the meteoric rise in the popularity of dirt track racing. This new sport had been introduced to this country in 1928, and a whole new business was created. The Douglas Company had been the first in the field with a specialist dirt track machine, the agency for which, in Birmingham, was held by Colmore Depot. The Rudge Company had responded with a very successful bike that had parallel valves with bolt-on rockers. Walter's friendship with John Pugh helped secure the Rudge agency and the business was successful in its first year in selling a large number of these dirt track machines. Sammy James, who had responsibility for this side of the business, could recall delivering these Rudges over a wide area including London.

So how good a businessman was Walter Handley? Geoff Davison wrote that in his opinion Handley was an astute businessman who could spot flaws in a balance sheet as quickly as a chartered accountant. Walter's brother, Tom Handley, agreed with the comment about his brilliance with figures, but had his reservations. Tom wrote:

> You ask me if I considered Walter to be a good businessman, you know that I have a great affection for his memory and also his personal character – but my answer must be a reluctant 'No' for reasons that one would consider to be an asset in his personal character, but a liability in the hard world of business.

He explained how he saw things:

> In business, experience has taught me that to be successful one often has to be ruthless and indifferent to 'hurting' people – and Walter was not that sort of person.

Looking back we can admire Walter for being enterprising. He opened a car business in Birmingham's Broad Street, a hairdresser's on the Stratford Road, and finally Hipwoods, an engineering business in Camden Street that he acquired three years before the outbreak of World War Two. His brother agreed that he was enterprising but felt that you had to be on hand to keep a watchful eye on your business, not just invest the money and leave it to others. He added, 'Walter was too kind and trusting of people's abilities.'

These businesses required closer attention than Walter was able and perhaps willing to give to them. This applied particularly to the business that bore his name because lots of motorcycle enthusiasts came to the showrooms hoping to meet their hero and went away disappointed. If flying gave Walter relaxation, his business interests gave him concern and prevented the full concentration of his energy and ability on the area where his true genius could have blossomed – the road racing circuits of Europe. Yet, it is only fair to point out that Walter was far from being a wealthy man who could afford racing as a pastime. Nor did the racing game carry with it anything like today's financial rewards. His aim seems to have been for his business enterprises to bring eventual financial security and the independence he cherished.

CHAPTER 20
ADVENTURING HOME AND AWAY

There was no evident sign of disappointment as the cheerful party from the FN works motored northwards from Adenau, the scene of the recent German Grand Prix. The new racing FN had not been ready for the 1930 Isle of Man TT and now it had been a non-starter at the Nürburgring after tests had shown that the steering of the FN at speeds over 100 mph had not been perfected. Hopefully the bike's high speed handling problems had now been ironed out in the Liège works ready for the Dutch TT. On they drove through the university town of Bonn and on to Cologne. In true holiday spirit they turned away from the industrial towns of Dusseldorf and Duisburg, to cross into Holland at Venlo. Then along a wonderfully straight road they reached Nijmegen, where they crossed the Waal on a huge steam ferry.

The next river crossing was effected by a flat bottomed boat driven by the flow of the water. The boat was anchored by a long rope secured some distance upstream in the middle of the river. Walter, who was enjoying every mile of this trip, watched incredulously as the ferryman, by manipulating the rudder, was able to get the unwieldy craft to drift from one side to the other. Their arrival at Arnhem was a pleasant interlude, the town's cleanliness with its smart villas and shops creating a favourable impression. The next day they continued their westward progress through Zutphen, Deventer, Zwolle and Meppel, to reach the Hotel de Graf in Assen. At last the FN was about to make its long awaited debut on the Circuit Van Drente in the Dutch TT.

The new FN attracted a lot of attention when finally the wraps were taken off. The 495cc overhead camshaft engine was built into a massive low slung unit construction with the four speed gearbox. Unfortunately, it was housed in quite the heaviest looking frame that spectators could ever recall seeing. The down tube alone had a diameter of two and a quarter inches. Another worry was the sheer complexity of the gear change. The operating pedal was attached to the shaft by chain, and moved the dogs through an ingenious hair spring selector mechanism. Apparently Walter called it 'the comic opera.' It was this gear change arrangement that brought Walter's FN debut in the Dutch TT to an early end. On the first lap his initial optimism was dashed, when he discovered he could not get out of second gear. None of the other three ratios were obtainable except by moving the layshaft by hand, very vexing but all in the game.

With the uncertain danger from the FN ended, the way was clear for the British riders and machines to continue their string of successes in continental Europe. In the 500cc race, Graham Walker (Rudge) repeated his victory in the German Grand Prix, while Simcock's AJS took the 350 class. The only foreign triumph was in the 250 class which was won by Arthur Geiss (DKW).

After the races, Walter and Dougal Marchant were motoring south on the road to Amsterdam, alongside a canal, when they were overtaken at speed by a young motorcyclist, evidently imbued with the desire to emulate the 'racers'. On rounding the bend, Walter and Dougal found the straight, narrow road empty of traffic for as far as the eye could see. Curious, they pulled up and looked into the canal and were in time to pull the slime covered motorcyclist and his poor pillion passenger out. All that was left of the bike were a few glug like bubbles as it sank.

A week later Walter and Dougal arrived in Spa for the Grand Prix of Europe, ominously scheduled for 13 July. This time they were confident that they had finally overcome the difficulties that had so far bedevilled the FN. Walter got away well in the massed start and had a good lead at the end of the first lap. Then on the second lap, the engine seized. A puzzled and disheartened Walter managed to get the engine going again to ride sadly into the pits. Dougal and Walter then held an examination and this is what they found. Someone had removed some screws from the crankcase and pushed, probably using a wire, some rag into the oil passages of the engine. 'There is no doubt whatever that it was done deliberately by someone who was hardly very kindly disposed towards me or my FN,' wrote Walter. They also found no less than one and three quarter litres of spirit in the oil sump, hardly the best lubricant. The saboteur was making quite certain that the FN would not go very far. The machine was dismantled before the FN directors and they were furious. It was thought that internal jealousies had prompted the foul play. At Liège, the company employed some 10,000 people, and it was impossible for Handley and Marchant to keep a check on everyone coming into the experimental shop. Every care was taken to guard the model before the race, but Walter believed that the saboteur had done his dirty work before the machine left the works. He was probably right, but it was generally acknowledged that security was more lax at continental events than in the Isle of Man. Walter was very upset. It was one thing to have technical troubles, but having one's hard work destroyed was past the limit of even Walter's stoical endurance. He gave expression to his feelings, 'Definitely I consider that such happenings are not in the game.' Fortunately sabotage is rare in the motorcycle road racing business.

Meanwhile, the races for the Grand Prix of Europe were another triumph for British riders and machines. The 500 and 350 classes giving further successes to Rudge and their winning riders, Tyrell Smith and Ernie Nott respectively. With Syd Crabtree (Excelsior-JAP) taking the 250cc honours, these Belgian races gave Britain a clean sweep. Motorcycle road racing is dangerous and lives can be lost. Syd Crabtree was one of the men willing to take up the challenge and face that risk. Four years later in the 1934 Lightweight TT, Syd, by then a TT veteran at the age of thirty-one, lost his life in a crash at the Verandah on his first lap in poor visibility.

Wherever Handley and Marchant went with the FN they became the centre of interest and speculation. It only took the entry of the Senior TT winner's name alongside that of the FN in a race programme to stir up anticipation of excitement to come. So there was considerable disappointment when it was announced that Walter's FN would be a non-starter in the Ulster Grand Prix. Excluding the TT races, Walter reported that he had only been able to complete three laps! Just as it seemed that

Flying down the Paris–Orleans road, near Arpajon, on the FN in 1930;
Wal Handley broke a number of world records.

his last chance to salvage something from the remainder of the racing season had gone, it turned out that Walter and Dougal had it in mind to go for some world records.

On 24 August, they arrived at the Arpajon Speed Trials with a specially prepared 495cc FN. Enclosed within the gearbox were extra large diameter gear wheels employed for the primary drive. Their target was world records on the 4-mile stretch of the Paris–Orleans road which the authorities had closed for the meeting. In perfect weather conditions the shirt-sleeved crowd waited expectantly. It was an international gathering with the Englishman Joe Wright attempting, on a supercharged 996cc machine, to wrest the World maximum speed record from the German, Ernst Henne, who was in the crowd watching. Joe came within a whisker of the record, just falling short of Henne's record of 134·68 mph with a best time of 134·51 mph. When Walter's turn came a buzz of interest greeted the streamlined FN, with its impressive monobloc gearbox. Walter was going to attack a number of world records. He was wearing a tight fitting black sweater with grey slacks taped up to reduce wind flap. He got his head right down, his body arched over the tank, and thundered down the straight so fast that the waiting photographers missed him on his first run! However, he too had just fallen short of his target, the 500cc Flying Kilometre Record of 122·23 mph. Perseverance brought its due reward and another four runs later Walter had broken the 500cc Flying Mile Record, raising it to 121·25 mph. At last the FNs were really ready and this was the first of some twenty-six world records that Walter captured over the next two months.

A few days later on 27 August at Montlhéry, Walter was in the process of taking several world records with the 495cc FN when he had an extraordinary piece of bad luck. It was one of Dougal's innovations to break speed records carrying minimum fuel, but this time he had evidently overdone it. Walter was moving briskly along averaging 115 mph when, with just a mile to go to complete 50 miles, his petrol ran out! So his own world record of 108 mph for the 50 miles, set up a year earlier on the Motosacoche, still stood. Nevertheless, at this meeting he had the consolation of capturing the fifty-kilometre record at 113·10 mph. This record in Class C took all the solo records up to 1000cc. As late as October the records continued to fall as first Walter would go out solo, and then follow this with a sidecar attached. Under the headline, 'A 350 Achievement', the *Motor Cycle* noted that Handley on his 348cc FN had taken the solo fifty-kilometre record at 109·18 mph in Class B about 2 mph faster than the existing record.

The new world record for the Flying Mile, set up by Walter, at 121·25 mph lasted only a week. Towards the end of September Ernst Henne was out on the Ingolstadt Road, near Munich, on his supercharged 735cc BMW, his aim to recapture for Germany the maximum world speed record. The new record had been captured for Britain by Joe Wright at Arpajon on his supercharged OEC at 137·32 mph. Then, Ernst Henne regained the record for Germany at 137·66 mph. At this meeting Henne switched to his 494cc BMW and covered the Flying Mile at 124·40 mph to also take Handley's record.

Undeterred, Wright went across the Irish Sea to Cork, and there on the 6 November, his supercharged Zenith V-Twin crackled down the Carrigrohane Road at 150·74 mph. The maximum world speed record was well and truly Britain's, at least for a while, with an increase of over 13 mph! As 1930 drew to a close, there was general satisfaction that Britain had triumphed in all three TT races, most of the continental events, plus a healthy haul of world records, that included those achieved by Wal Handley, with Wright re-gaining the maximum world speed record.

At the start of the new decade the movement of British riders and designers abroad drew a lot of comment. It was seen by many as a worrying trend that did not bode well for the future. We had falling home sales, and an apparent unwillingness by most British manufacturers to invest in new designs. When Handley and Marchant joined the FN Company in 1929 they found another Englishman waiting to greet them, George Patchett, who had been working for the Belgian firm since 1927. After Walter and Dougal had settled in at Liège, the former Brough Superior and McEvoy man joined the Czech small arms factory, Jawa of Prague. While there he designed unorthodox unit construction racing models, which were introduced to the TT in 1932. It was also Patchett, who designed the very popular single cylinder Jawa two-stroke, based on a Villiers 175cc engine. Today, known as Jawa-Cz, the Czech firm survived World War Two and the communist period to become the major

Czech motorcycle producer. Motorcyclists are a courageous breed. After the dismemberment of Czechoslovakia and the occupation of Prague by the Nazis in 1939, Patchett decided it was time for him to leave. Right under the noses of the German border guards he calmly smuggled out the Jawa plans for a new automatic rifle.

The gap left at Motosacoche by Handley and Marchant's departure was not long in being filled by yet another Englishman, Bert Le Vack. Bert had made a name for himself as a designer-tuner and world record breaker. Strangely enough he had ridden a Motosacoche in his first TT race in 1914, and now he found himself in charge of racing design and development at Geneva. Sadly, not long afterwards, he lost his life while testing a touring model. In accordance with his wishes he was buried near his beloved Brooklands in the old churchyard at Byfleet.

It was also at this time that the German NSU factory recruited Walter Moore, the man who had a hand in producing the first overhead camshaft Norton in 1927. Moore had been joined by that enterprising rider, Tommy Bullus, who it was thought would ride on an NSU in the 1931 TT. Actually he did not, but the NSUs were there plus other foreign challengers, Husqvarna, Motosacoche, La Mondiale and FN. As usual, Walter Handley was in the news. It was the FN entry that concerned the *Motor Cycle:* 'Handley is the real foreign challenge. Unless or until he retires or goes out with trouble every other competitor will be on tenterhooks.'

It was in April that Peter Chamberlain, writing in *Motor Cycling* dropped a bombshell. He reported a rumour going the rounds that the FN Company had decided that they would not be racing in the Isle of Man in 1931. Even more dispiriting was the report that the Belgian firm would not permit Handley to ride other makes:

> In other words [wrote Chamberlain] Wal Handley, who is indisputably the finest road racer in the world, may not be seen on anything in the TT this year. When he

misses one race it is bad enough, but Manxland without Walter would be like, I was going to say an egg without salt, but it would be worse even than that.

The feature concluded by expressing the hope that if the FN people were not going to race, they would be public spirited enough, 'to allow us all the sight of Wal Handley going round those 37 miles in the manner of which he only is capable. What about it, Mr Fabrique Nationale?'

Entered for the 1931 Senior TT, this is Dougal Marchant's FN with Walter in his 'civvies'. The bike was reputed to be the fastest machine in the race but it did not get beyond Quarter Bridge.

That there was some doubt about the FN entry was confirmed, when it was learned that Walter had taken the precaution of entering last year's victorious Rudge, that he had since acquired. However, the sceptics were confounded, and perhaps Walter himself was surprised, when the FN duly arrived in the Island, long after practising had begun.

The FN was distinguished by a large dark blue pistol grip shaped tank above the engine gearbox monobloc construction. On the handlebar was mounted a small triplex screen complete with hand controlled wiper. It was reputed to be the fastest machine seen in the Island up to that time, able to march all out at 110 mph on petrol benzole and some 125 mph on 'dope'. The *TT Special* had reservations reporting that although very fast it was top heavy, and 'apt to dispute who's in charge on corners.' Confirmation of this occurred when Walter set out to complete the first of the four practice laps needed to qualify. Fifty minutes later a tight-lipped Wal Handley parried the questions of waiting reporters who had noticed the broken handlebar. It transpired that the FN had steered him into a post on the mountain road, and the injury to his left shoulder was proving more troublesome than he was prepared to admit.

Riding through the rest of the practice period with, as he put it, 'one and a half arms,' Walter was luridly descriptive about the FNs navigational qualities. Thus arose the strange situation that whilst the journals were still respectful concerning the threat from the FN, amongst Walter's fellow competitors the chances of the previous year's winner and record holder were completely discounted. Yet, strange to relate, on the Senior Race day it was not the FNs steering which put Walter out of the race. In less than a mile he skidded to a halt. An incorrectly assembled gear sleeve had unscrewed on the descent of Bray Hill, completely jamming the 'cogbox' at Quarter Bridge.

'Handley has never yet started in a TT without providing a thrill,' said the *TT Special.* Only moments before the skidding halt, the crowds lining Bray Hill had witnessed Walter's hectic descent. The amazing battle between man and machine moved the *TT Special* reporter to comment:

> The huge machine is leaping, bucking, bouncing, but every incipient waggle is nipped in the bud, and the monster obeys the finest rider in the world.

Whether Walter could have mounted a challenge, given the FNs handling problems seems doubtful, but what is indisputable is the sense of loss experienced by the crowds who waited in vain for number 25 to appear.

Not that there was any lack of interest to sustain the spectators. Right from the start it was apparent that the Norton machines and riders were in the ascendance. This was the beginning of their dominance after their relatively lean spell since 1927. Now, with the Junior TT won earlier in the week their development work on the overhead camshaft engine was paying off. The 1931 Nortons appeared very workmanlike with Amal downdraught carburettors, four-speed gearboxes and semi slipper pistons. They had their own forks, and featured a quickly detachable rear wheel with a brake drum incorporated in the sprocket.

Jimmy Simpson led in the early stages gaining the distinction of being the first to lap the Island course at over 80 mph. On his fourth lap Simpson was still leading when he crashed at Ballaugh, with a seized-on front brake. This let Tim Hunt into the lead. Leading the pursuit of the Nortons was Freddie Hicks on the overhead camshaft AJS. At the end of his fifth lap he pulled in to refuel and learned that he was 41 seconds down on third-placed Jimmy Guthrie. Hicks, was shocked to find that lap after lap the Nortons had complete control of the race. Having put up the fastest time in practice he'd genuinely believed that he could win. It seems highly probable that the Norton team had not revealed their full potential in practice. Hicks set off determined to at least motor into the first three. On his fast approach to Union Mills, Freddie got too close to the left hand parapet on coming out of the right hand approach curve. In trying to correct, ready to bank to the left, he hit a sunken manhole cover which catapulted him across the road headlong into a stone post near the Post Office. Poor Hicks died en-route to hospital and so was lost one of the sports most gallant gentlemen.

The tragedy understandably cast a shadow over the race meeting, which was a pity for there was no denying the Norton achievement. The winner was the handsome, if somewhat temperamental, twenty-two-year-old Lancastrian, Tim Hunt, who had become the first rider to win the Junior and Senior TT races in one week. Tim (his actual name was Percival) was one of the great stylists of TT history. His graceful, almost leisurely performance was totally deceptive, he had just won the Senior Race at the new record speed of 77·90 mph. The Norton 1-2-3 was completed by Jimmy Guthrie and Stanley Woods, finishing second and third respectively. In the Lightweight TT the new radial four-valve Rudge model gave the company a well deserved consolation prize in the capable hands of the experienced, Graham Walker. At the time, no-one fully appreciated the significance of their reversal of fortune at the hands of the new Norton overhead camshaft design.

As soon as the TT was over, the racing fraternity quickly shifted its attention to the continent. British riders and machines made their way to the Montlhéry Autodrome for the French Grand Prix. It had been chosen for the 1931 European Championship. The Autodrome is situated on high ground, near the village of Linas, just over 12 miles southwest of Paris. The circuit, known as the Grande Piste Routière was carefully designed to be both fast and challenging. It was partly composed of nearly two miles of banked track, to which had been added in 1925 over six miles of road course. The races began in the Piste de Vitesse which, by virtue of the steepness of the banking, permitted much greater speeds than at Brooklands. The wide well surfaced roads were flanked throughout by greenery and colourful vegetation, the whole effect creating a pleasant vista for those who had time to admire it! Each bend and corner gave scope for riding skill whilst being forgiving to any possible error of judgement.

Tyrell Smith having damaged both himself and his Rudge during practice had recovered sufficiently to turn out as an interested spectator of the day's racing. Tyrell was cheered to see his team mate, Ernie Nott win the morning's 350cc race from Stanley Woods (Norton). The race was in the concluding stages when Wal Handley came round in about fourth place. The FNs were still giving him trouble in gear selection, particularly on the down changes. As he drew near the Faye hairpin, Walter found he could not engage the lower gears and ran well and truly out of road. Tyrell and his friends were seated on the inside of the bend facing the long tall grass in the fields beyond. Walter finally found a cog, and without stopping made a wide sweep through the grass, re-joining the road beyond the bend. Tyrell wrote:

> All we could see of Walter was his head and shoulders bobbing up and down in the tall grass, but Walter spotted us laughing fit to bust and the sheepish expression on his face at being caught in the act, was comical in the extreme.

Retirement inevitably followed when Walter found he could only engage one gear.

It was characteristic of Wal Handley that this incident, described by one official as, 'Handley out gathering strawberries in the woods,' should stiffen his resolve to go all out for the lead in the 500cc event. The starting line for the races on the Piste Routière was sufficiently wide, in front of the grandstand, to permit the riders to line up in one row. Within a few hundred yards the competitors leave the track at speeds approaching 100 mph, and dive through a narrow gate into the opening straight of the road circuit proper. There is thus a considerable advantage to be gained by an early lead, and this is exactly what Walter had in mind for the 500cc event.

The start of the 500cc race was awe inspiring as the field fairly howled off to converge on the gate. As they did so one figure detached itself from the pack and reached it first by a few yards, it was Walter on the FN. Then in the next few seconds all hell was cut loose. As Walter shot through the gate into the road circuit, his fuel tank filler cap came open, and fuel from a full tank gushed out over Walter and the FN. Walter put down one hand to secure it, but as he did so the FN hit a bump and got into a speed wobble. This caused him to trap the thumb of his other hand between the handlebars and the tank as the machine locked first one way and then the other. The sharp pain caused Walter to let go altogether. The FN continued its wobble unchecked and the inevitable happened, rider and machine parted company. They skated along the concrete drenched in fuel, and the sparks from the sliding bike set the lot on fire. Walter and the FN were completely obscured in flames and smoke.

As he slid along, Walter knew that with the rest of the field screaming along just behind, somehow he had to get clear. He managed to roll away from the fire into the long grass at the side, which quickly extinguished his burning leathers. Incredibly he came out of the incident with only an injured thumb. The other riders found themselves travelling too fast to avoid the widening pool of blazing fuel. They had no choice but to dive through flames and smoke not knowing what lay in it or on the other side. Some of them must have hit the blazing FN but amazingly not one rider came off. Amongst them was Britain's Tim Hunt (Norton) who went on to score his third international win in a fortnight at 71·26 mph. The charred remains of the FN were taken back to Liège, and so Wal Handley was without a machine for the next two races, the German Grand Prix and the Dutch TT races. Tyrell Smith could recall that after this race Walter always referred to any 500cc model he rode as 'the Fire Engine!'

It was not such a long wait before Walter's FN was ready for the Belgian Grand Prix at Spa on 19 July. Some believed that the 1931 event had one of the most dangerous massed starts of the decade. Try and imagine about forty riders hurtling downhill to an early sharp left bend. Now add to that rain pelting down so hard that it bounced a foot or so off the road. That's just how it was. Two riders broke loose from the pack and swept round that first bend in close company, Patchett on his new 500cc Jawa and Handley on the FN. Fortunately for the all British contingent, Handley and Patchett did not survive for long. Walter suffered yet again from gearbox trouble and Patchett had a 'busted' fuel tank. Partly due to the atrocious conditions fewer than half the competitors finished, but at least it was another British triumph, with Jimmy Guthrie and Stanley Woods making it a 350cc and 500cc double win on their Nortons.

There were mixed views on the subject of massed starts. The massed starts on the continent gave, in Walter's view, a definite advantage to those fortunate enough to be in possession of a fast machine, or those who were placed in a favourable grid position. Many riders would hang back disliking the role of early pacemaker, but where massed starts were concerned, Walter saw no objection to 'turning on the power.' An indifferent start could be a severe disadvantage. Even if you were able to eventually catch up with the leaders, it was no easy matter to find a safe opening to get through. Road surfaces in this period left a lot to be desired, and so it could be a painful experience to travel behind a bunch of riders going at 100 mph, blinding you with dust, grit and stones thrown up from their rear wheels. When the leaders throttled back for a bend, the charge from the riders behind, whose vision could be restricted, was often very dangerous.

At about this time, the *Motor Cycle* invited a number of well-known TT riders to air their views on the use of massed starts in the TT. Walter, in common with the majority of riders, made clear his preference for the interval starts system in the TT races that has lasted to this day. He felt strongly enough about the matter to write at greater length and advance more reasons in favour of the status quo than any of his contemporaries.

His dislike of massed starts never wavered. Being the supreme corner artist that he undoubtedly was, this can hardly be wondered at. His racing flair demanded that he take a bend by the shortest route. Riders bunched together served to baulk and prevent cornering in the same unrestricted style as when you were not riding in close company. Like Jimmy Simpson he did not relish the slower riders being able to get a 'tow'. Nor as a matter of tactics did he like his rivals in the massed start to know when he was 'getting down to it.' Yet in one respect his opposition to arguments favouring the massed start is curious, for the record shows that as a racer he had few equals in finding those gaps in the dangerous opening seconds of the race.

One of Walter and Dougal's last great efforts with the FN took place in September 1930 at the Avus Track near Berlin. The design of the Avus was peculiar, it consisted of two roads running parallel, each six miles in length, and joined at the ends

Wal Handley at the AVUS track in Berlin with his FN 498cc.

by two pear shaped curves. The layout stemmed from doubts concerning the commercial viability of a straightforward motor racing track, so the owners had opted for a dual purpose course that could also serve as a high speed test road. The controlling company was known as, Automobil-Verkehrs-und-Vebungs-Strasse, the initials giving the name AVUS. Translated it is the Automobile Testing and Trials Road Company.

It was hardly a promising venue for the trouble haunted

FN because in the early 1930s, prior to the alterations made by Adolph Hitler, the Avus was notorious for engine trouble. The two extremely fast straights were unusual in their length, and this, combined with the gradual slope caused the machines to be over geared in one direction and under geared in the other. Riders just waited in apprehension for the 'blow-up' as they roared up and down the two engine murdering straights separated by a strip of grass. Yet strange to relate it was the Avus that would have given a much needed victory to Walter's FN, but for a story of human fallibility.

Walter and Dougal arrived too late for practising, one almost writes, as usual, but no doubt they had their reasons. The FN was stowed away in the luxurious offices of the Berlin FN Agency. On the Saturday evening Dougal dismantled and checked over the engine for the last time, all the parts were carefully laid out on new white rag. Dougal was keen for Walter to have the clear run he needed to show the world what his FN design could really do.

The next morning Wal Handley, clad in a smart white racing suit, wheeled the gleaming FN to the start line. To his right and left were many 500cc and 750cc BMWs with famous riders such as Wiese, Bouvain, Kratz, Roese, Brudes and Huth. Notwithstanding this impressive array of talent it soon became clear that Walter's main challengers were Tom Bullus (NSU) and Arthur Simcock (Motosacoche), an Englishman and an 'Aussie'. Immediately on the fall of the flag Walter went to the front at tremendous speed. He increased his lead from lap to lap and although Bullus was doing his best, lying second, he was never in the picture. By half distance the Avus had taken its toll of the NSU and Tom Bullus was out of the race. Only 'Digger' Simcock was still anywhere in the picture, carefully nursing his engine and hoping for the best.

It was just before half distance that Dougal Marchant in Walter's pit gave his rider a sign that he was due to refuel on the next lap. Walter acknowledged the signal. He knew that everything was prepared for the stop on the following lap, the stop that never took place! Erwin Tragatsch, the distinguished Czech historian of the motorcycle industry was watching and remembered what happened:

> Flat on the tank at full throttle, Walter shot past the pits. He never even stopped to take in that essential fuel. The eyes of a despairing Dougal followed him. He was speechless as he put the stopwatches down on the table. 'Wal will never come back,' he said and he was right. Wal had not enough fuel for another lap and on the southern bend of the Avus, the fastest of the FN machines with the world's most famous rider in the saddle refused to go further without 'food'.

It was quite amazing, Wal Handley was okay, the machine was okay, but the tank was empty. Walter later admitted that he had so much enjoyed the riding that he just forgot to stop at the pits! As Erwin commented, it was a case of, 'Poor Wal, poor Dougal'. It was reported that Walter's average speed had been over 108 mph; eventually Simcock came in to win the race at an average speed over 20 mph slower. He did this on the overhead camshaft Motosacoche that had also been designed by Dougal Marchant, what an irony! There was only one other finisher, the remainder being victims of the dreaded Avus and the terrific pace set by Wal Handley.

Many years later I corresponded with Erwin and he wrote:

> Compared with other great riders of the past, Walter Handley was unique and in my opinion still the greatest of them all, especially on days, when he was in the right mood.

As Geoff Davison told me, 'Wal is, on his day, fearless, fantastic and unbeatable.'

CHAPTER 21
RACING UNDER PRESSURE

While Walter's two year engagement with Fabrique Nationale had certainly been packed with incident, in terms of racing success it was a disaster. Time and again Walter had been reduced to the role of spectator, watching his pals in the Rudge team battle to take their share of honours from the generally victorious Nortons. So when in August the opportunity had arisen for Walter to renew his brief but successful association with John Pugh for the coming season, he had accepted the challenge without hesitation. The news that Wal Handley was once again to 'ride British' came as a welcome tonic to his long suffering admirers!

What had happened in 1931 was that Arthur Carroll's redesigned overhead camshaft Nortons, allied to the skill of great riders like Tim Hunt, Jimmy Guthrie, Jimmy Simpson and Stanley Woods, were sweeping all before them, and it was not just a question of greater speed. It was said that a racing Norton would go just where you put it, their road holding quality was superb. It was noted that the new Nortons utilised more alloy metals, indicating much lighter weight, while the Rudges were still basically the 1930 design with an attempt made to try and improve the handling.

The Press were already speculating that the season ahead would be a Norton versus Rudge battle. Without the participation of Rudge-Whitworth the prospects for the 1932 TT would have been decidedly gloomy. Sales of motorcycles were falling continually as the slump deepened. In these circumstances costly road racing expenditure was inevitably being cut back. Few British firms were willing to spend thousands of pounds for what they saw as the doubtful privilege of serving as an outclassed background to the Norton stars. Rudges were the brave exception, the only manufacturer willing to mount a strong challenge to Norton Motors.

Wal Handley's first outing with the Rudge team came in September when he competed in the Ulster Grand Prix, after an absence of five years. In the Senior event the Rudge team was composed of Walker, Nott and Handley, while Nortons fielded Hunt, Simpson and Woods. What a battle this proved to be, as first Nott and then Woods held the lead with only seconds separating them at speeds averaging well over 80 mph. Walter had further justification for his dislike of massed starts with both he and Simpson receiving facial cuts and smashed goggles from stones thrown up in the opening maelstrom. With powdered glass affecting his vision Walter probably did well to come in fourth behind Woods, Nott and Hunt. This gave a race result of Norton-Rudge-Norton-Rudge. With the Junior race going to Jimmy Guthrie on his Norton, the Ulster battle honours had gone to Bracebridge Street, but the war was not over yet.

The following spring, the two rival camps again crossed the Irish Sea but this time they did not compete against each other. At the Leinster meeting only Nortons competed with Guthrie winning the 350 class. While in the North West 200 at Port Stewart, Nortons had the lone entry of Stanley Woods entered in the 500 class, Stanley was delayed on the opening lap and was left with a vain chase of the winning Rudge, piloted by Ernie Nott, while Walter won the 350 class. These meetings served as excellent testing grounds for the run-up to the TT. The lessons learned went into the final preparation.

With the 1930 races having produced a Junior-Senior double for Rudges, and this having been capped the following year by Nortons, the Press now looked forward to what was seen as a 'return bout'. Despite this exciting promotion of the contest in the journals, there was little real optimism in the Rudge team. Even so morale was high, and here the presence of Walter Handley was a not inconsiderable factor. He always enjoyed the company of the Rudge team. At the Sandyford Hotel in Douglas, where the team was staying, Walter provided comic relief by gaining the affection of what to everyone else, including its owner, was a particularly bad tempered hotel parrot. Within a short time he had the bird on his shoulder and was taking it on conducted tours of the lounge. As he did so the bird would pour forth a stream of rude words which, Walter quipped, it must have learned from Tyrell Smith or Ernie Nott! And so the good humour and backchat would continue amid the underlying pressure.

Tyrell Smith explained to me that whilst they recognised that the general handling and reliability of the Rudge was good, it was only in having a rider as brilliant as Walter Handley on their side that they felt themselves to be on competitive terms at all. This opinion was borne out during the practice period in which Jimmy Simpson had made the fastest lap in both the Senior and Junior classes, with Wal Handley second fastest in each case. Yet, whereas Walter's best lap on his Senior Rudge at 28 mins, 32 secs was just two seconds slower than Simpson, his best Junior effort was a full three quarter's of a minute slower. It looked as though Walter's best chance was in the Senior, but as so often happens that was not the way things worked out.

On Monday's Junior race a cracking pace was set from the start. All four members of the Norton team and Walter on his Rudge had beaten the lap record from the standing start, and lapped the course in under the half hour. Walter riding a superb race had managed to sandwich himself in the midst of the four Norton stars. Riding in the number 9 position Walter's second lap not only created another new lap record, but also he became the first man to do two laps on a 350cc machine in under the hour.

Meanwhile Stanley Woods, who led throughout, matched record lap for record lap. After Stanley's team mates had all

At Ramsey hairpin, Wal Handley makes a close turn
at speed on his Rudge 349cc, during the 1932 Junior TT.

Wal Handley flashes past the Grandstand in the 1932 Junior TT
in which he came second. Only Walter could get down to it like this.

Good sports! Runner-up Wal Handley (Rudge) congratulates
Stanley Woods (Norton) on winning the 1932 Junior TT.

A thoughtful-looking Walter talking to Stanley Wood's mechanic, Bill Mewis.
Jack Bayley, Walter's pit attendant (who is wearing the 'nine' armband), is listening.
This was after Walter had put on an electrifying display of high speed cornering that
gained him second place at 76.36 mph in the 1932 Junior TT; Woods won at 77·16 mph.

retired, there was the unexpected spectacle of the lone Norton being chased home by Wal Handley, shades of 1926 all over again but this time Stanley was gaining. Walter never gave up trying but he had not the power, he was about 30 seconds per lap slower than Stanley. Nortons also had a surprise in store, their riders only had to refuel once, whereas the Rudge riders had to make the customary two pit stops.

In response to the widening gap between himself and the race leader Walter put on a cornering display that left the crowds gasping. On his last lap he pulled out all the stops hurtling down the mountain, almost charging into the hotel at Creg-ny-Baa, just surging round in a wonderfully controlled slide. On that last lap he managed to clip 19 seconds off Stanley's lead, but the genial Dubliner still led comfortably by 2 mins, 10 secs at the end of the race. In third place, after a spill, came that other star from the Emerald Isle, Tyrell Smith over six minutes after Walter to give a Norton-Rudge-Rudge verdict.

The Rudge contingent had confidently expected to win Wednesday's Lightweight race. Their 250cc machines had romped home in 1931 to give Graham Walker his long awaited and popular TT victory. For the following year the bike had been slightly modified and under test conditions had developed 19 bhp at 6600–6800 rpm with a 9:1 compression ratio. Walter was the favourite to win, although given clear runs Walker or Nott were fully capable of bringing the Trophy back to Coventry. The odds on one of the Rudge trio winning shortened further when it was learned that two of their chief rivals, Ted Mellors and Syd Gleave, were non-starters. This left the twenty-four-year-old Wolverhampton garage proprietor, Leo Davenport, as the sole survivor of the New Imperial contingent.

By all calculations it looked a racing certainty for Rudge, but it's the unexpected in life that can so often happen. In one of the most exciting and hard fought contests in TT history, it was Davenport who emerged from the field to pilot his New Imperial to victory at the record speed of 70.48 mph. The men from Coventry must have wondered if they were undergoing some awful nightmare, as the leadership of the race changed five times and read, Handley, Nott, Handley, Davenport, Nott and finally Davenport. Excitement of this order in a Lightweight race was as welcome as it was surprising.

Wal Handley seems to have the gallery amused as he works patiently to get his 249cc Rudge moving again in the 1932 Lightweight TT, the time lost cost him the race.

Walter's lead at the end of lap one had been a handsome 43 seconds, but then he was slowed by of all things, whiskering plugs. He regained the lead and lost it again, making in all, three stops to change plugs. It was on the fatal fifth lap that he stopped on the mountain road for what must have seemed an interminable seven minutes, calmly prizing open the plug points with a knife borrowed from a spectator. This delay cost him the race and dropped him back to fifth place. Meanwhile Ernie Nott had a 'Go like hell' signal from a worried George

Making up lost time through engine trouble, Wal Handley
(249cc Rudge) swings round Parliament Square, Ramsey.

Hack, and he set off in pursuit of Davenport to such good effect that he entered the last lap 22 seconds into the lead.

After that final halt, Walter was able to go all out in the two final circuits. Perhaps this was the closest even Walter ever went to taking a motorcycle to its maximum limit. His sixth lap, completed in 30 mins, 34 secs at 74·08 mph created a record that lasted until 1935. Walter kept travelling very fast, fully determined to back up his team, knowing that even though he could not win, Ernie Nott could still save the day for the Rudge team. Then, as he approached Sulby, on the last lap such consoling thoughts were suddenly dashed. One incredulous glance was enough, there was the stocky figure of his fellow 'Brummie' Ernie stranded at the roadside waving frantically to Walter to 'Keep cracking'. This was dreadful luck for Nott who had now been cheated of victory in this race for the second year running.

On seeing Ernie's plight, Walter really flung himself round the course saving seconds here and there. It was just after Sulby that his tachometer recorded 7200 rpm with some assistance from the wind, before that too packed up. The combined effect of these two very fast laps was that Walter moved up smartly into third place, behind Graham Walker. The result, although it might have been worse, was a particular disappointment to the Rudge firm. They had hoped for a victory that would stimulate their sales in the ultra competitive small four-stroke market. Walter felt the disappointment as keenly as anyone and it made him all the more determined to put up a good show in Friday's Jubilee Senior TT.

Since the 1932 TT races were the twenty-first of the series, they were graced for the first time with a royal visitor. The youngest of the King's sons, HRH Prince George, reached the Island in time for the grand finale of the week, the Senior TT. Not for the first time in his TT career, Walter Handley had been allotted the conspicuous number one grid position. On this occasion it carried the honour of making him the first TT rider to be introduced to the future Duke of Kent, one of the ten TT winners competing in this race of the 'experts'.

Being the first rider sent on his way, Walter lost no time in extracting the full advantage from the open roads ahead. He was determined to, at the very least, drive a 'wedge' into the centre of this very formidable Norton team. At the end of the first lap it was apparent that he had done just that, and was lying third ahead of his team mate Ernie Nott, and Jimmy Guthrie's Norton. There was just eight seconds separating the first three riders, Simpson and Stanley Woods on their Nortons closely followed by Walter. The gap between himself and the leader had widened to 34 seconds after a record second lap of 81·5 mph from the leader, Jimmy Simpson. Shortly after this, Simpson was slowed by clutch trouble and was overtaken by the fast but steady Stanley Woods. When the times went up at the end of the third lap, it was apparent that Walter was not only overhauling the slowing Simpson, but he was also holding onto Stanley and gaining on Nott and Guthrie. It thus began to look as though Walter had an excellent chance of gaining at least another podium place.

In 1932 HRH Prince George, the first Duke of Kent, became the first member of the Royal Family to watch the TT races. He is being introduced to Wal Handley by Rev E. H. Stenning, the TT's padre. On the right is Professor A. M. Low, ACU Race Judge.

It was a cracking pace, the glare of the sun, the clouds of flies hitting the rider's goggles, and a testing breeze all added up to make this a most gruelling race. Walter was straining every nerve to hold onto the flying Nortons. On the straights he was tucked flat down, 'nose in the sorbo' was Wal's expression for

Wal Handley (Rudge) sweeps through Ballacraine in the 1932 Senior TT.
A few miles further on he had his only serious crash in the Isle of Man TT.

it. At the start of his fourth lap, the *Motor Cycle* reporter in the grandstand wrote:

> ... he was so flat down that his head seemed to be a knob protruding from a horizontal tank top, and the echo of his megaphone exhaust boom bounced deeply off the stands and hoardings; a cool 100 mph.

How he could get down so low for back-aching hour after hour, cutting wind resistance to a minimum, and still see where he was going was a secret known only to Walter. He was swerving and shaving through the bends getting ever nearer to the margin of safety when suddenly it happened, Walter had his first serious crash in ten years of wonderful competitive effort.

When Walter's pointer on the Grandstand Scoreboard failed to move from Ballacraine to Kirk Michael, a hush fell over the crowd, for a crash at such a fast stretch is a matter of some concern. What had happened? On the fast downhill approach to Kirk Michael there is an 'S' bend just short of the twelfth milestone between Cronk-y-Voddy and Baaregarroo. It was here that Wal Handley's crash at, what George Hack estimated to be 90–95 mph, put him out of what *Motor Cycling* called, '... one of the hardest cleverest races this wonderful rider has to his credit.'

It was a most unpleasant experience by any standard, he had not only an injured knee, crushed fingers on his right hand and a fractured wrist, but also bruising and abrasions to his back that left him lying helpless in the road unable to move and at the mercy of any oncoming machine. The Rudge was alongside, its engine still screaming away as petrol flowed all over the place, so that Walter was soaked in it. He was terrified that the pair of 'em would go up in flames before help arrived. But help did arrive and he rested in the front drive of a nearby cottage, soon to be named after him, and watched the rest of the race. 'If Walter didn't know how to fall off he'd have been killed a hundred times,' was the comment of Dougal Marchant.

Despite his injuries after the crash between the eleventh and twelfth milestones in the 1932 Senior TT, Wal Handley looks fairly comfortable as he waits for the end of the race and an ambulance. On the left is his pit attendant, Jack Bayley.

The race is over, the ambulance arrives to take Handley to
Nobles Hospital in Douglas and Handley's Corner is named after a great rider.

Today, a helicopter will lift off an injured rider from any part
of the course, but it was not always so. In 1932 Walter had to
wait, and just over two hours later the roads were opened, and
an ambulance was able to at last reach Walter, and take him to
Nobles Hospital in Douglas. There he was cheerfully making
light of the episode as a humorous incident! 'No wonder we
all thought the world of him,' was Geoff Davison's comment.
There were broad smiles when Prince George arrived to open
the new hospital wing. Imagine the Prince's surprise to find
himself again being introduced to the famous rider he had
greeted on the Glencrutchery Road, a few hours earlier. Walter
ruefully admitted that he would have preferred a renewal of
their acquaintance at the Villa Marina prize giving! The two
men were the same age, and sadly they were destined to lose
their lives within a year of each other in wartime air crashes.

Walter's exit from the race had made a Norton 1-2-3 victory
inevitable. Stanley Woods, riding a wonderful race, had
repeated Tim Hunt's feat of a Junior Senior 'double' to win his

fourth TT at the record speed of 79·38 mph. Stanley had been followed home by Guthrie in his first season as a member of the Norton team, and Jimmy Simpson who gained the record lap at 81·50 mph. The result was decisive and set the seal upon the Norton domination of the TT.

The high speed crash of a star rider gave the Press the chance for some sensational headlines. Three journals had Wal's toss as 30, 60 and 90 feet respectively! One paper even had him falling twice in a distance of three miles! Fortunately, initial Press reports that he had injuries to his spine were without

From right: Three great riders: Woods, number 27; Guthrie, number 22; and Simpson, number 15, triumph in that order in the 1932 Senior TT. Bill Mewis stands next to Woods with Joe Craig behind them. *Second from right:* Norton boss, Bill Mansell.

foundation, but he had hit a brick wall and undoubtedly had been saved by his helmet. Nevertheless, we think that perhaps the star prize should have gone to the headline, 'Steel Helmet Saves Star Rider's Life'. But what had really happened? Had Walter's 'inner pilot' of which he often spoke so feelingly deserted him on this occasion? To Walter, the reason for the crash was a mystery, so much for Press reports which spoke of his front brake locking on. He told his brother that he could not recall the crash and felt that he must have lost his usual concentration. From the description of a bystander Walter felt that there was a distinct possibility that he was off his usual racing line for a bend that had previously not caused him any real problems.

There are two further points of interest for the reader to bear in mind. First, Handley's Corner, or Bends, as it soon became known, is today a very different proposition from how it was in the 1930s. Tyrell Smith remembered the 'S' bend very well. He told me:

> It was a nasty bend, I was never happy about it and I was always glad to get past it. You couldn't take it too fast, about 75–85 mph. The farm gate on the left caused the road camber to dip on the outer edge of the bend.

Consequently if a rider was too far over to the left he would hit the dip on the rise and could go into a speed wobble. The second point concerns the steering problems of the Rudge. We now know that the steering was affected by the mistaken practice of 'springing' the engines into the frame. The holes for the engine and the front bottom lug should have been in line. Unfortunately this was not the case and the resultant stress took its toll. While it is true that the Rudge would hold a perfectly straight line and corner well at moderate speeds, this was not the case when it came to high speed cornering. Then you had to exercise great care.

Unfortunately the economic depression was about to claim one of its most famous and oft lamented victims. This race proved to be the last official TT entry of the Rudge Company. Early in 1933 it was announced that the Official Receiver had been appointed.

Walter had become the victim of intense pressure. He had reached the stage in his career when he was expected to either win or gain a top three finish. It had become a serious business.

At about this time his friend, Harold Willis of the Velocette Company, had remarked that the best way to win the TT is to have a 'plot' that goes quicker than anyone else's. Coming from Harold, a well-known humourist, it raised a laugh but it's not so wide of the mark. Walter's reported comment shortly after the crash that the Rudge, 'would only do 98 mph maximum,' is revealing. Although the really great racers come as close as they dare to the safety limit, it seems clear that Walter had been cornering just that bit too hard to make up for the lack of maximum speed.

While recuperating in the Queen's Hospital in Birmingham, Walter learned that he had been nominated as first reserve in the official Riley team for the RAC Ulster TT Car Race. Now he would be unable to go to Ireland. Yet, despite having to hobble around with a walking stick for the rest of the season, he was not forgotten. One admirer, after paying full tribute to Stanley Woods and the Norton team, wrote:

> I still fail to see a rider who could fill Wal Handley's shoes. In my opinion, there is not a man alive who could beat Wal, given machines of equal speed and a clear run.

Another wrote to *Motor Cycling*, 'Wal is a star in a class by himself; he could coax speed from a steam roller.'

CHAPTER 22
DECISION TIME

A period of great uncertainty was ushered into Walter's life when he learned, at the end of 1932, that the Rudge Company had decided to end their direct involvement in racing. He now had to start once again the process of getting fixed up for the TT races. He really needed the equivalent of a racing manager, but then he was such a fiercely independent character that he never could stand the idea of being managed.

In addition Walter had to contend with business worries at a time of economic slump. With Walter frequently away on the continent, it is no exaggeration to say that his Birmingham motor dealership was only kept alive by the herculean efforts of his brother, Tom. It was during this difficult period that the business was moved from Holloway Head round the corner into 144 Suffolk Street. Looking back one can see that Walter was trying to do too much; he simply had too many 'irons in the fire'.

The dominant factor in motorcycle road racing in the 1930s was the Carroll designed overhead camshaft Norton. The 'Norton Supremacy', as it became known, proceeded to win Isle of Man TT races with monotonous regularity. It was becoming more and more difficult to find British manufacturers willing to do battle against these all conquering Nortons. In the process many commentators felt that they virtually killed off the races as a proving ground for the British Motorcycle Industry. To Nortons, their racing programme was everything, but this was not reflected in their production machines. This dominance of the Norton 'single' had an important historic consequence. It meant that interest in multi-cylinder development became almost the exclusive concern of overseas manufacturers. Even at the time, it was a danger that did not go unnoticed. Freddie Dixon told Joe Craig, the Norton racing manager, in the bar of the Castle Mona Hotel, and in the presence of a crowd of famous riders, that Nortons were being too traditional. It went something like:

> Joe, I tell you a single cylinder is no good, a four is better than a twin, and a six is better than a four, you should be going one jump ahead and design a six.

He certainly made it very clear!

Walter had no intention of missing the TT races if he could possibly help it. Top priority was given to finding a machine to enter in the 1933 Senior TT. Approaches were made to AJS, Sunbeam, New Imperial, the Belgian Sarolea, the Swedish Husqvarna and the Swiss MAG. The responses were either negative or unattractive. With business disappointing they didn't want to incur extra expense. Another factor was the difficulty of reconciling Handley's oil contract with those of some of the oil contracts that certain manufacturers had agreed to use. All of this was in stark contrast to the attitude of the race organisers who were very keen to get one of the most famous riders in the world to enter their meetings.

In comparison to his difficulties in getting a chance to race in the Senior TT, the situation was much brighter for Walter in the Junior TT when it was learned that his friend, Harold Willis, had arranged for him to ride a Velocette. This provided Walter with an opportunity to challenge the Norton dominance. Contrary to what many believed at the time, and since, the 1933 Junior TT was not Walter's first race aboard a Velocette. There were two earlier occasions.

In only the second event ever held at Donington Park, the August Bank Holiday meeting of 1931, Walter, entered on a

350cc Velocette and won the All Star Invitation Race for TT Riders at 47·5 mph and carried off the £70 prize. It seems an incredibly slow speed but in those days Donington had a narrow winding track, thick with dust, quite a contrast to the broad macadamised surface of today.

Less than a year later, Walter made his second appearance on a 350cc Velocette, when he arrived in Italy for the Grand Prix of Rome. It was held on Sunday, 17 April, 1932 on the Littorio Aerodrome. The track was formed by concrete runways built to assist the take-off of heavy aeroplanes in bad weather! The runways were linked by banked curves reminiscent of Brooklands. As it was also the Grand Prix of Europe, a certain amount of ceremony was attached to the race with members of the Fascist government and the King of Italy present. Walter would have won comfortably but for one of the overhead rockers breaking, a familiar enough occurrence in those days but vexing all the same. Walter set off for the return journey in comfort having arranged for the bike to be despatched by the local agent. However, it was nearly five months later before the Velocette finally cleared through customs! It seems the belief that bureaucracy is far worse now than at any time in the past is just not true!

Early in 1933 Wal Handley's Junior Velocette TT entry looked straight forward. Appearances can be deceptive. The Velocettes were to all intents and purposes standard Mk IV KTTs, modified by the use of special alloys, with the overhead valve gear completely enclosed. Unfortunately, because the engine was taller the frame had to be modified to provide the extra head room. The result was a design that tended to be top heavy and difficult to handle. After the first morning's practice, Walter informed Willis that his difficulty was to hold the model on the roads when cornering at speed, especially with a full tank. In order to have a chance of winning he strongly urged that the Velocette be returned by air to Birmingham for alterations.

When once asked, which was the worst bend on the Isle of Man course, Walter replied, 'all of them.' It was an

Members of the Velocette 1933 Junior TT campaign. *Left to right:* Percy Goodman, Managing Director; Tyrell Smith; Ernie Thomas; Alec Mitchell; Harold Willis; and Wal Handley. They did not win the race but gained the manufacturer's team prize.

Wal Handley excelled on fast approaches into sweeping bends and here he is taking his 348cc Velocette through Signpost Corner. He estimated his 1933 speed into Signpost at 85mph in third gear, taking the corner itself at 30mph in bottom gear.

understandable reply coming from a corner specialist, because paradoxically, the nearer you get to coming off on these bends, the better racing man you are. Walter always seemed to take Creg-ny-Baa faster than most, and 1933 was no exception. He had given himself and early morning enthusiasts, spectating at this point, a thrill when on the first morning's practice, after approaching at terrific speed from Kate's Cottage, he banked the machine over steeply for the sharp turn only for the exhaust pipe to ground and spin the bike. The Velocette crashed into the hedge only inches below where Walter himself had been thrown backwards into the padded wall. Amid lurid comments all round, Willis had the exhaust pipe remounted higher, joking that touring bars might be necessary so that Wal could not scrape the new exhaust mounting on the road! However, no action was taken to modify the more serious weight distribution problem.

On race day the onward march of Norton dominance continued with the Junior TT ending, as had been expected, with the Nortons of Woods, Hunt and Guthrie finishing in that order. The race gave Stanley his fifth win at 78.08 mph by just seven seconds from his team mate Tim Hunt, with a pack of Velocettes taking up the next seven places and winning the manufacturer's team prize with their number one team comprising Alec Mitchell, Tyrell Smith and Wal Handley. A testament to the reliability of the black and gold Velocettes is that out of twenty-eight starters, only sixteen finished and out of these eleven were Velocettes. For the first four laps Walter was the leading Velocette rider in fifth place behind the Norton stars. If his bike had been only marginally slower, it is fairly certain that he would have once again got amongst his rivals. Then on the fourth lap something happened that very few noticed.

Since the second lap, Jimmy Simpson (Norton), number 22, had overtaken Handley, number 21, and was leading on the roads, yet on this fourth lap number 21 caught and passed Jimmy at Creg-ny-Baa and reached Governor's Bridge first. It was here, at the slowest point on the course, that Walter caught an oil patch and tumbled off. The whistle having sounded the imminent approach of Simpson, the policeman on duty stopped Walter from remounting until the Norton rider had passed. Walter eventually came in seventh and a study of the subsequent lap times show that this spill must have slowed him. Later he explained to his brother that with the enlarged Velocette tank he only had to refuel once during the race. The refuelling was scheduled for the end of his fourth lap, and so with a nearly empty tank he was no longer fighting gallons of petrol 'wafting' about, road holding improved and he could close in on Simpson. His friend Jimmy, who retired on the last lap with engine trouble, recalled the incident years later. He told of how he had been passed at the 'Creg' and chuckled at the recollection. He never thought it would be possible for anyone to pass him at that spot. Suddenly, there was a tremendous noise, and there was Wal finding space to slip past, 'I wondered what the [censored] was happening.'

Whilst it is true that Omobono Tenni's victory on a 250cc Guzzi in the 1937 TT was the first success by an Italian on an Italian bike, it was not until the arrival of Giacomo Agostini in the mid '60s that an Italian rider had real success. Earlier, the Isle of Man TT course had not been a happy hunting ground for the Italian stars. Its length and complexity, the uncertain weather, and to Italian eyes at least, the seemingly harsh enforcement of the rules had all combined to cause something akin to dislike. In mid week there was the prospect of the Lightweight race with Nortons not involved. If a distinguished British motorcyclist could be persuaded to ride the Moto Guzzi, a win for the Italian manufacturer might loom large. Walter Handley was much admired in Italy ever since that epic tussle with Tazio Nuvolari on his Bianchi at Monza in 1925.

Unfortunately, valuable time was lost in responding to the Englishman's enquiry due, to of all things, the illness of their translator at Mandello del Lario. On such apparent trifles can race results and even careers depend. When it came the initial offer to ride their much improved four-speed 246cc overhead camshaft Moto Guzzi proved disappointing. It reinforced Walter's belief, borne of long experience, that continental manufacturers were generally not interested in competing in the TT since their sales were more easily influenced by race results nearer home. Walter now became the victim of some unlucky timing. When finally a new revised offer came from Moto Guzzi, Walter learned just how keen they were to acquire his services for the TT.

The news arrived too late, he had already made a verbal promise to ride the new Excelsior-Blackburne. Having been badly let down in the past, by last minute productions, Walter made it a condition of his acceptance that the new Excelsior design must come through its tests satisfactorily. He had no wish to arrive in the Island with the new machine in an untried state. The new engine was being developed exclusively for the Tyseley firm by Mr H. J. Hatch of Burney and Blackburne. It was unorthodox in design and appearance, two thirds of the cylinder barrel being sunk into a crankcase of square looking appearance with the two camshafts placed fore and aft of the barrel. It had four radial valves actuated by pairs of pushrods, the two inlet ports were downswept and each had a carburettor. Its complexity and reputed 25 bhp deservedly earned it the nickname, 'Mechanical Marvel'. Although this commitment to Excelsior cast doubt on Walter's chance to ride the Guzzi, there was satisfaction in Genoa that the possibility still existed.

Any difficulties that Walter had experienced in the Junior TT on the Velocette were dwarfed by his problems in the Lightweight race. At the end of April he had been alarmed to discover that the Excelsior Mechanical Marvel, on which he was works entered, was still unassembled. In contrast the modified overhead camshaft Guzzi had been tested on the Monza track at around 90 mph. So feeling by this time worried that the new Excelsior might turn out to be disappointing he had, with the agreement of Georgio Parodi, privately entered the Guzzi without naming the rider. From now on much of the Press speculation would centre on who would be the rider of number 15.

Walter's great misfortune was the absence from the Isle of Man of the man with whom he had a good understanding, Georgio Parodi, who had been injured in an air crash. Without his steadying influence the willingness to listen to Handley's advice was sadly lacking. Again and again during practice Walter tried to impress upon the Guzzi camp that he could not ride their machine as long as the Excelsior was going fairly well because of his promise to the Excelsior Motor Company. The Italians kept insisting that either Handley ride the Guzzi or, failing this, another well known British star such as Ernie Nott, Tyrell Smith, Jimmy Simpson, Stanley Woods or Tim Hunt. Walter knew that all these riders had trade commitments which made it most unlikely they would be able to get permission to ride.

Valuable time was lost when first Nott and then Tyrell Smith rode the Guzzi and were refused permission by Rudge and OK respectively. All along Walter had kept urging that Alec Mitchell of Huddersfield, a man with no trade obligations, whom he considered a very good rider, be let loose on the Guzzi. Not until the last morning of practice did the Guzzi people relent and let Mitchell have a go. Alec did three good laps, appealed to the Stewards to overlook the fourth lap needed to qualify, but was refused. Walter was deeply sorry that matters had turned out so unsatisfactorily. His faith in Mitchell had not been misplaced. This rider had piloted his 350cc Velocette into fourth place in Monday's Junior TT, and in the Senior TT he came in sixth on the identical 350cc machine.

Moto Guzzi's anger was directed not only at the ACU but also at Walter. *Motor Cycling's* 'Cyclops' commented:

> I have a pretty fair knowledge of the troubles and complications which always seem to beset Handley in the Island, and can give my assurance that nine times out of ten it is not Walter's fault.

Walter was sorry for another reason; during practice he had

taken out the Guzzi, a fact that suggests he was not a hundred per cent happy with the Excelsior, and was very impressed with its speed. After the weighing in, Walter told Georgio's younger brother that he would have been far happier had he been riding the Guzzi, and he added prophetically that he was not sure that the Excelsior would finish the race. Although Walter was subsequently invited to ride the Excelsior on the continent, it is surely significant that he chose not do so, and Leo Davenport took his place in their works team.

The Lightweight race, run on Wednesday, 14 June, gave Syd Gleave his only TT win at 71·59 mph on another Excelsior-Blackburne. He finished two minutes ahead of Charlie Dodson (New Imperial). Whereas the Junior race had seen just two manufacturers, Norton and Velocette, take the first ten places, the Lightweight had more variety with four makes in the first six – Excelsior, New Imperial, Rudge and Guzzi. The favourite to win the race had been Wal Handley but for Walter it proved to be an exasperating experience. He had taken the lead on the

Handley pushing off at the start of the 1933 Lightweight TT with the Excelsior 248cc overhead 4-valve 'Mechanical marvel': he retired on the last lap with engine trouble after making another record lap of 74·08 mph.

first lap by one second, a sure sign to his supporters that all was not well. Throughout the rest of the race he steadily lost ground until by the end of the sixth lap he was lying third, 2 mins, 45 secs behind the leader. On the last lap his engine seized up near Sulby and that was that. Walter reported that he had found his Excelsior to be slower than during practice, and because it would not rev in the lower gears he had almost exclusively to use top gear. Reports from around the course indicated that he had once again made up for this lack of speed by cornering faster than anyone else. It was said that he came down the mountain like 'a skier in slalom.'

Walter was mystified by the bike's loss of performance which robbed the Excelsior Motor Company of a sweeping 1-2 victory. He wondered whether the magneto might have been partially retarded when the controls were taped up. There is another possibility. It is well known that the camshafts were easily accessible on these machines and later on the continent there were cases of sabotage. Handley was the clear favourite to win this race in the betting. Security was generally much tighter in the Isle of Man than abroad, but we do know that the Excelsior was the only one of Walter's three machines not garaged at the Nursery Hotel, Onchan, where he was staying. There is no proof either way, but Tyrell Smith with whom I discussed the matter felt that interference was quite possible in this instance. Although the victim of sabotage on at least one previous occasion, Walter was not naturally a suspicious person, he had lost the race, it was 'the luck of the game.' His only consolation was that his record lap of the previous year, 30 mins, 34 secs, was still unbeaten, it would not be decisively beaten until 1936 when Stanley Woods upped the record by 2 mph on the DKW.

The remarkable success of the Mechanical Marvel at the first attempt did not give the Excelsior Company any immediate commercial 'pay-off', for it never appeared on the open market. It was too costly and probably too difficult for the private owner to keep in tune. It was, however, the forerunner of the famous

'Manxman' model, both the two and four-valve versions which did so well in the capable hands of 'Ginger' Wood and Tyrell Smith before the outbreak World War Two. After the cessation of hostilities these bikes went on to win the Lightweight Clubman's TT for their private owners in the years 1948–1950.

Unfortunately there are two sad tailpieces to this Island race. Everyone had been saddened by the tragic death of that popular veteran, Frank Longman. This proved to be his last race, for he died from the injuries he sustained in the crash at Glen Tramon on the approach to Ramsey on his second lap. The winner, Syd Gleave, joined that adventurous band of pre-war racing motorcyclists who took up flying as a hobby. During the war he worked as a test pilot with A. V. Roe Ltd, and it was at Woodford in 1944 that he lost his life when a Lancaster bomber he was testing went unaccountably out of control.

Walter had an innate dislike of fan worship, and hated being fussed over at prize-givings. His self-mocking good humour would have made him the despair of the public relations experts of today. When things went wrong he never made excuses or attempted to explain himself, and sometimes he was totally misunderstood by the crowds. Yet when the full facts of a case emerged, a very different light would be thrown on the matter.

The public not knowing the inside story, had been puzzled by the non-appearance of Walter's Guzzi entry. On top of this came his decision to withdraw from the Senior TT. At the eleventh hour Walter's former boss, Ernie Humphries, had entered him on the OK Supreme-JAP, this machine was virtually a standard motorcycle. It had not been assembled until after the start of practising, and it is no exaggeration to say that it stood no chance. If Wal Handley had not been riding it no-one would have given it a second thought. His decision not to run caused a minor sensation. Yet he had not withdrawn because of the bike's lack of speed. Very few people knew that Walter's right hip and thigh were badly bruised in the hard landing that had resulted when the Excelsior had seized up in Wednesday's race. Feeling unfit he sacrificed the starting and entry fees, rather than tour round or retire with some imaginary trouble as he was advised to do from several quarters. It was typical of the man that he would not take the money unless he could put up a good show for the OK-JAP people.

Yet despite these periodic upsets and misunderstandings, he remained a very popular figure. His very personality seemed to attract, and so he was written about pretty freely. One of the men who did the writing was Bob Holliday of *Motor Cycling* he recalled that while Walter Handley had few close friends, he had a lot of acquaintances, people were proud to be able to say that they knew him.

On Sunday, 2 July, Walter returned to winning ways in the 250cc class of the Swiss Grand Prix at Berne. Making his first appearance on the Guzzi, he led from the start, being chased first by Charlie Dodson and then Ted Mellors, both riding New Imperials. Walter won at the record speed of 71·25 mph. Unfortunately, the entry of Moto Guzzi for the French Grand Prix at Dieppe on 16 July arrived too late for inclusion, so Walter shrugging off this disappointment, made his way to Spa for the Belgian Grand Prix. Clearly at this stage the upset during TT week had not soured Walter's good relationship with Georgio Parodi. He was still held in high regard in Italy.

The famous Belgian course is fast, beautiful and dangerous. Just south of Francorchamps village is the slow La Source hairpin which is followed by a winding downhill run to the pits. From here the rider negotiates an 'S' bend over L'Eau Rouge before the road winds upwards through the pine forests surrounding Burnenville. A curving downhill run leads to the sweeping right hand turn through Malmedy Corner. This is followed by a fast downhill straight leading to the acute bend near Stavelot. The road then climbs and twists its way back to La Source completing the triangular 9·25 miles with a steep wooded hillside on the left and a drop into meadows on the right.

Many times Walter had shown his skill on this, the most interesting and challenging of the continental races at that time, but never more so than on this occasion. 'How that man rode,' reported *Motor Cycling,* 'it was worth going to the edge of Belgium to watch him!' This time he made sure that his little red Guzzi took the lap record at 74·17 mph and in doing so his time of 7 mins, 32 secs was only 28 seconds outside the 350cc class record set up by Jimmy Simpson (Norton). It was in the final stages of the race that Walter's foot change mechanism started giving trouble. He almost had the tips of his fingers nipped off in the rear chain as he reached down, groping for the gears while travelling full bore. The last lap was completed in second gear with Ted Mellors (New Imperial) closing in on him. Despite this difficulty, Walter still managed to win at the record

On 23 July 1933 Wal Handley won the Lightweight Class
of the Belgian Grand Prix at record speed on the Italian Guzzi.

speed of 71·12 mph after 3 hrs, 7 mins, 23 secs in the saddle. As expected the Norton dominance continued with their stars winning the 350 and 500 class awards, as they had already done at Berne and Dieppe.

We British have always tended to have a bias towards those whom we consider to be the outsider. So it is hardly surprising that despite the high regard in which the name Norton was held, a break in the Norton run of victories came as a welcome surprise. On 19 August 1933 Walter, on board a Velocette, administered the first major check to Nortons invincibility by winning the 350cc class of the 'world's fastest road race', the Ulster Grand Prix at the record speed of 83.65 mph. In this race Walter had beaten Guthrie and Simpson fair and square. After a slowish start, Walter had joined the Norton party on the third lap riding alongside Guthrie, the pair being just one second behind Simpson. Harold Willis had evidently found some extra power since June and the Velocette rider surged into the lead with a fourth lap record of 85.91 mph. Safely into the lead Walter proceeded to steadily draw away from Guthrie with a marvellous display of consistent racing as these successive lap speeds show: 83.7, 84.0, 84.1, 83.3, 83.5, 83.6 – to take the chequered flag 1 min, 42 secs ahead of Guthrie. As one reporter wrote, 'To hold Walter when he has a slow motor is no joke; to beat him when he has the "goods" is impossible.' This Ulster victory marked the beginning of Velocette's virtual monopoly of the 350 class winning as they did nine out of eleven Ulster races between 1933 and 1950. The winner of the 500cc class was Stanley Woods who in gaining his fourth successive Ulster victory at 87.43 mph kept the Norton flag flying.

Meanwhile, Signor Georgio Parodi was delighted with Walter's successes at Berne and Spa on the red 250cc Guzzi and readily agreed to enter Walter for the FICM Grand Prix of Europe at Malmö, Sweden. It was to be held on 3 September on the Saxtorp circuit. Walter was confident of success, but it was during the practice period that his hopes were dashed when he had the misfortune to skid on a slow turn, and in falling he broke a bone in his right wrist. Hurried arrangements were made for Rolf Gulich, Malmö's Prison Governor, and a keen motorcyclist to take over the Guzzi entry, and after the disqualification of Ted Mellors, Gulich gained a creditable second place.

The race meeting had far reaching consequences for it saw the end of the great 500cc class partnership of Woods and Hunt. The two Norton stars were sailing round in close formation in their usual style. On the 13th lap Stanley had just slipped through a gap in a bunch of slower riders when, as Tim Hunt tried to follow suit, one of the FN riders, Erik Lindberg, swerved into the path of Tim. There was a terrible crash; the Swedish rider was killed instantly, while poor Tim was thrown against a nearby tree, breaking his thigh and forearm. It proved to be the end of Hunt's road racing career. He underwent several operations but his injuries took a long time to heal. He even undertook some rugged long distance trials riding in an effort to regain his fitness. Sadly it was to no avail and finally the damaged leg was set two and a half inches shorter than the other. Norton Motors had lost, in the opinion of many experts, one of their greatest discoveries.

The aftermath of Malmö was also to prove a turning point in Walter's career. In Italy Georgio Parodi anxiously scanned the signature on Handley's letters as Sunday, 15 October, the date of the Italian Grand Prix, drew nearer. Ominously the signature still was not quite regular even after Walter had the splint removed from his wrist. The Guzzi factory had three of their new 500cc V-twin machines ready for their debut in the Rome race and they wanted Walter to ride one of them. Walter's injury did not heal in time, but although the new twin did not win, it was quite clear that apart from a few minor alterations, it would have been victorious in the hands of an experienced rider. Walter was kept closely informed of the tests carried out at Monza which showed the 500cc twin consistently hitting speeds of between 105–111 mph, with power delivered on bench tests to the back wheel of 44 bhp at 7000 rpm.

The TT would be the major test. If the Guzzi was to beat the Nortons, Walter insisted it had to be not only quick, but what was equally important, it had to have good braking power and sound steering qualities. Parodi decided he would run the 500cc Guzzi in the 1934 TT if Wal Handley gave the Okay after testing it. Although no-one as yet knew it, the Guzzi factory had given birth to the 120 degrees 498cc V-twin destined to compete successfully until the early 1950s.

With the Hall Green factory working on their 495cc Velocette for the new season, the Norton camp could be excused for feeling uneasy. Wal Handley on the new Velocette or perhaps the new 498cc Guzzi twin would pose a formidable threat to Norton Motors. The injuries to Hunt had also cast a long shadow over the Norton team. It was becoming clear that Tim was very doubtful for 1934 and with Jimmy Simpson probably in his last season after joining the Competitions Department of Shell-Mex and BP Limited, Nortons felt they had to make a decision. It is interesting to speculate that by signing up their most distinguished adversary, they felt that the Norton supremacy would have much less chance of being broken.

The rush of events were now about to bring things to a head. Although Georgio Parodi and Walter confidently expected that they would continue their fruitful association in 1934, the two men had not seen each other for some time. The elder Parodi had missed the TT, through injury, and Walter's wrist trouble had kept him away from Rome. Then on Saturday, 11 November, Walter was confronted with the offer to ride for the Norton factory in 1934. It was all rather sudden, but after a few moments consideration, Walter said, 'Yes,' and shook hands with Norton's Managing Director, Bill Mansell. It was to prove the biggest mistake of his career although the decision was an understandable one. Today we live in a different world. Such a decision would not be taken by reaching across and shaking hands, the modern star would have his solicitor and barrister present questioning, advising and checking details.

It is not difficult to imagine what must have flashed through Walter's mind. He had witnessed the quartet of Woods, Hunt, Simpson and Guthrie win continental and TT races with unending regularity at a time when he could not even find suitable mounts for the larger class events. The Nortons not only had speed they also had the weight problem under control. He remembered the time he followed Tim Hunt in at the weigh-in on one of the continental events. Walter had been amazed when he heard the clerk call out the weight of the 500cc Norton at just over 300 lbs. This was very near the weight of his 250cc

Guzzi which, because of this, lacked acceleration out of slow corners. Months of pent up frustration led Walter to accept an offer he believed it would have been wrong to refuse.

At Olympia, just over two weeks after Walter had made his agreement with Norton Motors, Stanley Woods created a sensation by announcing that for the 1934 season he was leaving Norton Motors and would be riding Husqvarna, the make which had won the Swedish Grand Prix of Europe in Malmö. In the Lightweight class Stanley switched to the Guzzi that Parodi had originally expected Walter to ride. This was a surprise to everyone, including Walter, who had expected to partner Stanley in the Norton team for the new season. What no-one knew at the time was that all was not well in the Norton camp. Stanley Woods had realised that with Joe Craig, Nortons racing boss, showing increasing signs of favouring Jimmy Guthrie, it was time for him to move on.

Despite this unexpected development Walter viewed the prospects for 1934 with a great deal of optimism. The past year had been difficult for Walter, no less than for many other people in the racing game, but now it was ending on a bright note with the Birmingham star fixed up to ride the world's most successful road racing motorcycle – the Norton. Many people in the industry were glad to see the return of the 'World's Greatest Rider' – vide *Motor Cycling,* to race under British colours. Walter's only regret was that the hitherto friendly relationship with Moto Guzzi was at an end. His sudden decision to join Nortons came as a great shock to the Italians, they did not seem able to see his viewpoint in the matter and they never forgave him. This was the immediate price he paid for the Norton decision, and in the light of subsequent events it can be seen to have been a high one. It was a decision that had been made alongside his efforts to get into racing on four-wheels. Was it a case of simply trying to do too much? Whatever the cause, he was no longer the favoured rider with Moto Guzzi, that role would now belong to Stanley Woods, the popular star rider from Dublin.

CHAPTER 23
CAR RACING AMBITIONS

Over the years Walter had nursed a strong ambition to race cars. Yet through a variety of mischances, often resulting from his motorcycling race commitments and unfulfilled car racing promises, his racing experience on four wheels had remained limited. In 1934, the *Motor Cycle* journal commented:

> ... many of the best judges consider he nurses genius which nobody else can claim. But he has many irons in the fire these days, and is a little temperamental.

At this stage in his career Walter faced the same dilemma that others before and since have faced who, while famous in the motorcycling world, try to join the ranks of the car racers. He could point to racing and record breaking successes on all the major European circuits, but none of this had been achieved with cars. The main difficulty, in the opinion of those who knew him, was that he didn't have enough money to finance himself in car racing. These were the days when motor car sport was a closely knit fraternity, largely composed of wealthy amateurs. The motorcycle stars, men like Freddie Dixon, Syd Crabtree, and Walter had, in the opinion of many, greater skill but lacked the backing and were seen by the others as intruders. He made several approaches to the leading car manufacturers, but without success. As he once commented, 'car manufacturers are hard people to persuade to lend one a car.'

Walter Handley sits at the wheel of a works MG Magnette.

Walter did have more experience with four-wheels than might be supposed from the official record. He was familiar with the large Bentleys, TT Lea Francis, Rileys and the renowned 2 litre Grand Prix Bugatti. In 1930 he had acquired his own straight-eight Bugatti, a car capable of 100 mph. The famous TT rider was invited by the organisers of Birmingham's Perry

Barr Speedway to try to establish a 4-lap car record on their re-opening night of 28 May. This Walter duly did, broadsiding round the turns to register the very creditable record of just over 33 mph for the mile. A nice touch was added, for Walter's old friend Jack Parker, by now an established dirt track star and future world champion, joined him as a passenger.

Walter just knew he had the necessary skill, courage and determination to succeed. He wanted to win, he was no 'dabbler'. Five years earlier, he had performed the extraordinary feat of lapping Le Mans in a faster time than any of his fellow Lagonda drivers had been able to manage in a week of practising. He had done this on his first evening at Le Mans. Just when he was despairing of making a breakthrough, help arrived from an unexpected quarter. Amidst the letters and telegrams passing between Birmingham and Genoa, it soon became apparent that Parodi, the Guzzi chief, had a sympathetic understanding of the problem of a man who, while he had an exalted position in the motorcycle world, had the frustrated desire to become an established racing driver.

Georgio Parodi, the elder son of the Moto Guzzi President, was not only a founder of the firm, and an enthusiastic motorcyclist, he was also a shrewd businessman. He came from a wealthy shipping family, and had many friends in the Italian business world. He had met Walter Handley, admired his skill as a rider, and shared the Englishman's interest in aviation. He had flown in the Italian Air Force during the Great War, and it was through him that the Air Force badge of an eagle was chosen for the Guzzi trademark.

Parodi was aware that many Italian car drivers were former racing motorcyclists, such as Nuvolari, Varzi, Ghersi and the late Luigi Arcangeli, men whom Handley had out ridden on two wheels at one time or another. Considering all this, Parodi decided to speak about Handley to his friend, Count Carlo Felice Trossi, the President of the Scuderia Ferrari and himself a famous racing driver. The Scuderia Ferrari was the racing stable being run by the Modena garage proprietor, Enzo Ferrari. They had come to the fore following the decision in 1932 by Alfa Romeo to withdraw their direct participation in racing.

The timing of Walter's approach to the Scuderia looked promising. Although the Alfas had been winning races all over Europe, they were beginning to falter in the face of the challenge from first Bugatti and then Maserati. By the end of May 1933 Walter met Trossi and Ferrari in Milan. He told them about the new RAC Isle of Man car race 'round the houses' and indicated his keenness to enter a car. To Walter's disappointment it soon became evident that the Scuderia seemed more interested in entering Wal Handley in the Leghorn motorcycle races rather than introducing him into their continental car racing programme. Trossi sensed the Englishman's disappointment. Speaking perfect English, this tall likeable man calmly offered to lend Walter his own Alfa for the Island race. It was an unusual decision, for the Scuderia rarely entertained events organised outside the rich and prestigious European Grand Prix circuits. Walter felt buoyed up; here was his chance to drive the red Alfa with the familiar yellow shield and black horse, the insignia of the Scuderia Ferrari. It was a badge that had seen victory in every Grand Prix in the racing calendar.

After the prize-giving for his Guzzi victory at Berne in the Swiss Grand Prix, Walter quickly made his way to Milan for a meeting with Trossi and Enzo Ferrari. There he learned to his dismay that the promised 2·3 litre Alfa was no longer available. Two of these cars had been involved in crashes and the Scuderia was short. After much discussion Ferrari agreed to get one of their eight-cylinder 2654cc Alfas ready. The race was scheduled for Friday, 14 July, and everyone knew the car had to reach Douglas by the preceding Monday. Walter paid his entrance fee, reserved accommodation on the boat for the car, booked his hotel, and held himself in readiness to dash to Calais or London to hurry the car across to the Island. With just seven days to go a telegram arrived to dash Walter's hopes. Apparently the car could not be prepared in time. Walter was bitterly disappointed with a situation where he had done his best and was in no way to blame. He felt humiliated by what had happened because of the advance publicity his car venture had attracted.

The time between the Tuesday meeting in Milan, and having the Alfa ready for the last possible boat leaving Liverpool on Sunday midnight, was very short and perhaps impossible. Unfortunately, Walter was not in the mood to acknowledge this, and the story of the missing Alfa was a considerable embarrassment to him. A complicating factor was that Walter and the Scuderia each had contracted themselves to different tyre and oil manufacturers. Had the Scuderia succeeded in supplying a car for the Douglas race, Walter's contractors might have been agreeable to his racing in Italy, but with nothing to show for his efforts Walter declined to jeopardise the support he had by racing motorcycles at Leghorn. In refusing to go it may be that Walter lost the chance of being offered a racing car opportunity in Europe, where the Scuderia's interest was uppermost.

There is no doubt that Wal Handley's temperament was both his strength and his weakness. He was quite prepared to spend most of his time in Italy, as he had done in the recent past at Geneva and Liège, but he was not going to court Ferrari's support. Even if we disregard Walter's headlong reaction, it is quite possible that the situation was less favourable than Parodi had supposed. Italy was a fascist dictatorship and it was not unknown for Mussolini to take a close interest in Ferrari's plans. The Italians disliked seeing foreign drivers beating them in one of their own cars.

Parodi's immediate reaction to the Alfa debacle was to enter Walter on the 250cc Guzzi in the French Grand Prix at Dieppe, but as already related the entry was too late for inclusion. It is not too difficult to imagine Walter's feelings, there he was booked in at the Auberge de la Maison Blanche in Dieppe, still smarting from the Alfa disappointment, when the telegram arrives from Mandello del Lario advising him that he would not be allowed to race. It was due to this excess of officialdom that there were not enough entries in the following year, and the French Grand Prix did not reappear in the racing calendar until 1935.

With this feeling of being let down, Walter had decided that he was not going to jeopardise his tyre and oil contracts, nor was he in the mood to disregard the approach from Nortons, the world's most successful road racing motorcycle. At the end of 1933 he felt the clouds beginning to lift as his earlier enquiries into car racing were bearing fruit. MG racing driver and record holder, Captain George Eyston, advised him to go to Abingdon to see Cecil Kimber.

CHAPTER 24
THE LUCK OF THE GAME AGAIN

Just three days before the meeting with Norton Motors, Wal Handley arrived in Abingdon, the home of the only factory in the world at that time devoted exclusively to the manufacture of sports cars. MG (Morris Garages) had been formed out of the enthusiasm and skill of Cecil Kimber, who had been Sir William Morris's manager in Oxford. Patiently Kimber had established MG as an unofficial sports department of the great Morris empire, and eventually as a marque in its own right.

Despite an impressive string of racing victories, Kimber had seen his car sales dip in 1933. Hitherto MG's racing policy had been to rely on wealthy private owners who raced the cars at their own expense. In business you cannot afford to stand still. Kimber had decided he had to move forward with the formation of a works team, which he hoped would revive the public's flagging interest.

Handley's fame as a racing motorcyclist and his keen interest in car racing were well known to Kimber. By this time several former motorcyclists had successfully made the transition to cars, and in the opinion of many, had shown much greater professional skill than some of the more established car drivers; Black, Crabtree and Dixon were examples. Kimber was not a hesitant man, he was impressed with Walter as a person, and with the quickness of decision for which he was justly famed, he offered Walter a place in the official works team for 1934. For Walter Handley this was a considerable achievement in that he had reached this position without influential support. Inwardly he had never doubted that he had the ability to compete with the best, now his enthusiasm was fired at the prospect of driving in Captain George Eyston's team.

The *Daily Herald* gave the story prominence in a banner headline on 11 December, 'Speed Kings of Britain Challenge the World'. The report stated that the MG teams with official backing would, for the first time, take up the challenge of the continental manufacturers who, 'have refused to supply the latest Italian, German and French racers to British drivers.' This made good copy but in reality there was no chance of any British manufacturer producing cars to meet the requirements of Grand Prix formula. It was too costly without government support and there was no commercial incentive. Britain was not a country of big engine cars and the government's excise taxes, rising with increases in engine size, were more punitive than abroad.

Nevertheless the reporter's optimism was not entirely misplaced. In their class MG cars had already won every big international event within reasonable reach of amateur drivers. Eyston's record breaking exploits at Montlhéry had also shown that the company could produce small quality sports cars that were very quick. At the start of the 1934 season the development of the new supercharged K3 Magnette, that Eyston's team was to drive, was at an advanced stage. They had first come to notice in the 1933 Mille Miglia when K3s took the first two places in the 1100cc class. Later in the year a K3 in sports trim scored a resounding victory in the Ards TT; while a single-seater version had won the Brooklands 500-mile race. Considering the reputation they were to gain, it is surprising that only thirty-three of these cars were built.

The car's six-cylinder 1087cc supercharged engine was fairly conventional. The gearbox was operated by a four-speed pre-selector without a clutch. The two-seater body had the fuel tank forming part of the tail. The wheelbase came to just over seven feet and ten inches. The main weakness was that the solidity of construction made the K3 a heavy car at around 18 cwt. In a moment of exasperation Walter once exclaimed to Kimber that he liked the MG cars, but there was, 'too much lamp post iron in them,' not the most tactful thing to say to the MG boss but he had a point.

A great deal of interest was generated by the entry of the famous motorcyclist into the ranks of the car racers. The May 1934 issue of *Motor Sport* carried a feature headed 'Watch Handley!' After noting that racing motorcyclists invariably make first class car drivers, the writer paid tribute to Handley's uncanny genius as a motorcyclist. The piece concluded by expressing the view that, given the opportunity, Handley would soon become Britain's number one Grand Prix driver. The feature based this upon the fact that whenever Handley had raced against Nuvolari and Varzi, those fortunate enough to see these encounters had no doubt who was the better rider.

Unfortunately there was little chance of this expectation being put to the test. For while 1934 was to see the first serious challenge to the Grand Prix supremacy of the Alfa Romeo, it came not from Britain, but from the state subsidised Mercedes Benz and Auto Union teams of Hitler's Germany. The age of motor sport as a yardstick of national prestige was about to be ushered in. In such a climate the opportunity for British drivers to compete on anything like equal terms against the continental 'cracks' was virtually nil. Nearer home it was a different matter and some interesting racing was about to take place.

It was the Junior Car Club that had organised the first international Trophy Race at Brooklands in 1933 and they were the first to start using artificial 'road corners' on the track. The idea had been developed to such an extent that they were able to dispense with the complex handicapping systems usually requiring a stop watch and lap chart. The Club had in effect devised a scratch race to suit the wide variety of cars then racing in this country. The 1934 race had three parallel channels made from hurdles and oil drums laid out on the wide area of the Brooklands fork, where the old finishing straight met the outer circuit. The first of these formed an easy bend for the smaller cars; the three supercharged 747cc MGs and the larger un-blown Rileys and Bugattis. The second channel was more difficult consisting of a left hand bend followed by a right angle turn. This was the channel through which the supercharged MG Magnettes would go. The third channel had an even more acute right angled turn for the larger cars such as Lord Howe's Bugatti, the Maseratis of Whitney Straight and Brian Lewis, and the Alfa Romeos of Kaye Don and John Cobb. In theory if the leading car in each class went through the channels allotted to them, they would come out abreast.

It's a wet start for the 1934 International Trophy Race at Brooklands.
On the front of the grid in group two is Wal Handley, number 17,
and Norman Black, number 12, both driving supercharged MG Magnettes.

Two factors would determine the success of these arrangements. Firstly, had the JCC got its painstaking calculations right? Secondly, a lot would depend upon the courage and skill of the drivers. As they raced clockwise into the finishing straight at the end of each lap they faced an 'S' bend formed by the sandbags and placed before the channels. Since only one driver at a time could emerge from the 'S' bend it would be easy to select the right channel. The testing job for each driver was to try to reach the 'S' bend first, it was a task that required nerve to leave braking as late as possible.

There had been rain before the start and pools of water lay on the track. Walter took up a position on the front of the grid by virtue of his fast practice times. As the thirty-seven cars got away in the massed start, a great cloud of spray was sent flying. At the end of the first lap Walter emerged as the leading MG driver in third place behind the Maseratis of Whitney Straight and Brian Lewis. Momentarily the MG had gained the lead as the cars left the channels, only for the much bigger cars to overtake Walter out on the Byfleet banking. For the first few laps the order remained the same as Walter hung on trying to match the Italian cars for speed. One of Walter's fast laps was equal to 87·20 mph. Immediately behind Walter was Kaye Don's Alfa Romeo, then H. C. Hamilton's MG Magnette, followed by Lord Howe – no longer a young man but driving his Bugatti with the determination of his sailor ancestor.

Meanwhile another great individualist and former motorcyclist, Freddie Dixon, driving with great verve whipped his new Riley Six through the easiest of the three channels to take the lead after 30 laps. This did not last for long as Dixon was obliged to retire with, of all things, a fuel blockage. It was now that Walter's steady driving was rewarded as he regained third place at the half way stage, after enjoying a private battle with Hugh Hamilton, regarded at the time as one of Britain's most promising young drivers. It is sad to reflect that Hamilton was tragically killed later that year on the last lap of the Swiss Grand Prix.

By this time retirements had already taken their toll, early in the race Eyston had retired with clutch trouble and only seventeen cars were destined to finish. Walter's turn came abruptly, with his axle failing after 76 pounding laps on the simply awful Brooklands surface. The two Maserati's of Whitney Straight and Brian Lewis kept each other company throughout the race, finishing quite remarkably within four seconds of each other! The winning speed, of the twenty-one-year-old American,

Whitney Straight, being 89·62 mph. Straight, wealthy, talented and brave, had a distinguished wartime RAF career. Later he became Chairman of BOAC and Rolls Royce Limited. His decision to quit motor racing at the end of 1934 came as a surprise.

That the handicap system had tended to favour the larger continental cars was self evident, bearing in mind that they had taken six out of the first seven places. The MG Magnettes occupied the next four places. What was impressive from

Wal Handley (MG Magnette) selecting his channel at the fork during the 1934 JCC International Race. He was in third place when a broken axle forced his retirement.

Walter's point of view was that in this, his car racing debut, he had sustained his challenge amongst the larger cars for over 60 laps. It was evident that he was as bitingly competitive on four wheels as he was on two. He had successfully pitted himself against Britain's best drivers on, what Tim Birkin had once described as, the most out-of-date, inadequate and dangerous course in the world. Although the prizes were small and the drivers from Europe had not been attracted, nevertheless 100 laps of the notorious 2·6-mile outer track had proved as arduous as any continental race.

A moment during the 1934 JCC International Race. Out on the banking at Brooklands is Cyril Paul (Riley) closely followed by Wal Handley (MG Magnette), number 17.

CHAPTER 25
RACING ROUND THE HOUSES

It was the Monaco Grand Prix, started in 1929, that first captured everyone's imagination as the big glamorous 'Round the Houses Race'. Its twists and turns along the avenues of Monte Carlo is still with us today, a major event in the International Grand Prix Calendar. One of those modelled on the famous Monaco event was the contest organised by the RAC in Douglas, Isle of Man. It seems so long ago that it is almost forgotten, but not quite and for good reason! It was to be Walter's second car racing appearance and the crowds were expectant, knowing that Wal Handley could always be relied upon to deliver excitement.

There were no starting fees and the prizes of £200, £150 and £100 for the podium finishes were modest by the international standards of the day and there was therefore little attraction for the continental drivers. Nevertheless, the series had the support of the Manx Government and appeared more permanent than most. The races were known as the *Mannin Beg,* meaning 'Little Man' and *Mannin Moar* meaning 'Big Man'. In this the second year they were held, the 'Beg' was for cars with supercharged engines under 1100cc and unblown cars up to 1·5 litres, and the 'Moar' was for supercharged 1·5 litre cars and unblown cars over that capacity. Whatever these races may have lacked concerning money, crowds and the glamour of Monte Carlo, they more than made up for it in terms of fun and excitement.

Practising usually started at around 5AM. On the first morning's practice RAC officials forgot to wake up and were duly summoned from their rooms by a polite but insistent police sergeant. It seems amazing that they could have slept through the raucous whine of those supercharged cars! Well worth reading is Peter Chamberlain's novel, *Sing Holiday,* for it gives a truly hilarious account of an elderly widower who, seeking a quiet Manx holiday, finds himself caught up with the noise and hubbub of the car races.

The course was terribly bumpy and the story goes that the gentleman who looked after the roads, when asked if he had put down any material on a very uneven bit, replied, 'Yes, a little – about eight tons!' The course had been altered from the one used in 1933 so as to avoid disrupting the commercial centre of Douglas, but it was surely not for the faint-hearted. The route was packed with telegraph poles, tramlines, pillar- boxes, lamp standards and abounded with tight corners and eminently hittable kerbstones. The cars started from the Crescent Cinema on the Promenade from where they turned sharp right up Broadway Hill. They levelled out into York Road before dropping down to the Bray Hill hairpin. From the top of Bray Hill the road lay straight for a mile past the TT Grandstand before entering the Onchan hairpin. From here the road dropped steeply down Summer Hill to the sea front. The circuit amounted to slightly less than four miles, and with 50 laps it meant the cars would travel a distance of 185 miles.

There was tragedy on the Monday before the race. Kaye Don took his Magnette out for some testing with Francis Tayler, an MG works mechanic, as passenger. They set off late in the evening with no lights, number plates or insurance, and there was a collision. Both men were injured as the car lost a wheel and overturned. Sadly, Tayler died in the early hours of Tuesday, the day before the race. The subsequent court case was to bring MG unwelcome publicity, and it has been suggested that it was this event which began Lord Nuffield's dislike of racing and led directly to his decision, a year later, to end MGs direct involvement in the sport.

The day of the race, Wednesday, 30 May 1934, dawned bright and sunny with a slight mist over the sea as the nineteen starters lined up and came under starters orders. The front row on the grid consisted of Wal Handley, Hugh Hamilton, George Eyston – all driving supercharged MG Magnettes, and Freddie Dixon with his 1486cc Riley. They were the four fastest drivers in practice. Handley had made a strong impression being the fastest of all with a record practice time of 2 mins, 56 secs: 74·82 mph.

The moment the starter's flag dropped, Walter sent his brown and cream MG storming off into the lead for the sharp right turn into Broadway Corner all in the space of two hundred

At the pits during practice for the 1934 Mannin Beg 'Round the Houses' race. Walter is apparently not in a good mood.

yards. Behind Walter came the following cars in a snarling bunch, the sandbagged lamp-post in the centre of the road just escaping destruction. As the crescendo died away, the shaken flag marshal on this corner was so alarmed that he went to an RAC official demanding that the race be stopped in view of the danger. Meanwhile all eyes were turned towards Summer Hill at the Onchan end of the promenade. Less than three minutes had elapsed when the high pitched whine of a supercharged car was heard. It was the idol of the TT crowds, Walter Handley bringing his MG Magnette lunging down to the sea front and travelling at well over 100 mph. No other driver was in sight yet as Walter, using every inch of the road, swept through on the seaward side of the front. He had taken a seven seconds lead in less than four miles.

The mechanics in the MG pit had settled back to enjoy a hard earned respite. Their refreshments were neatly set out on the pit counter, when to their astonishment Handley's MG arrived much earlier than they had expected. They had just time to duck, as Walter, not bothering about white lines, screamed past within inches of the pit counter, sending up a cloud of dust, from the Douglas Corporation's earlier road sweepings, which completely smothered the sandwiches and everything else. 'Did we swear,' recalled one of the mechanics who told this story to Walter's brother Tom, 'but we were really sorry when we were told that Wal had not got safely round into Broadway.'

Walter had approached the sharp right turn too fast, braked and despite his efforts to straighten the resultant skid, the car slipped broadside on and its tail end smacked against the sandbags guarding the base of the lamp standard. Sand was sent flying from the burst sacks, the lamp shook, and whilst Walter's car was still vibrating the rest of the field careered round. Freddie Dixon managed to squeeze round by taking to the pavement on the wrong side. Walter's car, with a broken fuel tank and a buckled back axle was out of the race. Walter, who had been nearly thrown out of the car, was let off comparatively lightly with a bruised left arm up to the elbow. This did not bode well for Walter's TT debut on a Norton just two weeks away!

The famous lamp standard was destined to feature again in this race. On the next lap Dixon caused excitement by surging round on the other side of the lamp post, narrowly missing it. A little later, Pat Fairfield, also driving a Riley, struck the sandbagged lamp post but was able to continue. Another MG driver, Hugh Hamilton, was not so lucky. On the 23rd lap, his car in descending the winding Summer Hill, skidded and brought down a telegraph pole festooning the car in wires. Hamilton was unhurt, as he climbed out he found himself facing a poster which read, 'Why not Hire a Car and Drive Yourself'!

Into the lead went Freddie Dixon and with just four laps to go he looked a certain winner. Freddie's physical style of driving, his car frequently screeching into corners broadside on, was great fun for the spectators although his fellow competitors were noticeably less enthusiastic. Then with just 18 miles to go,

A sensational start to the 1934 Mannin Beg, Wal Handley
has gained an astonishing lead on the opening lap but catches
the sandbagged lamp standard at Broadway and is out of the race.

Dixon, for the second time in a month, had a fuel problem. This time he simply ran out of petrol on the far side of the course and was out of the race. Another ex-motorcyclist, Norman Black, came through driving a very steady race with his MG Magnette to win at 70·99 mph.

Walter's crash at Broadway had mystified onlookers. The Newsreel proves that he went into the turn with no other driver in sight. So what had induced Walter to throw away his chances in a race his practice performance suggested he had an excellent chance of winning? The answer lay with the well-known Handley temperament. To what fate was it due that on the morning of the race Walter lost his temper in an argument with a well known motoring journalist? The precise nature of the dispute is not now known, but whatever was said left Walter with a burning sense of injustice. Many years later he told his brother that, although bad luck had prevented him having more racing successes, the one exception was the Mannin Beg car race, 'I blame myself for that, I was at fault, I should have won that car race comfortably, but for my temper.'

Despite his injuries Walter had hoped to rejoin the MG team at Brooklands for the British Empire Trophy run on 23 June. Then just eleven days before the car race, he was injured again, this time in the Junior TT race riding a Norton. Nevertheless the depleted MG team made the Brooklands event another Abingdon triumph. Eyston, who was driving the EX135, won at 80·81 mph after Straight's Maserati and Dixon's Riley had fallen away when they had had victory in sight.

CHAPTER 26
THE NORTON DISAPPOINTMENT

There is no doubt that Walter approached the new season with Nortons in a mood of optimism. He had even entered the Birmingham Motor Cycle Club's early season Victory Trial on a 348cc Norton. It was an event he had not competed in since 1926. Spectators were treated to a Wal Handley spectacular climb of Dropping Wells in a series of controlled but spectacular skids. He was enthusiastic; it was 'game on'.

In the weeks leading up to the TT there was keen anticipation at the prospect of seeing Handley on a works Norton for the first time. The *Motor Cycle* commented, 'Handley on his day and in the right mood is still the most debonair and devilish of all motorcycle road racers.' Cyclops in *Motor Cycling*, went for a Handley win in the Junior TT explaining that despite, 'an undeniable tendency to fall off on occasion, to be what they call temperamental – I still think he is the finest rider in the world.' That such comments could be made after the sweeping successes of the regular Norton stars speaks volumes about the esteem in which Walter was held.

Yet Walter already knew that his supporters were likely to be disappointed. In the early season try-out in Northern Ireland, the North West 200, he had been shocked to discover that despite winning on corners in the usual style, his team mate Guthrie's Norton was miles per hour faster along the straights. The Scotsman went on to win the 500 class with ease, while Walter was obliged to retire early in the race. This suggested that the all powerful Joe Craig, boss of the Norton

Technical Department, had chosen Guthrie to succeed Stanley Woods as the Norton number one. This did not suit Walter at all; he wanted a fair and equal chance to win. He expressed his dissatisfaction and asked to be given the chance to prepare, at his own business premises, the Nortons he was scheduled to ride. It must have come as no surprise that the management of Norton Motors felt unable to agree to what amounted to a vote of no confidence in Craig. So it was in this unhappy frame of mind that Walter approached what was destined to be his last appearance in the Isle of Man TT as a competitor.

It might so easily have been a different story. Norton race policy in the Island differed from their continental practice in that there was no pre-conceived race plan. This would have suited Walter for he had no time for planned results, and wanted always to race, pitting his skill fair and square. Clashes of personality behind the scenes in the Norton training camp made this policy irrelevant from Walter's point of view. To the regret of the Norton back room, Stanley Woods a genial, charming and friendly person had sensed that he was no longer going to do so well after Guthrie joined the team, and so he had left to join Husqvarna. Walter was now also discovering that the atmosphere was not to his liking. On one occasion Craig referred pointedly to Walter's lack of interest in physical training, something Guthrie took very seriously. It provoked the riposte, 'You train the bikes, Joe, I'll ride 'em!'

Walter always believed that he was allocated the machines which vibrated the most, and it was true that the 1934 Nortons needed 'holding'. In June the *Motor Cycle* reported that the vibration at certain speeds gave the rider's hands a bad time. Walter had an additional disadvantage, the importance of which was not fully appreciated at the time, because of the Mannin Beg car crash he had to ride wearing a glove on his left hand with his arm blue with bruising up to the elbow. This was remembered by Bill Mewis, the Norton mechanic, who commented, 'How Wal rode for six laps in third place, I'll never know.'

In the race itself, Walter was definitely racing and giving every indication of his dissatisfaction with his third place behind Guthrie and Simpson. In view of the great physical strain under which he was riding, it was a wonderful effort. On the first lap only six seconds had separated the Norton trio, thereafter Walter fell back from the leaders despite his usual fast cornering and being reported as spectacular from all the main vantage points. At one stage Walter was battling to keep ahead of Ernie Nott's twin-cylinder Husqvarna, but as he came to the end of the sixth lap he was still holding a strong third place. It was a warm sunny day and in several places wet tar was presenting a hazard. It was at this point that Walter came off on the tar at Governor's Bridge. He was taken to hospital suffering abrasions to both hands and needing a stitch put in his nose. This mishap allowed his former Rudge team mate, Nott, to create a new record by piloting his Swedish Husqvarna-twin into third place. It was the first time a foreign machine had ever been placed in the Junior TT. Only nine seconds separated Guthrie and Simpson, the quiet unassuming Scot giving Nortons their fourth successive win in this event at the record speed of 79·16 mph.

It was unfortunate for Walter that his contract with Nortons meant that he was unable to ride in Wednesday's Lightweight race, his favourite event, because Nortons had made it a condition that their factory entrants were not allowed to race any other machines. With Walter unavailable Moto Guzzi had signed up Stanley Woods and the Irish flyer was a favourite for this race. Another star rider favoured to win was Jimmy Simpson, he was no longer bound by the Norton agreement because, since joining Shell, he was in effect a private entrant riding with the consent of his new employers. Shell was insisting that this was to be his last season. The way was now open for Simpson to enter the Lightweight TT as a member of Graham Walker's Rudge syndicate. Some of his friends recalled how unusual it was for Jimmy to refuse having a drink at the Castle Mona Hotel on the night before the race, he knew that this was going to be his last and best chance of winning a TT race.

This he duly did heading the Rudge trio with a winning speed of 70·81 mph, while Stanley on the Guzzi came in fourth after some early troubles. Yet, Walter's record lap for this race made on the Rudge two years earlier still stood. At last after twelve years of trying, Simpson had gained his only TT victory. It was a popular win, and Jim, just thirty-five years young, as the saying goes, was able to retire from racing on a high note.

In Friday's Senior Race, the two Jimmies repeated their one-two performance, but they had a battle with Stanley Woods' Husqvarna 500 twin, reputed to be the fastest bike in the race. Stanley had split the Norton pair before the 'Huskie' had run out of petrol on the mountain to let Simpson into second place. Walter was a non-starter because of the injuries he had sustained on Monday.

Walter had recovered sufficiently from his injuries to take part in the Belgian Grand Prix at Spa on Sunday, 14 July 1934. Riding with him in the 500 event as a new member of the Norton team was Charlie Dodson who, after the injury to Jimmy Guthrie in the Dutch TT, had been signed up to ride Nortons for the rest of the season.

In the continental events it was the Norton practice to plan the result in advance, and on this occasion Joe Craig decided that it was to be Dodson's race. This was absolute anathema to Walter who by now had other ideas. He was having a wretched season by his own high standards and by now he was convinced that he had been signed up to prevent the Norton supremacy from being seriously challenged. So with the memory of his TT disappointment fresh in his mind, Walter arranged to have molten lead poured into the handlebars of his Norton to deaden the vibration. The team manager's plan depended upon Dodson coming in to refuel first, learn his position and ride comfortably within himself and the machine. Walter decided to forestall this.

Away from the race track Walter was a slow moving individual who refused to be hurried. He always took up his position on the grid at the last possible moment, removing the familiar cap and calmly fastening his helmet. However, as the flag fell over the massed start he would become a very different being. With a steely deliberation he took the lead right from the start by leaving his braking into the hairpin as late as possible. After setting up an average speed of 85 mph, Walter came in first to refuel and waited for Dodson to join him. They agreed to ride together at high speed to make a spectacle for the benefit of the crowds lining the course. For the rest of the race there was never more than about three seconds between the two British

It's the 1934 Belgian Grand Prix and Wal Handley (490 Norton) is leading his team-mate, Charlie Dodson, round Francorchamps Corner to win the race; his only success with the Nortons.

riders. After just over three hours racing, Walter flashed past the line one second ahead of Dodson to win at the record speed of 84·09 mph. Although the result was hardly calculated to make Walter any more popular in certain quarters, he had made sure of his only success in 1934.

Walter Handley's final outing under Norton colours was in one of his old favourites, the Ulster Grand Prix. It was scheduled for Saturday, 17 August 1934. It is remembered in the annals of the sport because of the most stupendous pile-up involving almost all sixty riders, just half a mile from the start at Ballyhill. However, what was of much greater significance was the first victory for the new 495cc Velocette.

It is impossible to know exactly what happened in that opening mêlée. What we do know is that Jimmy Guthrie, riding for the first time since his misfortune in the Dutch TT, was at the centre of it. In trying to make up ground in the massed start, the Norton star ran out of space on the fast right hand

The Norton works team for the 1934 Ulster Grand Prix.
Left to right: Handley, whose 490cc Norton is in the foreground; Jimmy Simpson, who ended his career with a win in the 350cc race; Jimmy Guthrie; and Charlie Dodson.

sweeping bend, hit the bank at speed and cannoned across the road. There was little chance for those following to avoid the wildly careering Norton as first one rider and then another added to the pile-up. With engines screaming out their revs, and riders sprawled everywhere, the possibility of carnage appeared frightful, but amazingly the worst injury was that suffered by Alec Mitchell who broke his thigh. Nevertheless, this incredible opening was largely responsible for the fact that only fifteen out of the sixty competitors in the three classes run concurrently managed to finish the race.

Meanwhile, Walter being one of the riders in the van of the massed start had avoided the pandemonium and was chasing another Walter, the twenty-four-year-old blonde from Belfast, named Rusk. This local hero was riding Velocette's long awaited 495cc model upon which he had gained third place in the Senior TT. It was modelled on the famous 348cc model, the rocker gear was totally enclosed, there were two plugs and a twin-spark magneto. Rusk soon showed how well it could go as he became the first rider to clock a lap at over 90 mph in a European road race. As the leading Norton rider Wal Handley battled to remain on terms, so much so that at one point he ran off the course and broke both his fork girders. This was not discovered until after the race. Walter kept going and took the lead for some considerable time after Rusk had been obliged to stop and change a plug. Then in the latter stages of the race, Walter's Norton slowed appreciably and he was overtaken by Rusk and then his Norton team mate, Dodson.

On the last lap when a third place seemed certain, Walter had, as *Motor Cycling* commented, 'The bitter experience, not by any means new to him, of the engine going solid a mere 10 miles from home.' Walter Rusk, a rider of great courage and daring went on to win at the record speed of 88.38 mph. In the 1939 Ulster, Rusk gained the distinction of becoming the first rider in the world to lap an international road race at 100 mph. Sadly it was Rusk's last race for he died a year later while serving in the RAF. His victory in 1934 held in it for Walter a certain irony, for it had seen Rusk repeat Walter's own success over the Nortons in the same event a year earlier.

The stage was now set for changes in the new season. The time had come for him to approach his friend Harold Willis for the chance to ride Velocettes again. Walter notified Norton Motors that he saw no point in renewing his contract. The Norton episode, which had begun with Walter feeling very optimistic, was finally at an end.

CHAPTER 27
TWIST OF FATE

Walter's enthusiasm to get a foothold in the realm of motor sport was unabated, despite the early disappointments. He wanted a fresh challenge. It is a curious fact about motor racing that many a fine driver's promising start has been followed by the anti-climax, not of failure, but rather a lack of success caused by diverse circumstances. In the JCC International Race enough had been seen of Walter's driving to suggest that he had the necessary skill and verve. His enthusiasm was apparent, but various mechanical 'gremlins' continued to deny him success.

On Saturday, 1 September 1934, the Royal Automobile Club's International Tourist Trophy, a sports car race of major importance, was due to be run on the renowned Ards road circuit in Northern Ireland. It was an extremely challenging course, triangular in shape and about 14 miles long and driven clockwise. The drivers faced something of an ordeal for, although speeds would be much lower than in a European Grand Prix, the total distance was 478 miles and the race would last over six hours – twice as long as the average continental race. The start was on the straight stretch of road to the east of Dundonald, and just beyond it the road curved to the left round Mill Corner to rise up Quarry Hill and begin the twisting downhill stretch known as Bradshaws Brae. This led under a railway bridge into Newtownards, where a narrow sharp right turn permitted cars to squeeze by the Town Hall. A 2-mile straight followed ending with two bends and a level crossing before snaking into Comber. On under the railway bridge, the road passed through Ballystockart and yet another railway bridge to reach the Dundonald Hairpin, and the final stage uphill back to the pits.

It was a race strictly governed by a host of regulations, the RAC insisting that every car had to carry hoods, wings and screens, and be a standard production type. For this event, the seventh to be held on the Ards Circuit, the organisers had banned the use of superchargers. This ban was a major factor resulting in the absence of the foreign cars. Nevertheless, an estimated crowd of over half a million gathered early at various vantage points for what promised to be an exciting race. There were many cars present with a deserved reputation for going 'quick'. They included the Lagondas and Invictas, the Talbots and Singers, Rileys and Fraser-Nashes, Aston Martins, plus the Rolls-Bentley of Eddie Hall, to say nothing of George Eyston's MG team that included two motorcycle stars, Charlie Dodson and Wal Handley.

Since 1931 MGs had hardly ever raced without superchargers. To meet the ban, Kimber had ordered the development on the N-type Magnette to be stepped up. The power output was raised to an impressive 74 bhp at 6500 rpm. The six-cylinder engine was basically 1271cc, but listed as 1287cc. The manual gearbox was mounted on a rubber insulated sub-frame which was fitted into a tapered chassis. This resulted in the car having a slightly narrower track than the K-type.

Since the race was run under a system of both credit laps and time allowances, the cars were started in batches, and the N-type MG Magnettes would be the first away at 11am. As the MG team came to the line they knew that George Eyston's team plan might not work. Eyston had given Wal Handley the pace-making role and asked Charlie Dodson to keep as close as possible, while he, Eyston, would move up if anything went wrong. As the designated pacesetter Walter had an excellent chance if all went well. Unfortunately, Walter had found during practice that his car, number 26, was lacking in 'urge' and would falter as soon as it approached top 'revs'. Walter told the mechanics that he suspected that the cylinder head might have a crack. On the eve of the race the mechanics stripped the engine down but they could find nothing wrong. At 6 AM the next morning Walter was out on the course, but the car remained temperamental. Walter told Charlie that he was unhappy with the car and asked him to be ready to take over the pace-setting role. All that Walter could now do was to hope for the best.

Right from the start, Walter was unable to set the pace as planned. Any hope of the car quickly settling down to its work soon disappeared. The early order had been Eyston, Dodson, Handley, with Norman Black in another N-type close at hand. Later Dodson explained what had happened:

> On the rush up Quarry Hill, I was passed by Norman Black, our chief rival. I knew that it would be a bad thing if he were allowed to get away. I tucked in behind him, passed Handley and clung to Black all round the course. My idea was to pass him if I could, and then to let Handley go by and continue the good work after his own car had settled to its job.

At the Dundonald Hairpin Black ran wide and both Dodson and Handley got past him. Charlie waved for Walter to go in front, but the car still seemed below par and Black came up again and passed them both. Charlie explained:

> We chased Black down to Newtownards and along the straight to Comber, where he pulled up, we shot by, and Handley waved for me to go in front again, he felt that his machine was not motoring too well, and he wanted me to take his place and make the pace.

After this Dodson moved ahead, overtook Eyston and in response to pit signals kept going at top speed just keeping ahead of the challenge presented by Eddie Hall in the 3·6 litre Rolls-Bentley. Charlie Dodson went on to win the race by a mere

17 seconds from Hall after being at the wheel for well over six hours hard motoring at 74.65 mph. Although the MG Magnette had achieved a fast average speed, it illustrated the difference made by a supercharged car in the hands of a world class driver. In the previous year Nuvolari's supercharged Magnette had won at 78.65 mph while breaking the lap record seven times.

What had happened to Walter? After completing half the distance, he came into the pits at 2·15 PM. He had covered 17 laps averaging just over 73 mph. After three minutes, talking things over with the mechanics, he decided to call it a day in response to some queer engine noises, rather than risk causing any serious damage to the car. Gearbox trouble was given as the official reason. This race had eventually borne testimony to Walter's almost uncanny understanding of engines. In the run up to the Ards TT Walter had insisted that his car had a cracked cylinder head, but the available tests carried out in Belfast had been unable to locate the trouble. Yet when the car was later examined under more scientific conditions at Abingdon, Cecil Kimber was able to confirm that Walter's original diagnosis had been correct. A hairline fracture had been found on the cylinder head which opened up as the temperature rose.

This Ulster TT, the thirteenth in the series, had been unlucky for quite a few people. Out of the thirty-two starters, eighteen had been forced to retire. The MG camp had their fair share of problems. Bill Everitt's car had failed with a wheel collapse, Norman Black, who had won this event in 1931 with a C-type Midget, went out with engine trouble, as did George Eyston. However, it is results that matter and MGs publicity department could dwell with justifiable pride on the fast driving of Charlie Dodson and the reliable performance of the winning car.

The last big race of the season was the 500-mile race run at Brooklands on Saturday, 22 September. This event organised by the British Racing Drivers' Club took the form of a straight run around the outer circuit, with no corners and artificial bends other than those on the track itself. The race had an end of season atmosphere, and judging by the handicap times, fully justified its claim to be the world's fastest long distance event. Most enthusiasts tried to get the wheel of the fastest available car. George Eyston decided to use his 'Magic Magnette'. Its record breaking exploits in Class G included the Flying Mile at 128·69 mph and 120·88 miles to the hour. This K3 Magnette was built on to a chassis known as EX135. It had an offset transmission line in order to allow a low seating position. Eyston chose Wal Handley, whom he considered the fastest member of the MG team, to be his co-driver in this race.

By midday when the race was due to start, the rain was falling steadily and the track was awash. Eyston went into the lead on handicap right from the start averaging about 116 mph in spite of the appalling conditions. By 1·30 PM the rain was still falling heavily as Eyston continued to lead from Dixon's 2 litre Riley and John Cobb's 23 litre Napier Railton. Eyston, whose driving was of the imperturbable kind, was aware that the conditions favoured the Magic Magnette's handicap. A single-seater version of the K3, driven by Eddie Hall, had won the same event last year, so the auguries were good.

With almost clinical precision a rain soaked Eyston came into the pits at 2·15 PM, had the wheels changed, shock absorbers tightened, the car refuelled and handed over to Walter Handley. While this was happening, Freddie Dixon sailed into the lead. Shortly before 2·30 PM while Walter was off in pursuit the rain developed into what can only be described as a steady downpour. The wide flat un-cambered parts of the track could not drain easily. Flooding was to remain a problem throughout most of the five hours of racing.

It was at this juncture on Walter's third circuit, and the car's ninety-first, that the Magic Magnette, number 19, went into a long front wheel slide shortly after entering the Railway Straight. The car slid sideways off the track at well over 100 mph, nearly demolishing Eyston's private signalling station, complete with Ernest Eldridge and his assistants. The MG finally came to rest on the grass verge on the inside end of the straight. Walter emerged shaken but unscathed except for a minor cut on his forehead.

Charles Mortimer, the well known Brooklands motorcyclist, was one of the first on the scene, 'You okay, Wal?'

'Yes,' and then the familiar drawl, 'didn't think much of that at all.' He wanted Eyston to be told what had happened, Mortimer found Eyston making his way to the scene in a borrowed car. As he related in his book, *Brooklands and Beyond,* Charles deemed it unwise to tell Walter what Eyston said! Not surprisingly race reports tended to imply, even if they did not say so outright, that Eyston's co-driver had lost the race for him. In the November issue of the MG magazine, the respected motoring journalist, King-Farlow, appeared to lay the blame for the crash in the '500' entirely upon Handley. The article had, however, been written before any detailed examination of the car had been made.

In the January issue of the magazine King-Farlow, having learned the cause of the crash, was keen to exonerate Handley from any blame. He explained that a ball race in the near side rear wheel had seized locking the wheel and causing,

> ... an almost completely uncontrollable slide. Moreover, as the race housing had cracked it is improbable that the car, although drivable, could have continued at speed for any length of time.

The journalist asked that his letter be published in order to correct any wrong impression he may have given, 'concerning a very great driver.' Even Eyston, a skilled mechanic as well as a driver, who was most thorough in all his preparations for races and for record breaking, could not have foreseen this. These numerous and often inexplicable mechanical failures sowed the only seed of bitterness in Walter's otherwise generous nature, 'It would darn well happen to me,' he would say.

The 500-mile race was won by Freddie Dixon in his un-supercharged Riley, he finished the race in just under five hours at 104·80 mph. Not surprisingly, in view of the conditions, this was slightly slower than the winning speed of the K3 MG in

1933 – 106·53 mph and quite a lot slower than the speed Eyston's Magic Magnette had been averaging before the crash. A fast long distance event of this kind took a heavy toll on the racing machines which were generally much less reliable than today. Only seven of the thirty-two starters finished within the prescribed time, but since four of the seven finishers were MG Magnettes, the Abingdon factory must have felt reasonably happy with the overall result. The larger cars had great difficulty and John Cobb wisely withdrew his huge Napier Railton after getting into tremendous front wheel slides rounding the fork. At one stage Pat Fairfield's Riley Nine had been well in contention with Dixon, until he too went out of control in the Railway Straight and had ended up sliding backwards, demolishing a section of iron fencing on the opposite side of the track to where Walter had 'exited'.

It was an eventful end to the season, but Walter, who led an exciting life anyway, could not have been sorry to see the end of the 1934 racing calendar. He may well have reflected that his car racing was following the same disappointing pattern of his early years on motorcycles. If so, he had the incentive to remain as determined as he had ever been. His turn would surely come, but he needed more time.

What must have been Walter's thoughts as he piloted the twin-engine Monospar into Castletown, Isle of Man, on Sunday, 26 May, 1935? His first season in motor racing had been terribly frustrating, perhaps his luck was about to change? Over to his right he could make out the familiar crescent shape of Douglas Bay with its two picturesque headlands making a calm and sublime scene. In just three days time Walter would be one of the car drivers in the Mannin Beg car race, helping to shatter the peace and quiet of the pre-holiday season. The third and as it turned out, the last 'Round the Houses' contest, was about to begin. Walter wanted to win the Mannin Beg and he knew he could do so given a trouble free run, but was that likely? Privately he rather doubted the wisdom of the MG decision to concentrate their racing effort on the new R-type Midget.

Walter would have preferred the company to have continued its efforts with the already successful K3 in its various forms. The design change to the R-type had been dictated by the financial crisis. The small relatively inexpensive 'blown' MGR Midgets and Austin Sevens were virtually changing the racing scene in this country.

The MG Managing Director, Cecil Kimber, had been intrigued with the independent suspension systems of the new German Grand Prix cars, and wanted the possibility investigated. The response was a stiff backbone chassis with wishbone suspension to which was fitted a modified Q-type supercharged engine of 746cc. Although it depended upon the state of tune, this engine was capable of 110 bhp at 6500 rpm. Having magneto ignition meant that it was not necessary to carry a battery. The new car was announced on 25 April, at the remarkable price of £750. It was unique in that it was the only genuine single-seater MG ever offered for sale to the public. Unfortunately this enterprising design had a disastrous debut on 6 May, in the JCC International Trophy at Brooklands experiencing cylinder head cracking and trouble with the superchargers. These difficulties had to be put right if the MGR Midgets were to impress in the Isle of Man. The cars were known to roll a great deal on corners and later it was discovered that the frequency of the rear suspension was lower than that of the front, thus making the MGR unstable in pitch.

Meanwhile in the Isle of Man there were ominous signs that all was not well. The 1934 Mannin Beg winner, Norman Black, who had replaced Dodson in Eyston's team, sustained axle failure with a broken cardan shaft while practising. The next morning Eyston's car stopped on Bray Hill for the same reason. Several drivers were complaining about the bumpy nature of the course but there was little that could be done. In the MG camp these worries overshadowed the announcement that Sir Herbert Austin's new 750cc twin overhead camshaft single-seater cars would not be ready in time. This was a great disappointment to the motorcycling fraternity who had hoped to see three more of their heroes in action, Charlie Dodson, Pat Driscoll and Stanley Woods of the newly formed Austin team.

It was now apparent that the race was likely to be between the MGRs of Captain George Eyston's team, the two ERAs of Raymond Mays and Pat Fairfield, and Dixon's unsupercharged 1·5 litre Riley. This viewpoint seemed to be confirmed when it was seen that the fastest practice times had put Fairfield, Handley and Dixon on the front of the grid. Walter, whose driving was drawing much favourable comment, had in his 7 hp car equalled the best time put up by Fairfield's 1100cc ERA in

Walter with the MGR at the 1935 Mannin Beg 'Round the Houses' race in Douglas.

3 mins, 31 secs at 68·84 mph; Dixon's best time had been three seconds slower. The course was 4·03 miles, slightly longer than in 1934. The introduction of the new hairpin bend at Greensill's Corner gave spectators the attraction of a high speed double run along the promenade before a sharp left turn into Broadway. The rest of the course remained unchanged. The 'Beg' cars were limited to 1500cc or 1100cc if supercharged.

Walter, probably remembering his precipitate dash to disaster in the previous year, took up a strategic fifth position at the end of the first lap behind E. R. Hall (MG Magnette), Fairfield, Mays and Dixon. At the end of the third lap the order was Mays, Hall, Fairfield, Dixon and Handley. It was the last time that Walter came round. He was the first to retire when his axle snapped at the foot of Bray Hill. The MG team's hopes were finally shattered when Eyston retired with a faulty magneto, and Black, after just 15 laps, had his axle go again. Six of the thirteen starters were retired before half way; such was the rigour of 'Round the Houses'.

The early stages of the 1935 Mannin Beg race shows Freddie Dixon (Unsupercharged Riley 1486cc) closely followed by Wal Handley (Supercharged 746cc MGR). Wal retired after three laps with axle trouble, while Freddie was one of only two drivers to finish.

The race then developed into an ERA-Riley duel, with Dixon chasing home his former mechanic, the twenty-seven-year-old South African, Pat Fairfield, whose average speed of 67·29 mph gave him a winning margin of eight minutes. These two were the only ones to finish the 201-mile race! Fairfield went on to have a fair amount of success with ERA before he was killed at the wheel of a Fraser-Nash-BMW in a multi car pile up at

Le Mans in 1937. This Isle of Man Beg Race had given ERA (English Racing Automobile) their first victory since they had begun their quest with the 1934 British Empire Trophy Race. They were about to take over MG's racing mantle and they had two important advantages; their cars were designed from the outset as single-seaters, and they had a 1500cc engine available.

One can only guess at Walter's feelings. He evidently decided not to wait and see Friday's Mannin Mooar Race which Brian Lewis was to win for the third year running. Shortly after the Beg race ended, Walter's plane took off from Castletown and two hours later he landed at Castle Bromwich. Only that morning he had made up the front of the grid with Fairfield and Dixon, and been one of the favourites to do well, yet he was the only one of that trio not to finish. He was rediscovering, what he knew to be true, from his early motorcycle racing experience, that the margin between being brilliant and actually bringing home the results is so small as to be almost immeasurable.

In June 1935 all development work on the advanced R-type, single-seater MG Midget came to an abrupt end. Lord Nuffield, with his well known dislike of motor sport, finally withdrew Morris support for MG racing. The brief MG announcement simply stated that the company would cease building racing cars. The statement came as a bit of a shock when it was realised that this meant all racing, including events of the Le Mans and Ards TT type. Fortunately the Nuffield edict came too late to prevent Eyston's team from racing together for the last time on Saturday, 6 July, in the fourth British Empire Trophy Race. Only the year before George Eyston, in the K3 Magnette, had won this race, but if the MG camp was hoping to bow out with a repeat triumph from one of their drivers, they were to be disappointed. In the eight years of its pre-war existence, it is a fact that no driver succeeded in winning the Empire Trophy more than once, and no similar car twice crossed the line in first place.

In 1935 it was the turn of the 2 litre Riley's of Dixon, Edgar Maclure and Cyril Paul to score a sweeping 1-2-3 over the artificial road course laid out at Brooklands. Like so many races in this period it took its toll, and of the thirty-two starters, only fourteen managed to finish the 240 miles in the time limit. In many respects it could be said that the race degenerated into the story of oiled up plugs. The most likely cause arose from some very slow artificial bends which these highly tuned cars had to negotiate. This trouble began almost at once and it continued throughout the race. Walter suffered in the same way after going in front initially and leading his class for the first quarter of an hour. Then for some unknown reason his car suddenly went 'dead'. It happened in a most inconvenient position at the foot of an incline near the paddock bridge. In Walter's words, 'all electricity ceased.' It took some time for the mechanics to reach him, and when they did the trouble continued to elude everyone. Then, after about 30 minutes or so, the car sprang to life as mysteriously as it had earlier died, and Walter was off to try and finish. Meanwhile the ERAs and Eyston's MG were beset with misfiring, whilst Norman Black, who had in the closing stages looked as though he would gain third place for MGs, had finally to settle for fifth position after further plug troubles.

Once again Wal Handley had demonstrated that he was as brilliant on four wheels as he was on two, but at the end he had nothing tangible to show for his efforts. These unofficial times taken at 4pm, showed that he was the fastest exponent in his class: Handley 74·48 mph; Fairfield (ERA 1100) 72·97 mph; Letts (MG Magnette) 72·49 mph; Eyston 70·59 mph; and D. Evans (MG 'Q' Midget) 69·69 mph. When the time limit was imposed Walter had six miles or two laps still to do, yet allowing for all the delays, his actual driving time up to this point had been eight minutes faster than Freddie Dixon's winning Riley. Having magneto ignition had meant that it was not necessary for the MGR to carry a battery – a circumstance that in all probability lost Walter this race.

When the MG team left Brooklands for the last time, they already knew that but for the latest change in policy a new all independently sprung Magnette single-seater would have emerged. In closing down the Abingdon racing shops, Leonard Lord, Nuffield's new managing director, virtually guaranteed that the ERA would become Britain's foremost racing machine. It was to say the least an inconclusive and unsatisfactory end to Wal Handley's motor racing with MG. It was now time for Wal Handley to turn his attention to the Isle of Man TT races.

CHAPTER 28
THE INDEPENDENT RACING MAN

How Walter could swiftly move from racing cars to motorcycle racing in the TT is something only Walter could explain. He was certainly not ready to be numbered amongst the list of former motorcycle racing men. By now Walter had left Nortons and was entered on the new Velocette KTT Mk V for the Junior Race, and in the Senior he was mounted on the 495cc Velocette, first ridden in 1934 by Walter Rusk. In the Lightweight race Walter was to ride a new production racer, the interesting overhead camshaft 250cc Excelsior Manxman.

For the 1935 TT races there were fourteen manufacturers represented, including a sizeable foreign challenge from Guzzi, DKW, NSU and Jawa. To add to the interest there had been a good deal of stable changing amongst the star riders. Stanley Woods, who in 1934 had ridden Guzzi and Husqvarna in the Lightweight and Senior Races respectively, now rode Guzzi in both these events. After two years of development, the overhead camshaft 120 degrees, V-twin Senior Guzzi was at last ready and reputed to be very quick. Meanwhile in the Norton camp there had been wholesale changes; Jimmy Guthrie was the sole survivor from the previous year, he was now joined by newcomers, John Duncan, Walter Rusk and J. H. 'Crasher' White, a school teacher, due to ride in the Junior Race.

Walter felt confident that he could upset the Norton 1-2-3 pattern of success. After the disappointments of 1934, there could be no doubting his determination to 'mix it' with the Norton riders. The new KTT Velocette had a cradle type frame and the engine had been redesigned for greater rigidity. The lubrication system had been modified and the gearbox now had the famous, Willis designed, positive stop mechanism mounted internally, the complete gearbox assembly being no longer suspended from the frame but clamped between an extension of the rear engine plates.

Impressed with the Velocette's vast improvement in speed and road-holding Walter had 'pulled his punches' in the practice period so as not to fully reveal his hand. Nevertheless, when the *TT Special* reporters timed the stars over certain stretches of the course it was apparent that no-one was loitering! Between Ballacraine and Kirk Michael the recorded speeds were: Guthrie 500cc Norton 83·1 mph; Woods 500cc Guzzi 81·9 mph; Handley 350cc Velocette 81·8 mph. It was a similar situation through Hillberry where Walter's 350 Velocette held the 500 Nortons of Guthrie and Rusk; and on the Creg to Signpost section the 350 Velocette was slightly quicker than Rusk's Senior Norton! It took a long fast section like the Sulby mile for the superior power of his rivals to show to advantage; here Stanley Woods' Senior Guzzi notched up 112·5 mph to Walter's Senior Velocette's 109·1 mph.

It was here on the Sulby Straight on the last morning's practice, while motoring briskly, that Walter reached down to adjust the rear brake of his Junior Velocette. The wing nut being on the inboard end of the rod, his glove caught between chain and sprocket and he lost the tip of his left thumb. With the nerve ends affected he immediately realised that he would not be able to ride. He telephoned Willis and urged that he get someone else to qualify, he suggested Stanley Woods, who did not have a Junior mount. The loss of Handley was a severe blow to Velocette who had already lost Harold Newman, who was taken ill. Various contracts stood in the way of Stanley taking over Walter's bike and eventually Ernie Thomas and Doug Pirie substituted for Handley and Newman respectively.

In all the many disappointments that Walter experienced, I doubt if he came away from the Island more downhearted than after this incident. His brother was taken aback when Walter walked into his Birmingham office on the morning of the Junior Race with his hand in a sling bandage. 'I always thought the Sulby Straight a smooth speed section, but now I know it has got one bump at least,' was the wry comment. He just sat quietly listening to the sound broadcast of the race describing yet another Norton 1-2-3 for Guthrie, Rusk and White. 'We all kept out of Walter's way as he seemed so depressed,' recalled Tom Handley many years later. The Velocettes of Pirie, Nott and Thomas gained 4-5-6, a good show but probably a disappointment to the Hall Green company. Pirie, three times a winner of the September races, came in 3 mins, 45 secs behind Guthrie. Sadly it was Pirie's last result, for just 48 hours later he was fatally injured riding his New Imperial in the wet weather Lightweight Race.

As the week wore on Walter, listening in to the BBC commentaries, heard how his old rival, Stanley Woods, riding Moto Guzzi, had gone on to win the Lightweight and Senior races. The latter victory, by a mere four seconds from Guthrie (Norton), being one of the most exciting in TT history. It was a victory that must have given Woods great satisfaction to beat not only the Norton supremacy but also the man who had supplanted him. The upset to the Norton winning sequence by a former member of the Norton team contained a certain irony that could not have been lost upon Walter. Not the man to begrudge another his success, he would have been less than human had he not reflected that, but for the misunderstanding with the Guzzi personnel in 1933, he might have been there riding a Guzzi.

Although no-one realised it at the time, nor Walter himself, he had made his last racing appearance in the Isle of Man TT races. Yet while things had not worked out for Walter as well as they might have done, he had an Island record that any road racing star would be proud to own. In the thirteen year period between 1922 and 1934 he had ridden in twenty-eight TT races, and became the only man to win all four solo classes. He had also made nine record laps, was second on three occasions and was third twice. It is a remarkable fact that this outstanding rider had held the lead, at some point, in eight out of the seventeen TT races in which he had been obliged to retire. Yet he was not hard on his machines, everyone who knew him have been quick to refute this and point to his sensitivity and mechanical understanding. Leaving aside the race statistics, it will surely be his competitive ability and those resolute rides that will be remembered in TT history. The main thing about Walter as a racer is that above all he wanted to win. He wanted to be in front. In a massed start he would fight to be into the first bend in the lead. He was at his most formidable when faced with adversity – if he had been delayed you had to watch out! Then you saw what he really meant by those watchwords of his, 'Never give up, never despair.'

Walter Handley always looked right on a bike, no-one could tuck themselves away so neatly. In his generation he was outstanding. In the days when the machines still looked naked, this ability that Walter had to minimise wind resistance was very important. Like other TT aces before and since, Walter excelled on fast bends, not only in speed through the bends but also in the speed at which the subsequent section could be approached. The stretches through Braddan, Ballacraine, Kirk Michael, Creg-ny-Baa and Hillberry spring readily to mind. He claimed that he never took unnecessary risks, especially at the slow sections of the course, such as Quarter Bridge, Ramsey Hairpin, the Gooseneck and Governor's Bridge, where the gaining of an extra yard or so could so easily bring you off. Yet he had such outstanding judgement that he was willing and able to exceed that judgement, knowing that he was doing so. It is one of the paradoxes that, as Bert Perrigo pointed out, the closer you come to falling off the better racing man you are! In fact Walter was not alone in having more falls at Governor's Bridge than at any other part of the course. This often happened at a late stage in a race and was caused by the braking power having been steadily worn down.

It is worth remembering that Wal Handley had made his reputation in one of the strongest periods of competitive road racing in the Island. His contemporaries included some of the all time greats of TT history, Alec Bennett, Freddie Dixon, Howard Davies, Stanley Woods, Jimmy Simpson, Tim Hunt and Jimmy Guthrie. Unlike the last four Walter did not have the benefit of the all conquering Nortons. The rider Walter most admired was Alec Bennett, it was mutual, Alec once said, 'If Walter is in a race I know that I have a good chance of being second!'

With his sales and servicing business in Birmingham, his car racing and flying, people could be excused for thinking that Handley had deserted motorcycling, his first love. There was some truth on Ixion's side when he declared that for a year or two, 'Walter has been a comparatively dilettante road racer.' By 1935 his appearances had become quite rare. If he knew a machine was not good enough for him to put up a good show, he would rather decline the starting money than place in jeopardy his own reputation and that of the manufacturer concerned. This was in sharp contrast to the early days when he would enter any contest that gave him a chance to show what he could do.

However, there were still a few surprises in store. Just when some people had concluded that Walter's career had ended, he snapped right back on 24 August to win by 2 mins, 28 secs the 350cc Ulster Grand Prix at the record speed of 86·65 mph. It was the year in which the Ulster had been selected as the European Grand Prix, held on the Clady circuit, just outside Belfast. In a re-run of 1933, Handley, riding the 350cc Velocette, had once again routed the Junior Nortons on Irish soil. Guthrie helped restore Norton morale by winning the 500 class at 90·88 mph. This was the first time in motorcycle racing history that a road race had been won at over ninety. The Ulster had once again lived up to its reputation of being 'the fastest road race in the world'.

Walter was now thirty-three years of age, still young enough to stay at the top of motorcycle road racing for several years to come. Would he choose to do so? A clue to his outlook came at the prize distribution in Belfast after the FICM Grand Prix. He thanked those present for the wonderful reception they had given him, but he said he did not think it quite fair that only a select few of the prize-winners should receive all the applause. He reminded everyone that this select few had the wholehearted support of the factories behind them, and they were provided with the finest machines that this country could produce. The other riders were riding inferior machines and he felt that their riding abilities and efforts deserved every bit as much praise as the prize-winners themselves received. After a brief pause, he went further, and said that some of these 'also-rans' could have collected the principal awards had they been mounted on the machines the winners rode. It was probably the longest speech Walter had ever made. Usually he would say a hurried 'Thank-you' and retire quickly from the platform.

This speech is interesting, not just because it expresses his characteristic modesty, but because it shows his disenchantment with the way the racing game was developing. Walter had come to realise after his Norton experience in 1934, that in order to get the best motorcycle you had to be tied up with an organisation, and fall in with their racing programme. Organisation had now assumed a preponderant role. It was by now very unlike the days when Walter started in the 1920s, a time when you had to be mechanic and rider. Now the team manager could decide in the boardroom who would win, who would be second and who third. This sort of thing did not suit Wal Handley at all. It was his dislike of rigid team discipline that had led to his becoming a freelance rider. The note of exasperation in Ixion's, June 1933, comment is very understandable, 'On how many different makes of machines, from foreigners to home products, have we seen Walter Handley?' The answer, not surprisingly, was eight in the TT and ten overall!

Over the years the Isle of Man course had been developed, speeds had risen, and with it the machines had become more and more specialised, bearing little relationship to the mounts sold to everyday motorcyclists. Having been the last man to win the Senior TT on a virtually standard machine, the 1930 Rudge, Walter felt that the races were becoming too far removed from the requirements of the ordinary motorcyclist. With prophetic foresight he argued that a race for near standard production machines would not only put the 'Tourist' concept back into the Tourist Trophy races, but also once again place a premium on the skill of the rider.

Unfortunately the system was not about to change, and no home based manufacturers were prepared to challenge the Nortons. In June 1936 Walter issued a challenge through the letters column of the *Motor Cycle*. It was in response to an anonymous manufacturer who made the claim that they were, 'out to sell motorcycles and not to buy star riders.' That did it; Walter made one of his rare forays into print! He reminded everyone that the TT riders, including the stars, received no retaining fee from manufacturers, in other words they rode for nothing unless they won. Walter wrote:

> If buying star riders, is the difficulty which prevents this manufacturer from entering the TT, may I make him an offer ... if his firm can produce a machine which to my satisfaction is capable of giving the Nortons a run for the honours, I will ride it for them free, gratis and for nothing, and no doubt many other first class riders would be glad to do likewise.

Nothing came of this and so far as we know he received no serious offers from any other manufacturers. Since Walter was not someone prepared to dabble at the sport, the 1935 Clady victory turned out to be Walter's last appearance in a motorcycle road race. Viewed in retrospect his fifth Ulster victory formed a triumphant end to a brilliant career.

It seems clear that his happiest period was with Rex Acme in the 1920s, and with Rudge-Whitworth in the early 1930s.

His fight back after a long delay in the 1926 Senior Race on the Rex V-twin, his 1930 Senior Rudge victory in the rain, and his scrap with the Nortons in 1932 was particularly memorable. I asked Sam James why he thought he and Wal had got on so well together:

> I always did what he told me to do – it was no use arguing with Wal. If he said he would ride the 250 and then the 350, I would get the bikes ready in that order. I would fit the soft plug for him to get to the start and leave out the hard racing plug ready for him to change it.

Walter had been the epitome of the lone wolf, often scoring notable successes with little or no regular backing. Independence was one of his strongest character traits, over a period of twelve years he had ridden ten different makes of machine. One of his greatest admirers was Ixion – the Revd. B. H. Davies – who in almost despairing tones complained that:

> … one year Walter Handley gets the saddle of a fast, reliable machine, and finishes first in a style which makes everybody else despair. The next year he has a packet of trouble on a machine about which he cannot know very much, and either does not start or gets out of the race, or is out paced. But many of us suspect that if he had steadily associated himself with one good racing stable he might have made even Stanley (Woods) look almost ordinary.

Yet despite having a racing policy that prevented him from doing himself justice, he had, in addition to his TT successes, won eighteen International Grand Prix races in eight countries interspersed with track successes and world records – some of which he held for over ten years. These victories and his meteoric riding do not entirely explain his popularity and the affection in which 'Wally' was held. This was due to his remarkable personality. He knew that he was what is called a 'born rider', but he also knew that he had not achieved this through practice and perseverance, for apart from riding in races and going for world records, he hardly rode a motorcycle from one year's end to the next. Walter's friend, Harold Willis, was often seen driving him to the start of a TT race in his car. Abroad it was not unknown for Walter to land his Puss Moth alongside a circuit not long before the race was due to begin.

Walter once mused to one particularly persistent questioner:

> I seem to be a born motorcyclist. If this is so, I am lucky, this reflects no particular credit on me for I can't claim to have made myself faster than other men.

Such modest candour sat naturally upon him, and the Press and public loved him for it whilst no doubt reflecting that people who are modest generally have something to be modest about. Perhaps because he was the very antithesis of a latter day Muhammad Ali, he was very popular with his fellow riders. Graham Walker writing a few years after Wal's death wished that he might have known, 'What a grand chap we thought he was.'

CHAPTER 29
THE AUDACIOUS PARTNERSHIP

The sudden exit of MG cars from the racing scene had left Wal Handley without a car. To where would he turn? At that time the car racing scene was dominated by wealthy amateurs, men who owned and raced their own cars. Into this select world there strode quite a few of the motorcycle stars. Looking back, it is not so very surprising that two arch individualists like Walter Handley and Freddie Dixon should have come together, despite their very different personalities. The two men had raced against each other in the Isle of Man TT races, where it will be recalled, Freddie had gained his first and only solo TT win in the 1927 Junior TT on the HRD. This happened when, on the last lap, Walter's Rex Acme failed after having led the race throughout. They had a lot in common. Both men had suffered bad luck in the racing game, neither of them had any time for pre-arranged race results and they liked to play a lone hand. They came from humble backgrounds and they had begun their racing careers in a similar manner with speed trials and hill climbs. The two men had practical interests and understood engines. According to Sammy James, Freddie was one of the few men who would stand up to Wal and say, 'Well there it is, take it or leave it.' By the time Walter teamed up with Freddie, the latter had built a reputation as a Riley tuner and an audacious driver.

Freddie liked the Riley car design and having a Riley dealership he had found that the firm was willing to help him. Freddie had his own ideas about how to run a car and he was able to put his theories into practice. He gained extra power by employing one carburettor per cylinder. One of his techniques was to tune by running the engine in the dark and adjusting each mixture control until the exhaust flames were identical. With the 1935 Ards TT scheduled for 7 September, Freddie needed a second driver. Wal Handley was now available and a partnership was born.

By a coincidence it was here on the Ards circuit in 1932 that Dixon had made his own sensational car debut. On that occasion his black 1100cc Riley had led the race for four hours before being overtaken by Whitcroft, the eventual winner in another Riley. Dixon's indignant response was to stamp his foot down and roar off in pursuit. Not long afterwards the car hit the inside kerb of Quarry Corner, careered across the road, hit the bank, finally shooting into the air to disappear from view through a large hedge. Although his passenger mechanic was taken to hospital, the crowd witnessed this extraordinarily tough little man with just a few bruises getting back on his feet.

Now, just three years later, it was Dixon's reserve driver, Walter who, as race day approached, proceeded to steal the headlines. On the preceding Thursday, Walter took out the new 1496cc four-cylinder Riley and put in an electrifying final practice lap of 10 mins, 20 secs, to record 79.31 mph – a record for its class. It was the second fastest time of the day, only the 3255cc Bugatti, driven by Brian Lewis, managed to beat the Riley's time by just two seconds. It was Lewis who described Handley's wonderful lap:

> I was close behind Handley, it was next to impossible to catch the little blue Riley which was going round the corners at tremendous speed. Time and again the car went almost broadside on corners, but Handley controlled it magnificently. It was really brilliant driving.

On this showing Walter had improved on the handicap by 32 seconds and so it followed that the drivers of the larger cars, Earl Howe, Brian Lewis, Charlie Dodson and Eddie Hall would have to average speeds of around 85 mph to beat the Riley. Consequently Dixon and Handley were firm favourites to win. Walter's participation in a Dixon TT victory would be popular with the people of Belfast who, only a fortnight earlier, had seen the famous motorcyclist win the 350 class of the European Grand Prix on the Clady Circuit. Would Dixon be strong enough to drive throughout? In the previous year Freddie had crashed at Donington breaking several ribs at the time. In February he had been involved in an aeroplane accident that had put him in hospital. Since then he had come back to win the British Empire Trophy at Brooklands, but this Ulster TT Race of nearly 500 miles lasting just under six hours was a severe test of any man's strength.

There was no sign of any waning of physical powers as Dixon raced his Riley across the line, averaging 76.9 mph after nearly six hours at the wheel. He had beaten Eddie Hall's second placed Bentley by 1 min, 13 secs. It was a remarkable achievement by any standard. It was typical of Freddie to continue, he had an iron constitution. He was remarkable in this respect, only he could have done this, but for the man waiting patiently in the pits for his chance at the wheel it must have been very frustrating. Walter had not come over to Belfast just to be a spectator, as the white-helmeted figure of Dixon drove on relentlessly to glory and the 'bags of gold'. It is not known why Dixon decided not to use his reserve driver. He may have been determined to prove his level of fitness after his earlier injuries or he may have got carried away with the excitement of the race and just kept going. Another possibility is that he wanted to avoid being outshone by the younger driver.

Two weeks after the Ulster Ards TT came the world's fastest race, the seventh international 500-mile car race of the BRDC, held at Brooklands. It lived up to its reputation. The tremendous pace set by the leaders, averaging around 125 mph was a major factor in causing incessant tyre failures that became a feature of this race. Time after time the cars threw treads sky high and at the finish the concrete was strewn with rubber. The Rileys suffered an amazing number of tyre failures. Whoever was at the wheel was liable to become the 'whipping boy' as the treads flew off like rifle fire. The physical punishment and the constant high speeds ensured that this time all the reserve drivers came into the action. On the Monday following the race, Tom Handley remembered being shown by Walter, who was not a demonstrative person, the bruising and discolouration of his arms and shoulders caused by tyre whipping.

High speed was not the only cause of tread stripping. Alarm spread as the track began to break up high on the Members' Banking. In a little while stones were being thrown down the banking as the cars thundered past. The position of the two parallel gulleys, which had opened up, was right in the path of the fastest cars right on the black line. There was roughly a passage about a car's width above the topmost break and the lip of the banking. Most drivers, including John Cobb (Napier Railton), Marker (Bentley), Seaman (Duesenberg) and Bertram (Barnato Hassan), dived below the hazard, but in doing so they not only lost some speed but by taking the lower line they probably increased tyre wear. There was also the risk of being hit by the loose stones scattered across the track. A flying stone caught the favourite to win this race, John Cobb in the face and, with blood streaming from the cut, he brought his enormous 23.5 litre Napier Railton into the pits and handed over to Rose-Richards.

Brian Lewis consistently placed his 3.3 Bugatti straight across the gashes, later he explained that with his low seating position he could not see the trouble spot! Walter, who was sharing the driving of Dixon's 2 litre Riley, got the headlines again. The *Sunday Express* reported that:

> Only one driver dared to take this passage, it was Walter Handley who had taken over Dixon's car and in trying to get into the lead he took the narrow passage, tight-roping at over 120 mph.

Again and again Walter took Dixon's Riley within inches of the top of the banking. Between them Freddie and Walter performed prodigies of speed putting everything in the shade with both drivers putting in several laps at around 130 mph, 15 mph up on handicap, as they tried to make up the lost time for eleven stops caused by wheel changes.

By the late afternoon Walter had brought the Dixon Riley into fourth position for the first time, and was closing down on the leaders. The Aero-engined Napier Railton still looked set to win, but the battle for second and third places was far from over in a race that had seen cars on and off the leader board with bewildering rapidity. By 4 PM Von der Becke's factory entered Riley was in second place, over a minute ahead of the fast gaining 3.3 Bugatti driven by Brian Lewis. Just 37 seconds behind the Bugatti came Walter driving at tremendous speed. Some 25 minutes later Walter was on the same lap as Lewis and gaining on Von der Becke's Riley when, with just nine laps to go, disaster struck. A con-rod went through its base, and Riley, number 21, rolled into the pits trailing oil and with smoke billowing forth. It was hard luck for Freddie Dixon, last year's winner, but for Wal Handley it was extremely upsetting to retire when so near to gaining, if not second place, a certain third. 'So ended a gallant drive against big odds,' was the comment of *Sporting Life*.

Although none of Dixon's three cars had finished, they had recorded the lowest time aggregate on formula and were rewarded with the team prize. Dixon's second Riley had been driven by Cyril Paul and Charles Brackenbury, and the 1100cc Riley Nine by A. C. Hess and E. K. Rayson. It had been a most destructive race with only six cars finishing inside the time limit. John Cobb and 'Tim' Rose-Richards were comfortable winners of the 'five-hundred' after a fairly trouble free run in the Napier Railton at 121·28 mph. They were followed in by the 2 litre Riley driven by Von der Becke and Edgar Maclure and the third placed 3.3 Bugatti of Earl Howe and Brian Lewis

Meanwhile there lived in Derbyshire, a man whose ambition

it was to promote a full length race for single-seater cars under contemporary Grand Prix rules. He was another ex-motorcyclist and his name was Fred Craner, the Secretary of the Derby and District Motor Club. The beautiful but difficult Donington Park Circuit, surrounded by woods and avenues of trees was becoming established as England's first mainland road racing course. It was the early success of the first two motorcycle meetings in 1931 that persuaded Donington's owner, John G. Shields, JP, that Craner and the Club might have a point in wanting to develop the road circuit to take car racing. By 1935 Donington Park had been lengthened, widened and resurfaced. There was a paddock, pits and a grandstand. Parking space was ample and the provision of footbridges gave spectators easy access to favourite vantage points. A public address system kept everyone informed of the race situation.

Donington's success was rewarded with the realisation of one of Fred's great ambitions. On Saturday, 5 October 1935, there was in prospect a race according to the International Grand Prix formula. The cars would go off together without any of the usual handicapping complexities. The length of 306 miles comprising 120 laps of the 2·55 mile course was about right for a Grand Prix. Even the weight limit of 870 kilograms was very close to the official international limit of 750 kilograms. It was a just reward for Fred Craner's energy and enthusiasm. Nothing was too much trouble for Fred. An example of this was the help he had given members of the MG team with their experimental testing. He knew Wal Handley from the days when he too had ridden Rex Acme, Fred simply asked Walter for a few days' notice so that he could arrange for cattle to be removed from the adjacent fields and for the two entrances to be closed!

For the big road race Craner had managed to attract a promising field. It was to prove the forerunner of those classic battles of 1937 and 1938 when the powerful German teams thundered through Donington Park. In 1935 the foreign element was less dramatic but full of interest. The Scuderia had brought over two Maseratis, the very latest 4·5 litre V8 driven by the favourite Dr Guiseppe Farina, and for Gino Rovere there was a 3·7 litre Tipo 34 model. Alongside Farina on the front of the starting grid was the Frenchman, Raymond Sommer, who had his ex-works 2·9 Alfa Romeo Monoposto. Pitted against these all foreign challengers were three 3·3 litre Bugatti Type 59s, driven by Earl Howe, Charles Martin and A. H. L. Eccles – the lap record holder. Shuttleworth had his 2·9 Alfa Romeo Monoposto, while Harry Rose drove an older 2·3 litre two seater model. There were also two 2·9 litre Maseratis driven by Featherstonhaugh and Dobson. Among the smaller cars was a new 1·5 litre ERA driven by the young Siamese Cambridge undergraduate, Prince 'Bira'. It was a twenty-first birthday present from his cousin Prince Chula Chakrabongse.

To complete the field there were four 2 litre Rileys. They were to be driven jointly by the Maclure brothers; Dobbs shared with Von der Becke, Brian Lewis with Cyril Paul and Wal Handley with Pat Driscoll. The last two cars were entered by Dixon, who was absent, having lost his appeal against a charge of reckless and dangerous driving in the course of which he had assaulted a police officer and was bound over for twelve months. He now had to serve a prison sentence of three months. Pat Driscoll, an experienced ex-motorcyclist who had successfully made the transition to car racing, was contacted in London by Brian Lewis around midnight and was asked to take Dixon's place and drive with Wal Handley. Driscoll drove up from London and arrived early, five hours before the start, in the hope of practising but he found that already large crowds were spilling onto the course and so practising was not possible.

Although the smaller cars were at a disadvantage because of their limited engine size, they had the further difficulty of being the only 'unblown' cars in the race. It was calculated that supercharging gave a car a 30 per cent greater capacity over a car without. Freddie's Rileys were always 'unblown' because he disliked using superchargers and much preferred to tune his normally aspirated cars, making them go very fast.

Such was the attraction of the race that, despite lashing rain and a lowering sky, thousands of car headlights could be seen in the morning gloom moving very slowly along the nearby Ashby–Nottingham road. Enthusiasts were determined not to miss seeing England's first real road race. Mercifully the rain eased off before it was time to remove the covers off the cars. Ahead lay nearly five hours of motoring. From the start the cars enter a sharp left turn at Red Gate Corner from whence the course bends round through Holly Wood. A drop downhill is followed by the dangerous hairpin turn. Sweeping under a bridge the cars bend their way through Coppice Wood encountering the sharp right turn known as McLean's Corner. The road then rises up to Coppice Corner, a right angle turn leading into the fast straight which descends to Starkey's Corner, the hairpin turn and the finish.

Under an overcast sky and amid clouds of spray thrown up by churning wheels, fifteen racing cars leaped forward on the stroke of 12·30pm. As expected Farina's smooth and powerful Maserati surged into the lead. Sommer held his 2·9 Alfa in second place, followed closely by Martin's 3·3 Bugatti. After only seven laps Farina was about to lap Brian Lewis, who was finding it difficult to cope with a car arranged to suit Freddie Dixon's physique. Walter Handley had the same problem, compounded by a drastic reduction in the Riley's braking efficiency. A mechanic had incorrectly fitted standard brake shoes. On an early descent of the hill to the hairpin bend, Walter found the Riley's brakes were not responding, and in sliding round he charged the first aid enclosure, going through the fencing backwards! Without stopping he drove out again and on to Coppice Wood. The wet and muddy track saw several drivers sliding onto the grass. The ERA of Prince 'Bira' shot off at Red Gate, while Shuttleworth, Martin and Featherstonhaugh all enlivened the proceedings at Starkey's Corner.

After a while Walter, who had won the toss and had started first, brought the car in, saying it was a pig! Somewhat mystified by Walter's obvious disenchantment, Driscoll set off and at once was very impressed with the car's smoothness and power, but it was not long before he too was in trouble, going off the road several times at corners. He soon realised the cause, Fred had very short legs and had made late alterations to suit him. The bottom section of the steering wheel had been cut away to give Freddie more room. Walter and Pat found that with their longer legs, when they tried to brake, it was quite impossible to turn the wheel as the cut part of the rim would stick into their legs about four inches above the knee. In effect you had to choose between steering and braking! Although Handley and Driscoll completed 115 laps they were, race reports notwithstanding, not running at the finish having decided it was hopeless to continue. It was a great pity that neither man had been able to practise; had they done so they would have been able to make the necessary adjustments. None of the Rileys were placed, but their speed and reliability were thoroughly convincing. On learning the outcome, Dixon was sorely disappointed.

The crowd, estimated at about 10,000, had a race of absorbing interest with the lead changing on four occasions. After 40 laps Farina's Maserati came round no more, a broken axle half shaft had put paid to the favourite. Raymond Sommer took over the lead, but then to his apparent fury another axle failure ended his race. Just when it looked as though Charles Martin (Bugatti) had the race in his pocket, his brakes gave out obliging him to take the escape road at McLean's Corner. While he struggled to get restarted, Shuttleworth swept by in his 2·9 Alfa Romeo, and driving with a steadiness, which he had not always shown, the race was his at an average speed of 63·97 mph. It had been so exciting that even the BBC allowed their commentary to stray into Children's Hour for 20 minutes. 'If the modern kiddy is what we think he is he didn't mind a bit,' commented the *Light Car Journal* totally ignoring the possibility that little girls might also be interested.

Whereas two weeks earlier, the Brooklands 500-mile race had taken a terrific toll of engines and tyres, this Donington road race had been remarkably free from such troubles. With its tightly packed twists and turns, it had, in complete contrast, played havoc with brakes and transmissions. Although engine size had had the final say, England's first mainland road circuit had proved itself to be rather more than just a high speed test.

A fast Walter Handley MGR in the early stages of the 1935 Mannin Beg race.
A broken axle puts him out of the race when up with the leaders.
Note the proximity of the unprotected spectators lining the Douglas promenade.

CHAPTER 30
EXCEEDINGLY BRAVE

In 1936 the British Racing Drivers' Club decided to transfer the British Empire Trophy Race from Brooklands to Donington. The move served to highlight the trend which, by the outbreak of war, had firmly established the East Midland Circuit as Britain's premier road racing venue. On Saturday, 4 April, a record crowd of about 17,000 had gathered at Donington to see the fifth race in the series. A bitterly cold east wind, blowing strongly across the course, hinted at some of the difficulties which would face the competitors in a contest lasting nearly six hours and covering 100 laps, approximately 255 miles.

The success of a handicap race hinges on whether the organisers have got their sums right. In this race the method used was to allocate time allowances based on the grouping of different classes. The first group was made up of just four cars. There were three privately entered R-type MG Midgets fitted with double overhead camshafts, and a lone un-supercharged 1100cc Riley. These small cars received a 6 mins, 40 secs start over the 'scratch' group. The second group consisting of fourteen cars was the largest. There were five ERAs based on the touring Riley engine with its two high camshafts, three Fraser-Nash cars, a Maserati and a bored out MG – all supercharged 1·5 litre models. Completing this group were four Rileys, the only 'unblown' cars in the race. Two of these cars, 1·5 and 2 litre, were works' entries. The other two were privateers – H. G. Dobbs had his white offset 2 litre model, while Freddie Dixon brought his familiar aluminium car to the start line. Sharing the driving with Freddie was Walter Handley. All the cars in this group received five minutes from scratch. Behind them came a group of six supercharged cars up to 2·7 litres receiving 3 mins, 20 secs. Prominent among these was Richard Seaman's black Maserati, raced by Whitney Straight before his retirement, and now lineared down to 2·6 litres, but no less formidable for all that. Four Alfas and a rather slow 2·3 Bugatti completed the group. Bringing up the rear was the 'scratch' group of three supercharged cars. Martin and Staniland had their 3·2 and 2·9 Alfas while Eccles drove his 3·3 Bugatti.

Walter arrived at Donington on Thursday, 2 April. He immediately put in a practice lap that placed the Dixon Riley on the front line of his group, alongside the ERAs of Prince Bira and Fairfield. Despite this encouraging omen Walter remained concerned that on a course like Donington, the supercharged cars had a tremendous advantage in acceleration. This applied particularly in picking up speed out of the bends. Dixon, whose dislike of superchargers was well known, was anxious to retain the Trophy he had won a year earlier, now decided to try and find some extra speed. On the eve of the race he locked the differential, thus making the Riley's axle solid. It was a somewhat futuristic idea. In motor racing a semi-locked differential was subsequently evolved that had within it a limited self-operating slip clutch.

In the early stages of the race, Prince Birabongse, better known under his racing name Bira and still a newcomer to the sport, took his six-cylinder ERA to the front. However, by quarter distance the ERA had lost its tune and had dropped back. As he did so, stop watches showed that Seaman, averaging 67·55 mph was leading the race on handicap. All this tended to confirm the views of those who said the allotted times favoured the ERAs and the cars in the 2·7 litre class. In the windy conditions the cars were sending up swirling clouds of dust. This and the dry slippery road surface made driving difficult. Some cars went spinning round to end up facing the wrong way, others thudded into the safety banks or overshot the bends. Freddie had his moments in the Riley, surging round in a thrilling series of violent skids.

At 2·52 PM Dixon came into the pits and handed over to Walter. Freddie had, since the start at 1·30pm, completed 35 laps averaging just over 66 mph. The Riley was now in third position having been overtaken by Pat Fairfield in his ERA, although some reports suggest that Freddie may have slipped to fourth or even fifth position. With great coolness Walter pulled the Riley out right in front of his old Brooklands rival Chris Staniland, who was bearing down in the 2·9 Alfa Romeo. A collision seemed certain but the Riley's acceleration was sufficient. As he swung into Red Gate, Walter glanced across the track noting the position of Seaman's Maserati number 28. Challenging large supercharged cars meant a nerve tingling fight against telling odds, but Walter was used to this.

By now Staniland was going really well in his ex-Raymond Sommer car, but try as he might he could not get past Handley in the Riley. Respect for the Riley grew as it appeared for two successive laps still in front of its supercharged rival. At the end of each lap Walter glanced across to check Seaman's position and noted with satisfaction that the race leader was not creeping away. Walter was responding to the smooth power of the Riley, there was no fear, just a confident feeling of adventure. Speed into each bend was essential, if Staniland's supercharger was not to leave him, on coming out of the bends. Walter went round Starkey in what appeared to be one long slide. Then on his third lap, disaster struck, it happened at the infamous 45 degrees turn known as the Hairpin.

The Riley took the rise into the turn and as it did so, slewed round right under Staniland's wheels. The Riley was seen to hit the inside barrier, leap high into the air and roll over in a cloud of dust. Such was the phenomenal speed of the crash that no-one could be sure how many times the car turned over, but turn over it did. From the Newsreel it is possible that the car spun over three or four times. Mercifully the car ended upright with the limp figure of Walter hanging over the side. The crowd was silent, fearful for the driver's life in the face of such a petrifying crash. Just a few seconds after help had reached him, Walter regained consciousness. His rescuers found him most uncomfortably wedged in by the steering wheel. It was so difficult to free him that before they had succeeded, urgent messages were sent to Dixon for a mechanic who knew how the wheel came off. After receiving first aid for his facial cuts, Walter sat in the car and smoked a cigarette. Then unaware that he had serious spinal injuries he eased himself out of the car and tried to walk away, only to collapse. After this he was immediately removed by ambulance to the Derby Royal Infirmary.

The injuries Walter had sustained in this race kept him out of racing, cars or motorcycles, for the rest of the season. Just over six minutes driving had ended with Walter receiving three compressed fractures of the spine, two cracked ribs and three stitches across the bridge of his nose. The car had rolled over with the result that Walter's back had supported three quarters of a ton. In many respects it was a lucky escape. Four years earlier Walter's life had been saved by the hard helmet he was wearing when he crashed in the 1932 Senior TT, but when it came to car racing, Walter, in common with the other drivers only wore a soft helmet. This was a time when the drivers were not at all well protected. Typically they wore a thin tunic boiler type suit and a linen helmet. There were no safety belts and the cars did not offer much protection. There were no real barriers between the racing cars and the thousands of spectators lining the track. Medical facilities were minimal. If you wanted to race you knew that you were taking risks. Not until the 1960s did things begin to improve, eventually leading to safer cars and safer circuits, better medical support, fireproof clothing and very efficient marshalling.

What were the principal causes of this frightening crash? On the face of it the main reason appeared to be excessive risk taking. Yet, as is so often the case, a full knowledge of the circumstances will often vindicate the driver. An important

The 1936 British Empire Trophy Race at Donington shortly after Handley's high speed crash in Dixon's Riley. The car had somersaulted over the earth barrier at the hairpin bend and ended upright. The unconscious figure of Walter can be seen hanging over the side.

Although the Riley was virtually undamaged, Wal Handley suffered serious injuries that kept him out of racing for the rest of the 1936 season. A few seconds after this picture was taken he was smoking a cigarette and talking to his friend Graham Walker.

factor, not generally known at the time, was Freddie Dixon's alteration to the car's differential on the eve of the race. This had meant that the car had in effect a solid axle and there had been no time to practise without the usual differential. Walter's entry into the Hairpin had been fast, perhaps too fast. As the inside wheel lifted, the other wheel kept on driving, whereas a differential would have broken the action and allowed the car to drop. Walter believed that in normal circumstances he would have controlled the skid. There was another factor picked up by the *Autocar,* when it complained that the 750s and the 'unblown' Rileys had been completely disadvantaged by the time limits they were given. In their view the race had become a 'scratch' affair by quarter distance.

Strange as it may seem, the Riley was far from being a 'smoking wreck'. According to the *Autocar* report on 17 April, the car was virtually undamaged apart from a few dents and was raced again at Brooklands less than a month later. With this dramatic end to Dixon's entry taking place just before 3pm, the order on the hour was one, Seaman; two, Fairfield; three, Staniland. The latter was driving the car which became the basis of the distinguished Multi-Union that reappeared at Brooklands in 1938. Chris Staniland pulled out all the stops, and at one stage was in second place before going out with a broken axle. After this the race was between Fairfield and Seaman. For a while it looked as though Fairfield's ERA might spring a surprise, but eventually the inevitable happened and the 2·6 litre Maserati finally overtook the 1·5 litre ERA. Seaman went on to win his first race in Britain by 42 seconds at 66·33 mph. For Dick Seaman, twenty-seven years of age, this was the start of a great season that was to lead ultimately to his joining Alfred Neubauer's Mercedes team. Sadly, only three years later this talented young driver lost his life racing at Spa in Belgium.

It was not long after the race before Walter Handley began to get restive in the Derby Royal Infirmary! Walter hated inactivity and he never took kindly to hospitals and was deeply distrustful of doctors. After the x-ray he was told that he must stay in the hospital for several months. Walter had other ideas. With the help of a friend he slipped out of the Derby Hospital on the Thursday evening. Urgent messages were sent out to find the man with a broken back encased in plaster. On Saturday he was finally tracked down driving his car in the centre of Birmingham. This was exactly one week after his tremendous crash. At the local Queen's Hospital he was promptly refitted with a new, much more restrictive case. Poor Walter was not only in plaster down to his waist; his head was kept well back in a collar. Later propped up in bed at his Sheldon home, he told a reporter, grinning as he did so, 'They had to crucify me in plaster to make sure I didn't get away again.' Three months after the Donington crash Walter, never an easy patient, was still at home in this very uncomfortable plaster case.

On 10 July came the proverbial last straw. Walter's doctor informed him that he had to stay in bed for another twelve months! What made it worse was the realisation that he was making desperately slow progress. It was at this critical juncture that along came Walter's friend, the trials rider Harry Perrey, with an offer of help. Harry had been impressed with an orthopaedic surgeon, Dr Wilson Stewart, who had masterminded his own complete recovery from injuries sustained in a recent trials riding accident. Harry wanted Walter to meet the specialist. 'I can tell you he helped me,' said Harry, who met with the irritated response, 'He'll be like all the others I suppose.' Suddenly Harry had an inspiration, he knew that Walter regarded himself as an 'engineer', and had a high regard for engineering skills. 'Wal, I can tell you this man is something of an engineer.' Walter brightened up, that was different; all right he would meet the surgeon.

Just over a week later the plaster case had been replaced by a less restrictive body support. Walter was delighted, but the surgeon was uneasy concerning his new patient. Somehow he must have learned of Walter's extraordinary exploit in flying his Puss Moth GABIA to Liverpool while still in the old plaster case. Taking Harry on one side, the surgeon spoke with heavy emphasis, 'See that your friend, Handley, does no flying, a landing could kill him.' Harry did his best, and it was not until September that Walter flew again.

CHAPTER 31
THE BIRTH OF THE 'GOLDIE'

In the 1930s Walter had often enjoyed visiting central Wales with his friend Harold Willis. But now, with time needed for recovery from his injuries, those fishing expeditions, and the speedboat racing across Tremadoc Bay must have seemed a rather distant memory to the impatient convalescent. The 1936 racing season came and went. Guthrie and Frith won the Senior and Junior TT Races for Norton Motors, while the Lightweight race went to Bob Foster on his New Imperial. With Walter injured and not available, Stanley Woods had taken his place in the Velocette team and in the Senior TT Stanley had pressed Guthrie so hard that at one stage it had looked as though he might repeat his victory over Guthrie of the year before. By 19 September Walter was well enough to visit Brooklands where he watched as Freddie Dixon and Charlie Martin won the 500-mile race in the Riley. Only two weeks earlier Dixon, supported by Charlie Dodson, had also won the RAC TT run for the last time on the Ards road circuit. But for his injuries Walter might have shared in some of these successes.

In the late summer Walter's recovery was going well and he was able to spend a few days on the Welsh coast near Llanbedr. Throughout the 1930s he would often visit this beautiful area of central Wales. Sometimes he would stay with his friend Harold Willis in the village of Llandanwg. The two men got on well. They had both raced in the Isle of Man TT. They had a common interest in engineering and they both loved aviation. They were also great humourists with that priceless ability of being able to laugh at themselves. Walter had a sense of humour that, coupled with a seemingly inexhaustible fund of racing anecdotes, would keep everyone amused. It would be told in that quiet voice with just a suggestion of a lisp. For his part, Willis could be said to have coined a new motor trade language, some of which has lasted to this day. Plugs were 'candles', valves were 'nails', a piston was a 'cork', a horse was a 'hay motor', and one that has survived, a cam was a 'knocker' so that a 'double knocker' was the Willicism for a double overhead camshaft.

By the start of the 1937 season Walter had fully recovered and wanted to race again. He was upset to learn that Velocette had not kept a place for him in their team. There is no evidence to support the idea that Walter had opposed the inclusion of Stanley Woods in the Velocette team. After his injury at Sulby in 1935, while practising on the Junior Velocette, he had immediately telephoned Willis and suggested that he try and get Stanley to qualify. Earlier when, because of various contracts, he could not ride the Lightweight Guzzi, it was Walter who had recommended Moto Guzzi to try and get Woods to ride. So although Walter and Stanley were very different personalities, there is no doubt that they held each other in the greatest respect. For their part the Velocette management were astonished to learn that Walter wanted to race again after the injuries he had suffered. He even turned up at Donington with the intention of driving Manders' R-type MG in the sixth British Empire Trophy Race. The stewards decided that he had arrived too late to practise and so he was not allowed to drive. Motor racing is a difficult business without strong financial backing, but there could be no doubt that Walter Handley was made of sterner stuff than to withdraw from racing just because of a crash, however violent it had been.

Understandably, Walter was feeling dispirited when, on 4 June, his determination was rewarded from a totally unexpected quarter. He was asked by the BSA Company to race a works prepared 497cc Empire Star model at a Brooklands meeting and get for them a 'gold star' by lapping at over 100 mph. Apparently

Jack Amott, a member of the BSA competition team, had approached the company boss, Mr D. W. Munro and urged upon him, 'Get Wal Handley if you can, he is the one man to achieve success.' Just five days later, Walter arrived at Brooklands and went out and tested the BSA on the track achieving a speed of 108 mph. He was satisfied and informed BSA that all was ready. In the preceding November, the Empire Star, had been amongst the new sports singles on display at Olympia, others in this category had included the Matchless Clubman, the Ariel Red Hunter and the Triumph Tiger. Val Page, the former Ariel and Triumph designer, had now joined the BSA design team and his influence could be detected in the simple uncluttered appearance of the new BSA designs.

Machines like the Empire Star can be seen as a response to the improving economic situation. In design it was straightforward, having a four-speed foot-change gearbox, dry sump lubrication, and a modern looking chromium tank. There were other more adventurous designs at Olympia. Phil Irving's Vincent-HRD 998cc Rapide was the forerunner of the post-war 'Black Shadow' and 'Black Lightning' models. In the meantime, designer, Edward Turner, having joined Triumph, was busy preparing his new brainchild, the attractive Speed Twin. These new models were barely adequate in the face of the ever increasing threat from the Italian and German 'multi' designs. Hitler's government was prepared to pay the equivalent of a £10 subsidy for each machine sold abroad. With such an incentive the German BMWs, NSUs and DKWs were streaming forth from the factories.

It was against this background that BSA decided on an exploit designed to give their new sporting single, planned for 1938, a novel publicity launch. The BMCRC had the custom of awarding a little gold star lapel badge to any rider who topped 100 mph during one of their meetings. Success in this venture would provide a ready made name for the new BSA, it would become the 'Gold Star'. There would be the advantage of linking Wal Handley's name to the resultant publicity, coupled with the absolute certainty, as Bert Perrigo related it to me, that Walter would achieve it. In fact he had already won a gold star on a Rex Acme twin back in 1926 in the 750 class.

On Wednesday, 30 June 1937, Wal Handley startled everyone by appearing on the start line of the BMCRC 3-lap all-comers outer circuit handicap event, with the specially prepared 497cc overhead valve Empire Star. The bike had a special high compression piston, special cams, a racing magneto, a modified riding position and was methanol fuelled. It was reputed to develop 34 bhp. BSAs were rather looked down upon in the racing fraternity and many were puzzled that such a famous rider, known for his selectivity, should be persuaded of its race

potential. Despite having to give nine seconds start to the limit man, he had no difficulty in carving his way through the field and winning at an average speed of 102·27 mph. His second lap had been covered at 107·57 mph, thus winning the coveted gold star.

On June 30th 1937, Wal Handley made a surprising reappearance at Brooklands on a BSA Empire Star. He won his race at an average speed of 102·27 mph with one lap at 107·57 mph to win the coveted Gold Star and the BSA had a new name.

The direct result was the introduction of the new 497cc BSA M24 Gold Star model in the following year. Unlike Walter's specially prepared Empire Star, the new model had a light alloy cylinder head and barrel. Its price, advertised at £65·75, sounds reasonable but the average working man's wage of about £3 per week meant that it was not cheap and the competition model was listed at £82·50. However, its speed and reliability ensured its reappearance after the war. The 350cc version won the ACU Clubman's TT, a race over the Isle of Man course for amateur riders in four successive years from 1949 to 1952. To general regret the last 'Goldie' was produced in 1962. Today 'Gold Star' clubs still thrive in this country, Australasia and in the USA.

Unfortunately, there was an unhappy sequel to Walter's success in winning the gold star for BSA. The next race was for two laps only. Walter was put back over six seconds behind scratch. At the end of the first lap Walter was already passing those ahead of him. Holding the BSA well down the banking with those very strong wrists of his, he was streaking through at well over 100 mph when a slower machine, he was about to overtake, suddenly swerved down from high up on the banking, where slower machines should not be, out of control. Walter just failed by the narrowest of margins to avoid the ensuing crash. The back wheel of the 498cc Excelsior caught the front of the BSA, tearing at the rim and tyre. The Empire Star was damaged beyond repair. The Excelsior wobbled to a halt in the Finishing Straight, its rider suffering a broken ankle. Wal Handley was less fortunate. Thrown from his machine at well over 100 mph he lay motionless on the track. He was rushed to Weybridge Cottage Hospital with serious head injuries only a year after his great Donington crash. This accident naturally put a 'damper' on what should otherwise have been a celebratory occasion for BSA's achievement.

Walter had a fractured base of the skull and for several days was too ill to receive visitors. On about the fifth day, the hospital telephoned Tom Handley in Birmingham, saying that his brother wanted some cash. A relieved Tom noted in his diary, 'sounds better!' Having regained consciousness Walter asked for newspapers to catch up on what had been happening. This request had been turned down flat, 'Head injuries do not permit reading.' So having obtained some cash Walter decided to take the matter into his own hands. Unfortunately he was spotted by the matron returning up the hospital drive in his dressing gown and slippers. Under his arm he had a bundle of reading matter obtained from W. H. Smith in the High Street. Was there a bother! Shortly afterwards one of Walter's friends, Charles Mortimer, tried to visit him and was refused outright by this formidable lady. He was told that Mr Handley was a terrible nuisance, an utterly irresponsible person and she would be grateful when the time came for his discharge.

The matron had her wish much earlier than expected. Walter set about discharging himself on Sunday, 11 July. He had arranged for Harry Perrey to come and collect him, but it was not as simple to get out of the hospital as he had supposed. Before Harry could help Walter into the back of his Armstrong Siddeley, the matron required him to sign that he was responsible for his friend's life! Walter objected to this, 'I can sign that myself.'

Matron retorted, 'No, you are not a responsible person.' They could accept no responsibility for his life, if he insisted on riding or driving in the state he was in.

'Well, it's my head and so it's up to me,' was the exasperated response. Twelve days later the managing director of W. L. Handley Limited was at his desk in Birmingham, and by 5 September he was flying his beloved Puss Moth again.

Over a year later Walter was at Donington practising on a works entered Gold Star for the August meeting. Twice he returned the machine to the Small Heath factory asking for certain improvements to be made affecting the general performance. When he found that these had not been done he decided, to the great disappointment of the fans, not to ride. It was the same decision he had made a number of times before. He would rather miss out on the starting fee, than ride a machine in danger of damaging the manufacturer's reputation. He was very aware that with Wal Handley in the saddle expectations would be high; an indifferent showing would cause knowledgeable spectators to look askance at the BSA.

So it came about that his 1937 Brooklands foray on the Empire Star was the last time that Walter raced. There is no doubt that had a suitable opportunity arisen he would have raced again. Suggestions that he had retired do not seem to be borne out by what we know. The continual comings and goings of well-known personalities to his Birmingham office, right up to the outbreak of war, bore silent witness to his strong interest in the racing world; Dougal Marchant, George Eyston, Freddie Dixon, Charlie Dodson, Billy Cotton, Kaye Don, and his old friends Jimmy Simpson and George Patchett were amongst the callers.

CHAPTER 32
ALL THINGS POWERED

As the 1930s drew to a close, something attracted Walter back to the setting he knew so well – the Isle of Man TT races. In 1937 he flew to the Island in his Puss Moth and watched Guthrie and Frith win the Junior TT and Senior TT respectively for Norton Motors. This was the last time Walter saw his old rival, Jimmy Guthrie, for later that year the heroic Scot was leading the German Grand Prix at Sachsenring when, on the last lap, he crashed and was killed.

Walter was never really reconciled to the role of spectator, and when in 1938 he returned to the Island for the last time, he was offered and accepted the job of Travelling Marshal. In the Lightweight Race on Wednesday, 15 June, the German and European champion of the 250 class, twenty-nine-year-old Ewald Kluge, riding a DKW, was building up a huge winning margin over 'Ginger' Wood and Tyrell Smith, both mounted on the two-valve overhead camshaft Excelsiors. Walter, watching this display of German supremacy, was growing restive. It will be remembered that at this time the attitude of the Nazi regime was causing sport to be used as an instrument of German propaganda. Walter, waiting in the pits with his 'Manx' Norton idly ticking over, decided to have a bit of fun. As Kluge roared passed the pits towards Bray Hill, Walter swung into action. At Braddan the crowds leapt to their feet as Kluge appeared, hotly chased by the Travelling Marshal. Walter passed Kluge near the Highlander, and so it went on right round the course with the German now chasing the Travelling Marshal. The crowds were thrilled and the broadcasters amused by it all.

Some people believe that Handley did this out of sheer exuberance, but his brother was certain that he had made the mental resolve to show this German a bit of riding! What Walter had done was typical of him. It was naughty but he had been careful not to impede the race winner, and after it was all over he was quick to compliment Kluge on his success. Such an episode served to confirm the public's image of Wal Handley as the man of action. They saw him riding the front

Walter *(right)* acquired his Bristol Fighter jointly
with his friend Harold Willis *(far left)* and Jack Rowley
(middle), a friend and member of the Midland Aero Club.

wheel only and not caring a hang where the back one went. So they could be excused for imagining such a man to have been a rather wild 'tear-away'. Nothing could have been further from the truth. Away from the glare and tension of the race track, he was a different being. His mild easy going manner and his thoughtful brown eyes tended to mask the fact that you were in the presence of a road racing genius. Only the jutting jaw hinted at his practical ability.

His character was indeed complex. Not an easy person to get to know, but once accepted as a friend he would remain steadfastly loyal and was very generous. His slightly acidulated sense of humour was a delight. Often he would have his listeners convulsed with laughter as he converted one of his hair-raising experiences into a humorous tale. By nature he was modest and quiet, almost shy. At a club dinner or dance you would not find Walter, to use a phrase, 'prancing among the highlights,' but rather tucked away in a corner chatting with an acquaintance.

However, Walter also possessed the mercurial temperament of the true artist. His mood could change suddenly. His friend, Harry Perrey recalled that he could start by telling you an amusing story, usually against himself, and then switch to something intent or serious:

> He was fiery at times, but it never bothered me, we never fell out. He rarely spoke about his upbringing but he did mention his father dying of cancer when he was a boy.

There were times when his temper would get the better of his judgement. His old friend Geoff Davison wrote:

> Walter was a man with many friends and only one real enemy – himself. He would have had far more success in life had he been less morose in manner, less bluntly and directly accusing when ill-used.

Despite those not always predictable moods, the people who knew him always emphasised his great personality, his generosity and kindness. Reporters found that unlike some of his contemporaries – who were allegedly easier to deal with – he never dodged awkward questions and would do his best to give a straight answer. Nevertheless he was not an easy person to interview; wizard with machinery that he was, words simply did not flow from Walter Handley.

It was his remarkably sensitive handling of engines, almost amounting to a sixth sense, which made him master of the situation whatever the elements. On one occasion Walter joined Geoff Davison in the latter's boat, reputed to have been the Admiral's Pinnace of the German warship *Hindenburg*. They were situated off Milford Haven with a decent gale blowing. In describing what followed Geoff wrote:

> He and I were in the wheel-house, with others of the party, some of whom were rather queasy, below. He was at the wheel. He looked towards the open sea, where the real stuff was to be found, with a questioning glance. I nodded, for I knew my boat, and enjoyed that sort of thing. We headed for the ocean. He had never handled a boat of that size before [fifty feet in length] yet it was obvious that he was the complete master of her. Pitching and rolling we staggered on, and as we ran into big seas he eased back the throttle. As we hung on by our eyebrows we laughed at each other, just as we had laughed in the Belgian Grand Prix some fifteen years before. But when cries for pity reached us from the passengers below, he growled a curse, assumed the customary Handley scowl, and turned her about through heavy waves – a tricky job – as if he had been handling her for years.

He possessed superb judgement and it was this that made him so great on two wheels or four, but he was always willing to exceed that judgement, knowing that he was doing so. His lightning reflexes allowed him at times to chance the impossible. As a result he had more crashes, than most, usually because he was prepared to take that extra risk. In his time he broke many bones, including his back and had a fractured base of the skull. Yet none of these accidents affected his nerve. Geoff Davison wrote, 'His quickness of thought and action was incredible, and early in his career he had reduced high speed crashing to a fine art.' However, it was said that as a flyer he was a different being. If not satisfied with an airfield, it was not unknown for him to spend the best part of an hour examining it before take-off. As he once commented, 'I never take chances with planes; one usually has only one accident with them.' It was Walter's incredible quickness of thought and action which saved his own and his friend Davison's life. On this occasion Geoff was bringing his newly acquired twin-engine monoplane into a left hand circuit of the airfield before landing. He had the left wing properly down when, without warning, the left engine cut. In a flash they were in a power spin, with 'mother earth' about three

Wal Handley was, by 1932–33 when this picture was taken, a keen airman.
He had just acquired G-ACAC his Bristol Fighter.

seconds away. Walter snapped the throttles back and said quite casually, 'All right Geoff, I've got her,' and as he said it he pulled out of the spin with about twenty feet to spare.

It was with Geoff Davison, in rather different circumstances, that once again Walter's ability 'at the stick' saved the situation. It was in March 1933 that Geoff, excited by his new purchase, a DH 60 G-Moth, suggested a week's flying holiday. Walter, never loath to get away from his desk, said simply, 'Ah, Okay,' and it was settled. Two days later they set off on a route that was to take them across France to the Mediterranean coast. It was on the return journey that the weather changed abruptly. The little plane had to complete the Dijon–Le Bourget stretch in cross winds gusting up to 50 mph. After a two hour buffeting, the two men were happy to reach the warmth and comfort of Le Bourget's lounge. A short while later they saw 'Heracles' – the forty-passenger liner of Imperial Airways, the largest and heaviest in the world at that time, come in and land. That did it, Walter finished his cognac and said, 'Are you ready? If that packet can fly, we can.' It was no use arguing, Walter was set for home, and Geoff, who as he said later would cheerfully have sold his new aeroplane for the fare home by train and boat, had to follow. They made it – just, but it took six men to hold them to the floor at Lympne, where they learned that the wind speed had reached over 70 mph. Rather too strong for a small Moth, but not when Walter Handley was at the controls!

This makes Walter's adventurous life sound like lots of fun, but unfortunately the 1930s were a worrying decade and Walter was not exempt from various troubles. Business took up an increasing proportion of his time and trade was so poor that in 1939 he took the brave, though not necessarily wise, decision to end motorcycle sales and to concentrate on cars. In view of this change of policy, it was perhaps appropriate that he should manage to slip away and compete in the seventh and eighth RAC Car Rallies in 1938 and 1939 with Geoff Davison. They shared the driving in Geoff's powerful 14 hp Triumph Dolomite and in the 1939 Rally they won their class. So as the war clouds gathered, Walter capped his career with a Rally success.

CHAPTER 33
PRELUDE TO WAR

By the late summer of 1939 the signs of war were there for all to see. By August the tide of events was moving with incredible speed. Civilians were being encouraged to volunteer for a variety of emergency services. Blackout exercises were commonplace and, most sombre of all, school-children were being evacuated to country areas.

In London moves were afoot at the Air Ministry to set up a pool of experienced civil pilots ineligible, on account of age, for operational or, at that time, non-operational flying in the RAF. Their tasks, it was thought, would be the movement of dispatches and medical supplies as well as ambulance work and co-operation with the police and fire services. This embryo organisation was to be called Air Transport Auxiliary (ATA), and was attached to British Airways, soon to be merged with Imperial Airways into BOAC, for administration and finance. One of their directors, thirty-three-year-old Gerard d'Erlanger, a member of the banking family, became the driving force behind the idea.

On Thursday, 31 August, the crisis assumed stark proportions as an Air Navigation Order came into force banning all civil flying over the UK without a special permit. A shocked Walter realised that he had flown his latest acquisition, an Avian Monoplane – GAAYW – for the last time. Meanwhile he, in common with other selected 'A' Licence holders, aged twenty-eight to fifty years and having at least 250 hours experience, were being circulated by d'Erlanger. Walter quickly responded and thus became one of that small intrepid band of ATA founder members known as the 'first twenty-eight'. Of course he need not have volunteered, particularly as three years earlier he had acquired Hipwoods, a small engineering business that would be requisitioned for war work. One can be certain that such a consideration would not have crossed his mind.

At 11 AM on the morning of Sunday, 3 September 1939 the country learned that it was now at war with Germany. Shortly afterwards d'Erlanger received authority to put his great idea into operation. Telegrams were sent to the selected applicants asking them to report to Whitchurch Aerodrome, Bristol, for an interview and flight test. On 6 September Walter was checked out for basic flying ability in a Tiger Moth, and interviewed by d'Erlanger and A. R. O. MacMillan, the Chief Flying Instructor of British Airways. Following the test, Walter was told to return home and await further instructions. A week later he became one of twelve pilots offered contracts as first officers. This resulted from his having over 700 hours flying time accumulated since 1928, and sufficiently varied experience to handle twin-engine passenger carrying machines. Walter's salary, in line with that paid to British Airways own civil pilots, was to be £350 plus 3s and 6d an hour flying pay. We now entered the period that became known as the 'phoney war', but for the pioneers of ATA the waiting was about to end with an unexpected and rather challenging telegram.

Less than three weeks after his test at Whitchurch, the telegram reached Walter. It read: 'Report to Central Flying School Upavon for test with view to ferrying RAF Aircraft.' This was a real surprise and no mistake. The original idea had been that the ATA pilots would fly light aircraft, ferrying people and medical supplies across the country and generally maintaining communications. Yet within twenty days of the outbreak of war, the decision had been taken to give selected amateur pilots the chance to show whether they would be able to fly 'hot warplanes'. Although, we were still in the period of the 'phoney war', it was already apparent that before long, the

Captain Walter Handley in ATA uniform, the two stripes denoting that, shortly after the outbreak of war, he is a First Officer, the RAF equivalent is Flight Lieutenant.

operational squadrons would become much too busy to use their own pilots for ferrying duties.

On Tuesday, 26 September, Walter reached the Central Flying School (CFS) on Salisbury Plain and presented himself at the OC's Office. There he was introduced to a member of the

Refresher Flight, the 'chunky' Rupert Leigh, who had been on the instructing staff since 1937, and was soon to take command of No. 66 Squadron. He led Walter across to a bright yellow coloured aeroplane which turned out to be a North American Harvard, used by the CFS as an advanced trainer. Walter was invited to stand on one wing, while his instructor stood on the other and introduced him to an amazingly neat and colourful assortment of dials and knobs. There was talk of pitch controls, toe brakes, retractable undercarriages, flaps, boost gauges and a few other things, some of which Walter had never heard. Before sending Walter off to be issued with a parachute, the Squadron Leader paused and mentioned that the aeroplane had a most unpleasant and vicious stall, 'but then,' he added with a disarming grin, 'You mustn't let it stall.'

It had already been made clear to everyone in the ATA that there was no question of people being trained to fly these potentially lethal aeroplanes. If Walter did not succeed in being 'converted' in a reasonably short space of time, he would be politely sent home. Everything would hinge on a fifty minute dual flight over the Wiltshire Downs in Harvard N7186. After the aerobatics, during the last half hour of which the Harvard had rarely been the right way up for more than a minute or two, the instructor took charge preparatory to landing. As they crossed the boundary perimeter Walter saw the throttle lever move to the closed position. A moment later he almost jumped out of his skin as a deafening Klaxon Horn went off just behind his head. Walter turned and queried what was happening. Apparently this was a device which warned the pilot that his undercarriage was still retracted and would go off as soon as his airspeed dropped. Walter was happy to lower the wheels as quickly as possible, remarking as he did so that he thought it was a bit early! The frightful noise then stopped and the dashboard lights changed from red to green.

This little incident illustrates the point that the CFS was seeking pilots who could operate in the RAF manner. Ferrying combat aircraft was going to demand technical concentration at all times. Everything must be done correctly and in the right order. After the landing Leigh climbed out and told Walter that he could go off and do an hour on his own. Before Walter left Upavon he was somewhat astonished to learn that he had been cleared to fly all operational singles.

Six weeks later Walter returned to the CFS for conversion to twin aircraft. His week's flying included not only the Harvard and the Battle Bomber, but also dual instruction on a short nosed Bristol Blenheim Mk I. Amongst other things he quickly learned how, with one of the twin Mercury engines 'dead', he could keep the bomber on a straight line during take-off and delay the climb until the engine failure safety speed had been reached. Walter was now cleared to fly solo in bombers of the Whitley, Hampden and Wellington class; the latter being the largest aircraft flown solo by ATA at that time.

Events now moved quickly. All the ATA pilots were summoned to report for 'Auxiliary Air Duty'. They came together in the Royal Hotel, Bristol, to hear their future leader d'Erlanger outline their awesome task. He had received a signal from the Air Ministry stating that his thirty or so pilots were urgently needed to assist the RAF in ferrying trainers, fighters and bombers from factory and store to the various air force stations. The prospect of flying some of the RAFs fastest aircraft was viewed with trepidation by some and with delight by others. In fact, nearly all these 'Ancient and Tattered Airmen' adapted to the new situation surprisingly quickly after their conversion courses.

CHAPTER 34
HEROIC DAYS

The next move by Gerard d'Erlanger was to allocate twenty or so of his pilots in equal proportions to No. 1 Ferry Pool RAF at Hucknall, near Nottingham, and to No. 2 Ferry Pool at Filton, Bristol. On Monday, 16 October, Walter joined the party of pilots sent to Hucknall. In command of these civilians in uniform was the Canadian, F. D. Bradbrooke. Before the war, this naturally gifted leader founded the Winnipeg Aero Club and he later became a staff journalist with the *Aeroplane*. He was a brilliant pilot and one of the most experienced amongst the 'first twenty-eight'. When the all civilian ferry pool at White Waltham was first formed, it was 'Brad' who became the flight leader. Everyone felt a great sense of personal loss when, over a year later, the news came through that he had been killed while serving in the Atlantic Ferry Service.

In the beginning at Hucknall, Bradbrooke and C. S. Napier, son of the car and aero engine designer, were the only pilots cleared to ferry both singles and twins, since the CFS had a limited training capacity. Until his CFS course in November Walter was confined to singles, while others in the group were only permitted to fly training aircraft. The pressure of work was so great that training on station was virtually non-existent. Sometimes the RAF pilots would squeeze in an hour's instruction at the end of the day, but more often the ATA airmen had to learn as they went along. On 24 October, Walter had his first solo flight in the outdated, but still operational, dun coloured Battle day bomber, powered by the greatest piston engine of its

316

day, the Rolls Royce Merlin. No dual instruction was possible in the Battle and so the Officer Commanding 'C' Flight was only able to explain a few things to Walter before leaving him to get on with it.

Five days later Walter had his first solo in the faithful Anson taxi aircraft – 'Annie' to the grateful pilots tired out at the end of a long day ferrying complicated aeroplanes. Because it involved the safety of up to ten other pilots, the Anson was often reserved for the senior members of a pool, and Captain Handley would become very familiar with it over the next two years. The first three months of that terrible winter of 1939–1940 saw the ferrying of many unfamiliar aircraft types providing a nerve racking adventure for the ATA pilots. They had to work with half remembered cockpit procedures, check out weather reports and make estimates of daylight time remaining. Occasionally Walter would get a relaxingly familiar DH Tiger Moth Trainer, but such diversions became increasingly rare. One day he would fly a Harvard to Lossiemouth, next he would ferry a couple of aircraft manufactured by Blackburne for the Fleet Air Arm – the Roc two-seater fighter and the Skua fighter dive-bomber. Much more common were the Avro Ansons; Fairey Battles; Bristol Blenheim IVs and Hampdens. They were soon followed by Beaufighters; Wellington Bombers; Hawker Hurricanes and, of course, the Spitfire. By the following spring, his brother said to Walter that he felt he had a dangerous job. Walter agreed in the sense that his job was much more varied than that of the RAF lads because they were usually specialists on one type of aircraft, a fighter or a four-engine bomber, whereas the ATA had to fly so many different types, in his case he had already flown over twenty different aircraft.

All the ferry pilots, civilian and service, were working through the short daylight hours, and sometimes into the dusk, delivering thousands of aircraft from the factories to the RAF Maintenance Units where guns were sighted and harmonised, and radio and oxygen gear tested. Until about mid 1940 it was usual for the RAF pilots to fly the completed aircraft from the MUs to their final destination. However, with the onset of the Battle of Britain, the ferry pilots of ATA took over this added responsibility. On any day during the war it has been estimated that between 400–1,400 aircraft were in the course of being ferried.

The first winter of the war often produced a log jam of ferry movements as virtually every airfield in the country was in turn snowbound, icebound, mud bound or waterlogged. The smoke haze and dense fogs of the North Midlands compounded the difficulties at Hucknall. Bradbrooke wrote almost despairingly, 'Most of us have "Hucknall Throat" and our entrails ache with coughing, we yearn for the South and our own Pool.' Bradbrooke's wish was to be fulfilled much earlier than anyone had anticipated.

On Friday, 9 February 1940, d'Erlanger collected a Tiger Moth in Bristol and set course for White Waltham, near Maidenhead. This airfield, just about 30 miles from London, had been chosen as the new home of the ATA organisation. The next day Walter joined the other pilots in the move to Berkshire. With the RAF still in full possession of most of the airfield, they initially had to occupy the wooden hut known as the 'Cuckoo's Nest'. Here the forty-two male pilots settled into their cramped quarters, but no-one minded. By now a great sense of camaraderie had developed and the atmosphere was that of a flying club. The tradition has survived because today the airfield is the home of the largest flying club in the UK, the West London Aero Club.

The twenty or so, who had worked at Hucknall and Filton, now formed the nucleus of an organisation banded together in a common enthusiasm to do a job nobody had really believed they could do. Experience was being built up and each day that passed added to their confidence. Casual informality vanished and quiet purpose took over as the message came, 'Will all pilots report to the "Ops" Room for their chits.' Maps and helmets were sought out, followed by a weather check and the latest as to balloons and airfield serviceability. Taxi pilots checked their itinerary and got the engine of the Anson, Stinson Reliant or

Airspeed Courier started and warmed up. The day's work had begun and as the pilots walked out carrying their parachutes and overnight bags, no-one really knew what the day might bring or how long they would be away.

A dramatic example of the unexpected occurred, one warm afternoon in May 1940, a few days before the Dunkirk evacuation. The story is told in *Brief Glory* by E. C. Cheesman. Walter was one of five or six pilots returning in an Anson at the end of a day's work. As the machine taxied to a halt, d'Erlanger opened the door. For just a moment there was silence broken by the CO saying, 'I want some of you fellows for a job to France,' everyone volunteered at once.

'When do we go sir, first thing in the morning?'

The CO looked grim, 'You are needed at once.'

Within half an hour the Anson was on its way to Hullavington, near Chippenham, to collect Fairey Battles – the only operational aircraft available. This done, the eight airmen set off for Andover where each plane was armed. The ATA men were introduced to an RAF Flight Lieutenant who was to lead them to their destination, 'somewhere in France'. They explained that they would have to follow him closely for, besides possessing no 'Mae West' life saving suits, they had no maps either. 'Oh, that's all right chaps, neither have I.' After a wide sweep of the English Channel, during which time their flight leader struggled to get the right compass bearing, they flew over Northern France. They landed in what can only be called a large ploughed field near Troyes. With the help of providence and some remarkably skilful piloting every one of the eight Battles landed safely, although by this time it was nearly dark.

They were very disconcerted to find that the Squadron Leader in charge was definitely not pleased to see them. He had had to move six times in eight days in the face of the swift German advance. The enemy was hourly drawing nearer and the countryside was seething with fifth-columnists. The Battles were no sooner landed than attempts at camouflaging were undertaken. It was all to no avail. Walter was still there, when shortly afterwards, everyone dived for cover as attacking planes roared overhead. When the attack was over, Walter was angered to see the delivered aircraft blown up and in flames. It was in moments like this that Walter felt most keenly his greatest regret. He just wished that he had been a few years younger so that he could have had a 'crack' at the Nazis in the air. In the midst of the chaos the ATA pilots were left to fend for themselves. They split up into two groups and set off in a westerly direction. It was not unknown in these circumstances for some of the ATA to get back by flying un-serviceable Hurricanes. Some of these aircraft were made good in time for the Battle of Britain. Since only sixty-six of the two hundred and sixty-one Hurricanes sent to France got back to Britain, it can truly be said that each individual effort counted in the desperate situation that was unfolding.

On 10 May 1940 just eight days before ATA flew to France; various Panzer groups had crossed the Belgian and Dutch frontiers. Holland held out for only five days and the allies, finding themselves in danger of encirclement, were in full retreat. Already German armour had attacked through the Ardennes and was racing across France at alarming speed. As he flew across Northern France, Walter could see the roads teeming with refugees. Long before the news became public, Walter had told his brother that France had collapsed. Over four long years of war would pass before ATA returned to Europe.

It has been said many times that we British are at our best in the face of adversity. So it is perhaps not surprising that during the darkest period of the war there should come one of ATA's best stories. The fact that it happened to feature the irrepressible Wal Handley is not really surprising. It happened when he was in command at Hawarden. Walter set off with two other ATA pilots to collect three Spitfires from somewhere 'down south' for delivery to an RAF station. After collecting the Spitfires his two colleagues left ahead of Walter who stayed awhile. As he flew north he was looking ahead scanning the skies for a sign of the other two. Soon he was relieved at sighting the distinctive elliptical wings of the two Spitfires but was astonished to see them doing rolls, dives, loops and general 'gymnastics'. 'What do those two reckon they are doing? It's most unlike them.' Then, thinking, 'Ah well, anything they can do so can I,' he decided to join in the fun. He was amazed at what they were doing but really enjoyed it. However, it did seem a bit hectic; so after a bit Walter decided to leave these two to their antics and get back to base. He would certainly want to know what the other two thought they were doing instead of obeying instructions

Walter Handley sits in his favourite aircraft, the Spitfire,
he was not alone in admiring this wonderful fighter.

and returning directly. When Walter got back he found his two pilots already there, they were wondering what had happened to the 'gaffer'. He soon found out! Apparently, he had unwittingly joined in a highly secret demonstration of the latest Spitfire's capabilities before a lot of high ranking RAF officers. 'Phones had been ringing wanting to know who the uninvited pilot was who had joined in the display. Walter had rather spoiled things by keeping up with them in the old model!

Important changes in the ferrying programme became apparent during April 1940. Possibly Walter had advance knowledge that changes were about to happen for it was on 6 April that he asked his brother to take over the job of Managing Director of his motorcycle business in Birmingham. Shortly after this, White Waltham first learned from the Air Ministry that, from 1 May, the ATA was to ferry all new aircraft between the factories and the Maintenance Units. In order to cope with its own expansion in responsibilities, the ATA decided to disperse the White Waltham Ferry Pilots Pool so as to reduce taxi and ferrying distances. On Saturday, 25 May, Walter joined sixteen other pilots in the move from White Waltham to Hawarden airfield in northeast Wales, near Chester. At the same time another twelve pilots moved to Whitchurch, near Bristol, to set up two new civilian ferry pilot pools. Hawarden was named as ATAs No. 3 Pool and initially came under the command of H. A. Taylor – formerly Assistant Editor of Flight. It was the pool chiefly responsible for clearing the factories in the northern area, especially the Wellington bombers from the Vickers Armstrong Factory on the airfield. Other ferrying duties in those early days consisted mainly of Blenheims from the Rootes 'Shadow' factory at Speke, Handley Page Hampdens from Preston, Hereford bombers from Belfast, and Hawker Hurricanes from nearby maintenance units (MUs).

With the formal end of hostilities in France on 22 June, the country braced itself for the anticipated invasion. At Hawarden, the airfield was taken over by Fighter Command, and No. 7 Operational Training Unit was formed. Here at Hawarden some of our best fighter pilots would undergo their training. At the same time the RAF's No. 48 Maintenance Unit and the ATA Ferry Pool became lodger units on the aerodrome. Churchill had invited his friend Lord Beaverbrook to take charge of the new Ministry of Aircraft Production and had given him overall control of the ferrying programme. British industry, newly galvanised by Beaverbrook's Ministry was, by the time of the Battle of Britain, turning out Hurricanes and Spitfires at the rate of nearly 500 a month. ATA's role thus became the vital one of moving the much needed fighter planes not only from the factories but also, in some cases directly to the Battle of Britain airfields.

The fighting, which began over the English Channel on 9 July, carried on with hardly any let up until mid September when the Luftwaffe, exhausted by the summer battles, turned its attention to night bombing. Throughout this period the ferry pilots proved tireless. Frequently when delivering aircraft they had to chase the front line squadrons from place to place. It could and often did get quite desperate. At the end of a long summer day the exhausted Hawarden pilots, having been collected from numerous airfields by a taxi Anson, would head for home. It was time to forget the 'wheeling dog fights' they had seen and the smoke trails across the bright blue sky which signalled victory and defeat; life and death. Soon the reassuring sight of Shropshire's Wenlock Edge and the Wrekin would come into view. Ahead were the gleaming shapes of the Dee and Mersey Estuaries. At 1,000 feet or so Hooton Park aerodrome could be seen. Just 15 miles away to the north was Speke, its environs closely guarded by the ominous points of the Liverpool balloon barrage. While ahead and below were the aircraft assembly sheds of RAF Hawarden and beyond, a little to port, was the twin aerodrome known as RAF Sealand. As the Anson taxied to a halt, its Cheetah engines at last silent, the exhausted occupants would tumble out in grateful anticipation of a few hours 'kip'.

Although the RAF ferry pilots bore the brunt of flight movements during the Battle of Britain, they could not have coped without the help of the fast growing ATA organisation. Some accounts seem to have overlooked this, but in 1945 Lord Beaverbrook was in no doubt:

> Just as the Battle of Britain is the accomplishment and achievement of the RAF, likewise it can be declared that the ATA sustained and supported them in the Battle. They were soldiers fighting in the struggle just as completely as if they had been engaged on the battlefront.

By the end of the war ATA had ferried over 300,000 aircraft to the squadrons.

CHAPTER 35
WALTER TAKES COMMAND

It was during October 1940 that a change of leadership occurred at the No. 3 ATA Ferry Pool, Hawarden. This happened when First Officer H. A. Taylor was finally accepted for a vacancy in the test flight at RAF Hawarden's No. 48 MU. The leadership of ATA immediately responded by promoting First Officer, Captain Walter Handley, to become the Officer Commanding the Hawarden Ferry Pool. Walter's experience and his outstanding qualities as a pilot and leader of men had made him the natural choice.

The first HQ of No. 3 Ferry Pool was a semi-detached cottage, situated on the edge of the great aerodrome. In this small unpretentious building, almost in the shadow of the nearby Vickers sheds and approached by a narrow bumpy track over a level crossing, the foundations were being laid for what was to become ATA's largest Ferry Pool. Walter, 'Wally' to most of his pilots, was a good organiser. He was already working the transformation, holding the reins loosely, and allowing his thirty or so pilots to get on with the job of moving aeroplanes free from unnecessary interference. One of his first tasks was to assist First Officer A. W. Vincent in setting up the sub-pool at Ringway, Manchester. The embryonic No. 14 Ferry Pool was left to handle most flight movements of Ansons and Blenheims from Woodford, Proctors from Trafford Park, and Beaufighters, Fulmars and Swordfish made by Fairey Aviation at Ringway.

By now the Hawarden Pool had developed into a great team effort. From the Pool Commander, who spent as much time in the air as his most junior pilot, there was a happy spirit. When the weather was too bad for flying Walter would sometimes amuse his pilots, cooped up in the little cottage, with stories of his 'lurid past' on road and track. Somehow he managed to do all this and still find time for dealing with cash sheets, requisitions, billeting papers and planning. Despite a recurrence of his old ulcerated stomach trouble, induced no doubt by the continuous strain of his job, his private life was not so displeasing. He took out a lease on Warren Bank, a comfortable and spacious residence set in an elevated rural setting just inside Wales near the Cheshire border. He had servants to wine and dine

Warren Bank, the home of Captain Walter Handley OC of ATA Ferry Pool No. 3 in northeast Wales near the Cheshire border. The car is Walter's two-seater Jaguar SS100.

his visitors. He was never known to buy a new car and true to form he acquired, at this time, a good quality two-seater Jaguar SS100. Sometimes he was away for days at a time, but whenever he returned, Warren Bank offered a semblance of normality – a place to relax with colleagues and friends. He was a man who valued his independence and many of his friends surmised that it was unlikely that the idea of marriage ever occurred to him. During his racing career he had always maintained that it would not be fair to get married because of the danger racing presented. He had enjoyed travelling and leading an adventurous life so that the idea of buying a house and settling down was not something that had appealed. Now that he was comfortably settled at Warren Bank, and in command of thirty to forty flyers, his friends expected him to get married, but for some reason this did not happen.

What direction would Walter's life have taken had he survived the war? There was some speculation that he might have made a career in civil aviation. My brother Graham reminded me that Walter had met a recently recruited eighteen-year-old ATA Flight Engineer, 'Young Freddie Laker' early in 1941; who knows what might have been.

During the summer of 1940 following several close encounters with the enemy, ATA decided to recruit twenty air-gunners for the protection of taxi and ferried aircraft. The armament usually consisted of a Lewis or Vickers gun, and ammunition was obtained from the RAF. After a brief course of instruction the gunners proceeded to their new Ferry Pools. One of the Hawarden air-gunner recruits was summoned after a few weeks to the local Ministry of Labour to prove that he was engaged in an essential occupation. Apparently the interview went somewhat as follows:

'You say you are employed by the ATA at Hawarden aerodrome. What do you do there?'

'My job is to look after a Lewis Gun.'

'Oh, you mean you work in the Armoury?'

'No, I'm an air-gunner.'

'Oh, I see; you're in the RAF. We thought you were with the ATA.'

The air-gunner confirmed that he was indeed with ATA.

'I'm afraid there must be some mistake. You say you're in the ATA, who are civilians, and yet you're a gunner. What do you do?'

'I sit in the back of the Anson and fire the gun.'

At this point the official lost patience and rang up Walter Handley, by this time commanding the Ferry Pool. 'We've got a chap here who says he's with you and fires a machine gun. He must mean he's in the RAF at Hawarden.'

'No, he's not, he's with us and we're jolly glad to have him these days!'

'Well, what the heck do I put him down as – Licensed Bandit?'

This term 'Licensed Bandit' was pretty accurate. During the late summer any marauding aircraft were discouraged with gunfire from the turret of the taxi Ansons. No-one seemed to worry that this arming of civilians was a breach of international agreements. One of ATA's best loved characters was the Irishman, Oliver Eric Armstrong, known as 'Paddy', an experienced airman who, on joining ATA, was posted to Hawarden and served under Walter for a year before opening up the new Belfast Ferry Pool. He was piloting a Blackburne Botha across the Irish Sea, when a destroyer opened fire. Suddenly puffs of white smoke came up, followed by a bang as some shrapnel penetrated the floor. The ATA air gunner peppered away furiously with his machine gun. After things had quietened down, he went up to see how the pilot had taken it. Paddy was red in the face with rage. 'These bloody English,' he roared, 'they'll have me in the war yet!'

The ATA pilots of Hawarden soon became accustomed to the Irish Sea, crossing from Short and Harland's factory in Belfast to the MUs on the mainland, and by September 1940 the first of the four-engine heavy bombers, the Stirling was being ferried by ATA. Walter, being a Class V pilot was able to fly any aircraft in No. 41 Group. In fact he was one of the first to fly this aeroplane of great character. With a steeply angled overall length of eighty-seven feet, the pilot was seated twenty feet above the ground. Although it was very manoeuvrable, three point landings were not easy because of the Stirling's attitude and height. Not long after this, the ATA pilots were introduced to another four-engine bomber, the Halifax. At the same time the Lockheed Hudson twins were beginning to arrive from across the Atlantic. The Hudson took some getting used to because of its tendency to swing on landing runs. Good three point landings were very desirable because the Hudson had its fuel tanks directly above the undercarriage struts and a heavy landing could lead to ruptured tanks and fire!

Amongst this varied assortment of aircraft there were the Master types, the famous 'cloak and dagger' Westland Lysander, and some fairly odd types that had to be flown 'off the cuff' with no handling notes or even first hand advice for guidance. All these aircraft had to be flown without radio or other forms of navigational aid. This meant that once contact

The map of the local area was kept in Walter's office. The three stripes denote that he is an ATA Flight Captain, the equivalent of an RAF Squadron Leader.

had been lost with the ground, i.e. rivers, landmarks, railways, or even roads, there was no way of ascertaining your position and organising a safe return to contact flying. From Hawarden the ferry pilots had to give the Liverpool, Widnes, Warrington and Manchester balloon barrages a wide berth. The only means of crossing into Lancashire was through a corridor about four miles wide between the Liverpool and Widnes balloons. If you passed through this gap into low cloud and rain, you were in an area rather lacking in landmarks. In these early days of the war it was not allowed to mark balloons or new airfields on maps. So the master map, kept under lock and key in Walter's office, had to be memorised before take-off. Walter once said, with some feeling, that if you could fly in Britain you could fly anywhere.

The second winter of the war was truly appalling, the grim weeks of fog, and the low cloud and rain caused many of the new airfields to be a foot deep in mud. The rains turned to snow and Hawarden had drifts over five feet deep in parts of the airfield. There was little ferrying being done anywhere. First the runways got snowed up, then as the snow melted a period of fog and low cloud would set in again. Fortunately the bad weather hindered the enemy as much as the RAF. As late as March Hawarden was still un-serviceable, the only flying possible was being done from the all weather track belonging to Vickers Limited.

During this long winter of 1940–1941 plans were being drawn up for a new ATA HQ to replace Hawarden's little cottage. The Pool Commander was sceptical. To a visitor, Walter quoted the wonderful total of aircraft ferried by his thirty pilots under conditions of acute discomfort and in all weathers. These figures were at that time proportionately the highest in ATA:

> I'm all against it myself. Look at it here. Things are so blasted awful that they've got nothing else to do but go out and fly. Give them comfort and what'll they do? Sit down by the fire and read the paper!

Officious bureaucracy was something Walter could not tolerate. Once he resigned after receiving a letter from White Waltham demanding to know why a job application form had not been completed by a part-time cleaning lady. Was the Pool Commander furious? Yes, he certainly was, he stormed down to White Waltham and before his startled superior officers he dumped his uniform on the table. With tightened lips he told them that he was trying to help fight a war, and the last thing he needed were daft letters from a lot of 'blasted stooges' and walked out. For a week he regularly attended his business in Birmingham, dressed in civilian attire, ignoring all telegrams and telephone messages asking him to report for duty immediately. Then, as he calmed down, he relented, missing no doubt the happy camaraderie of his Ferry Pool. Paddy Armstrong, 'Brookie' Smith, Percy Lane, 'Joe' Ellam, Bert Yardley, Greenhalgh, Lingard and Woolcott, names that will always be associated with Hawarden's early and heroic period; they were all much relieved to see their fiery but popular little skipper back at the helm. Although his intolerance of red tape would occasionally get the better of his judgement, Walter never spared himself and was one of the most hardworking and respected Pool Commanders in ATA.

CHAPTER 36
THE FATAL FLIGHT

By May 1941 ATA pilots were doing virtually all the home ferrying. As the summer wore on they were being confronted with many more American military aircraft with their neat rows of switches and sundry gadgetry. One of these aircraft was the Bell P39 Airacobra. It has been called the back to front fighter because its supercharged V-twelve Allison engine was mounted amidships, behind the pilot. The power was transmitted by a ten foot shaft which ran underneath the pilot to a propeller reduction gear in the nose. The plane also had 20mm cannon that fired through the propeller hub. The unorthodox position of the engine permitted another unusual feature, an electrically operated tricycle undercarriage.

The American Bell P.39 Airacobra: the Allison V-12 engine was housed behind the pilot, this led to it being called the 'back to front fighter.'

By October several Airacobras had been received at Hawarden for modifications. They were destined for No. 601 County of London Squadron which was converting to the Airacobra from Hurricanes. Walter Handley, never the desk bound OC, took the opportunity to try out what was one of the most heavily armed single-seater fighters of its day. Upon his return he declared that he did not think much of the Airacobra, but added, 'It would make a damn good racing car!' Rather an apt comment in view of the automobile type entrance doors, the cramped cockpit, and the fast and long take-off run, about seven hundred and fifty yards getting up to 150 mph!

It was in truth a masterly piece of understatement, for the Bell Airacobra was a distinctly unpleasant aeroplane. It was said that should the tricycle nose wheel fail to lock in position, then on landing the engine would plunge forward into the pilot. Since vibration at idling speed was a problem, pilots were advised to run the engine at over 1000 rpm while taxying. You had to drive quickly along, holding the aircraft in check by using the pedal brakes. This reduced the fearsome whip and rattle that came from the shaft running at engine speed between the outstretched legs of the poor pilot. Amongst other things everyone was advised not to use the cabin ventilator because the air admitted was warm!

On the morning of Saturday, 15 November, Walter seemed in a pensive mood as he gazed out of his office window at an airfield bathed in sunshine. These conditions were most welcome for all movements of aircraft had been held up by bad weather for several days. He turned and looked at the duty rota for the day. His eye noted the collection, by one of his pilots, of an Airacobra AH 598 from FPP No. 16, the last ATA pool to be formed and situated at Kirkbride, near the Scottish border. He told his Operations Staff to cancel the instruction and substitute his own name. He knew that the Airacobras were proving troublesome and he decided to deal with it. As he left the cottage HQ he remarked that he would take advantage of

such a nice day and have a break from office routine. He took off
from Hawarden in an Anson and turned for the north.

After a spell of bad weather, there's a certain magic in
blue skies and near unlimited visibility even if there's a cold
easterly wind blowing. Gone are the nagging fears of getting
lost in a sea of unbroken cloud or of tangling with hidden
balloon barrages. So Walter sat relaxed in the Anson, scanning
the instruments or squinting in the unaccustomed brightness.
Flying to the north he set course for the coast. Over to the west
he could see the clouds which topped the Isle of Man's Snaefell.

One of the last pictures taken of Walter, he is at the controls of the Anson.

Did his thoughts go back over the years to the TT races, the
scenes of so many of his triumphs and disappointments? He
had come a long way from that humble beginning in his native
Birmingham. Now at thirty-nine years of age, wearing the
dark blue uniform of which he was so proud, he was entrusted
with the delivery of warplanes, aircraft that he had certainly
never been taught to fly and now he was in charge of ATA's
largest and busiest ferry pool.

By taking the coastal route to the Solway Firth, Walter avoided the dangerous beauty of the Lakeland fells, before turning due east for Kirkbride, one of the ATA's loneliest outposts. Meanwhile the operations staff at Hawarden had alerted No. 16 FPP of the imminent arrival of their Pool Commander. When the news reached the lads of the adjoining RAF MU No. 12, there was a buzz of excitement at the prospect of meeting a 'real speed merchant'. In spite of a bitterly cold easterly wind many of them were waiting as the Anson taxied to a halt and duly escorted Walter across the aerodrome. Walter talked for a while and smoked a cigarette with the adjutant. It was nearly 4 PM when, having signed the necessary clearance paper, he walked out to the Airacobra. The ground crew had started things up in advance. He climbed up, opened the door and squeezed into the cockpit. With a casual hand salute he taxied to the long central runway. After a short pause he turned to face due east into the wind and commenced take-off.

Everyone who knows about flying agrees that this is the most critical period of flight. Trouble at this point can spell disaster, for there can be no turning back. We know from RAF witnesses that Walter's take-off from the aerodrome was perfect. But while still climbing, the engine started making a revving or surging noise. Two miles away, standing in the yard of Studholme Farm, was local man Percy Bulman. Hearing the sound of an aeroplane moving 'hard', he looked above a line of trees to the south and saw the fighter heading due east at about 1,000 feet. As he watched he saw a sooty plume of black smoke start from the tail. A few seconds later, as the aircraft passed from his sight, he heard the engine splutter and die out. There was a brief silence followed by an explosion like a loud backfire.

At the aerodrome they had heard the Airacobra's engine making an awful din, and watched in horrified silence as the black smoke began pouring from the exhaust. The aircraft was only about three miles away when they heard the explosion. According to E. C. Cheesman in his book *Brief Glory* a sheet of flame was seen to envelop the rear of the aeroplane and parts of the aircraft were seen to fly off. The Airacobra then turned about 45 degrees to the north, away from the village of Little Bampton, before going into a dive from which it never recovered. The woodlands near Fingland hid the scene of the disaster, but a rising pall of black smoke marked the site of Hawarden's first great tragedy.

Percy Bulman was one of the first to reach the burning aircraft. There was nothing he could do, Walter would have died instantly. The scene he described to me was one of utter desolation. There had been a massive fire and the smell of the burnt aircraft lingered on for days. The Airacobra was a charred wreck. Both wings were torn off, the fuselage was half buried, and debris lay scattered across the ploughed field. Nearby was the broken extension shaft. The branches of trees, on the edge of the field, were snapped off where the starboard wing tip had caught them in the sudden plummeting descent.

One curious fact was that the aircraft had almost made a complete turn and was pointing south towards the Little Bampton road. Had Walter, in those last desperate moments, put the Airacobra into a turn before the explosion? Realising that his engine was on fire, Walter would be fighting to save himself. In those last moments Walter's eyes would be searching, his hands, feet and brain flying what remained of the aircraft by instinct born of long experience. Running directly across his flight path was a long straight road leading past the village of Little Bampton. Was his last action to try and land the small fighter in the lonely country road?

In this remote corner of England died, to quote Cheesman's *Brief Glory*, 'an endearing character and a very gallant airman.' Captain Walter Handley was one of the last people the ATA leadership had expected to lose. It certainly alerted everyone to the Airacobra. Gerard d'Erlanger's Accident Committee began its investigation immediately. The initial finding 'cause unknown' remained unchanged in its essentials after deliberations lasting over six weeks. Everyone agreed that major fire had occurred in the engine but what had caused it?

As the aircraft climbs in the take-off, the barometric pressure falls. The supercharger compensates by impelling air into the engine increasing combustion, just as one does by blowing air into a fire. Unlike British aircraft at the time, the Airacobra's boost control was manual; it had no overriding atmospheric control. One theory put forward by the committee was that the pilot had allowed the limitations to be exceeded, thus over boosting and over revving the aircraft. Yet, we know that Walter had previously flown the Airacobra in addition to other American aircraft, such as the Hudson which also had no boost control.

Another possibility has been highlighted in *Wings Across the Border* by Derrick Pratt and Mike Grant. In their book, First Officer Ken Day, states that the Airacobra having boost, the throttle gate was wired off to stop over-boost. It was found in Walter's aircraft that this wire was not present so he could have pushed through the gate causing the engine to explode. If this is what happened, it looks as though Walter may have been the victim of slipshod maintenance. Like all airmen he was aware that aeroplanes can 'turn and bite'. He once said that while he would be prepared to take a known chance with a bike or car, he would never do so with a plane.

This brings us to a second possibility considered by the committee. They agreed that the aircraft may have been run up with the mixture control in full rich. RAF witnesses agreed that AH 598 had been left idling quite a while before Walter taxied off. So Walter may have unwittingly taken off with a machine containing gaseous mixtures tantamount to having a bomb at his back. Perhaps the safest and simplest thing to say is that there had been complete engine failure. Only one squadron, No. 601 based in East Anglia, was ever equipped with this American fighter. After making the switch from Hurricanes to Airacobras, the flight logs show that a high proportion of their flights resulted in forced landings. Less than a week after Walter's accident, an RAF pilot had scarcely become airborne when a violent backfire ensued and the Airacobra's engine cut. Fortunately, the pilot was able to land uninjured, but understandably he was severely shaken! The RAF never liked the Airacobra and in December 1941 they withdrew it from service on the grounds of its un-serviceability and its operational limitations in the ground-attack role. It was not until 601 Squadron had re-equipped with Spitfires that they were said to be 'back in business'. The remaining Airacobras either reverted to the USAAF or were sold off to the Soviet Air Force.

Walter Handley became the first Pool Commander to meet his death while serving with ATA. Having come through the two worst winters of the war, in an organisation that had only one third of one per cent of its total flights resulting in accidents, Walter can truly be considered very unfortunate. His loss came as a great shock, not only to ATA but also to his many friends and admirers in the Royal Air Force. The Hawarden based, No. 7 OTU gave him full military honours in an impressive but sad little ceremony at Broughton Church, near Chester. Spitfires, Walter's favourite aeroplane, roared overhead and dived in salute as the procession led by an RAF detachment, including a firing party and a band, approached the Church.

Two days later the interment took place at Yardley in Birmingham. It was a cold windswept day. Despite wartime conditions, with many of Walter's friends away on active service, the cemetery was very full. The coffin, covered with the Union flag, was borne to the graveside by six of his brother officers in ATA. Lining the rain soaked pathways were over one hundred wreaths from trade personalities, manufacturers, friends in motor sport and aviation, and many others. Tommy Rose, of Cape Record fame, who had taught Walter to fly, was one of many who felt deeply moved:

> He was always the same Wal, the man I looked forward
> to seeing more than anyone I know. He was the bravest
> and yet quite the kindest man I have ever known.

This was very true; behind the sometimes scowling exterior there was the idealist, a kind hearted gentleman who always had sympathy for the less fortunate.

It seems that Walter Handley will never be entirely forgotten by motorcyclists amongst whom I think he was most at home. This applies particularly to his long and happy association with the Isle of Man and its people. Out on one of the fastest sections of the TT course we have Handley's Corner, marked on race weeks near the twelfth milestone, where he crashed in 1932 in

The Walter Handley Memorial Seat is situated near the Quarter Bridge Road. It was unveiled on 8 June 1948 by Graham Walker. Standing behind Graham, wearing a badge, is Geoff Davison. Tom Handley stands next to Canon E. H. Stenning. On the right is Mayor of Douglas, F. Corkill. The last line of the inscription reads: "None ever passed this way more bravely."

pursuit of the flying Nortons. However, many people feel that his real memorial came when the Borough of Douglas accepted on 8 June 1948 the gift of a Memorial Seat, donated by his brother, Tom Handley. Whatever favoured TT star gets the accolade of the 'greatest rider' can never be settled, as Mike Savage says in his book, TT Heroes, but the inscription on the Memorial Seat says something that is true and cannot be disputed for Walter lived his life bravely and to the full. No matter how great the discouragement, his watchwords remained constant, 'Never give up, never despair.' His memorial is situated on the TT course at the junction of Alexander Drive and faces the Quarter Bridge Road. Designed and made of Burmese teak by local craftsmen, it features a runic cross. The unveiling ceremony was performed by Graham Walker, a fellow TT winner and competitor who knew Walter well, editor of *Motor Cycling*, BBC commentator and Murray's father. The bronze plaque bears the inscription:

In Memory of Walter L. Handley,
Maker of Tourist Trophy Race History,
Killed, Serving His Country, 15 November 1941
None Ever Passed This Way More Bravely.

Later that day on the BBC Home Service, Graham said:

Well, perhaps the greatest tribute I can pay to Walter's memory is to say that no-one who competed against him ever expected to finish higher than second as long as he was in the race. None begrudged him his successes because we knew him to be the finest rider of our time.

APPENDIX

Isle of Man TT Race Record of Walter Handley between 1922–1934
(including race numbers where known)

Year	Race	Bike and Race No.	Result	Average mph	Lap Record
1922	Lightweight 5 laps	OK No. 26	Retired leading on second lap broken inlet valve.		44 mins, 24 secs 51.01
1923	Junior 6 laps	OK	Retired first lap, Bray Hill, valve rocker fracture.		
1923	Lightweight 6 laps	OK No. 36	Eighth leading up to fourth lap, various troubles.	47.8	41 mins, 58 secs 53.95
1924	Junior 6 laps	Rex Acme No. 22	Retired leading on third lap: flywheel trouble.		
1924	Lightweight 6 laps	Rex Acme No. 5	Retired on third lap early-lead, broken rocker.		
1924	Ultra-Lightweight 3 laps	Rex Acme No. 7	Retired on third lap when in lead. Burst oil tank.		
1925	Junior 6 laps	Rex Acme No. 50	First. 3 hrs, 28 mins and 56 secs.	65.02	34 mins, 23 secs 65.89
1925	Ultra-Lightweight 4 laps	Rex Acme No. 7	First. 2 hrs, 49 mins and 27 secs.	53.45	41 mins, 52 secs 54.08

Year	Race	Bike and Race No.	Result	Average mph	Lap Record
1925	Lightweight 6 laps	Rex Acme No. 17	Retired third lap in the lead, puncture.		37 mins, 36 secs 60.22
1926	Junior 7 laps	Rex Acme No. 1	Third after early lead, gearing loss. 4 hrs, 10 min and 6 secs.	63.37	
1926	Lightweight	Rex Acme No. 1	Retired fourth lap after being second, broken valve.		
1926	Senior	Rex Acme No. 2	Second, after long delay – plug trouble. 3 hrs, 59 min and 2/5 sec	66.31	
1927	Junior	Rex Acme No. 32	Retired on final lap when in lead, cracked piston.		32 mins, 44 secs 69.18 mph
1927	Lightweight	Rex Acme No. 22	First. 4 hrs, 10 mins and 22 secs.	63.30	
1928	Lightweight	Rex Acme No. 2	Retired on sixth lap when lying second engine trouble.		
1928	Senior	Rex Acme No. 29	Retired on first lap water-in magneto.		

Year	Race	Bike and Race No.	Result	Average mph	Lap Record
1929	Junior	AJS No. 22	Second. 3 hrs, 48 mins and 45 secs.	69·29	
1929	Lightweight	OK Supreme No. 2	Retired at end of fourth lap lying fifth. Engine trouble.		
1929	Senior	AJS No. 15	Retired on first lap after helping at accident scene.		
1930	Lightweight	Rex Acme No. 13	Retired on third lap when in lead.		33 mins, 52 secs 66·86 mph
1930	Senior	Rudge No. 28	First. 3 hrs, 33 mins and 30 secs.	74·24	29 mins, 41 secs 76·28 mph
1931	Senior	FN No. 25	Retired on first lap, gearbox trouble.		
1932	Junior	Rudge No. 9	Second. 3 hrs, 27 mins, 35 secs.	76·36	
1932	Lightweight	Rudge No. 8	Third after twice leading, engine trouble. 3 hrs, 46 mins and 53 secs.	69·86	30 mins, 30 secs 74·08 mph

Year	Race	Bike and Race No.	Result	Average mph	Lap Record
1932	Senior	Rudge No. 1	Retired lying third when injured after crash on fourth lap.		
1933	Junior	Velocette No. 21	Seventh, steering difficulties.	74·98	
1933	Lightweight	Excelsior No. 24	Retired on last lap lying third after early lead.		
1934	Junior	Norton No. 19	Retired sixth lap lying third injured after fall at Governor's Bridge.		

In 1935 Walter Handley was due to ride Velocettes in the Junior and Senior TT Races and an Excelsior Manxman in the Lightweight but he was injured on the 348cc Velocette during practice and had to withdraw.

Shortened summary of Walter Handley's successes
This summary does not include the races in which Handley had to retire –
often when leading. He had success with every make he rode.

Year(s)	Event	Result	Manufacturer(s)
1925, 1925 1927, 1930	Isle of Man TT	Four firsts	Rex Acme, Rudge
1926, 1929, 1932	Isle of Man TT	Three seconds	Rex Acme, AJS, Rudge
1926, 1932	Isle of Man TT	Two thirds	Rex Acme, Rudge
1922–1932	Isle of Man TT	Nine record laps	OK, Rex Acme, Rudge
1923, 1925, 1929, 1933, 1934	Belgian Grand Prix	Five firsts	Rex Acme, MAG, Moto Guzzi, Norton
1922, 1923, 1926, 1933, 1935	Ulster Grand Prix	Five firsts	OK, Rex Acme, Velocette
1928, 1935	European Grand Prix	Three firsts	MAG, Velocette
1928	Austrian Grand Prix	First	AJS
1929	German Grand Prix	First	MAG (Motosacoche)
1929	Algerian Grand Prix	First	MAG
1929	Royal Italian Grand Prix	First	MAG
1928, 1933	Swiss Grand Prix	Three firsts	MAG, Moto Guzzi
1928	German TT	First	AJS
1929	Dutch TT	First	MAG
1924	Welsh TT	Two firsts	Rex Acme
1932	Irish NW 200	First	Rudge
1925	Leinster 100	First in class	Rex Acme
1929	Klausen Pass Climb	First in 350 class	MAG
1925, 1926, 1927	Brooklands BMCRC	Three firsts	Rex Acme

Year(s)	Event	Result	Manufacturer(s)
1925	Brooklands two-hundred-mile	Solo first	Rex Acme
1927	Brooklands two-hundred-mile	Sidecar first	Rex Acme
1937	BMCRC outer circuit handicap race at Brooklands	First (gold star)	BSA Empire Star
1935	BRDC five-hundred-mile	Race Team Prize	Dixon Riley
1922, 1923, 1925 1926, 1927	Brooklands	World records	OK, Rex Acme
1930	Arpajon, France	World records	FN
1930	Montlhéry, France	World records	FN
1921–1927	Speed Trials and Hill Climbs	Approximately forty firsts	OK, Rex Acme
1920–1926	Reliability Trials	Approximately seventeen medal wins	OK, Rex Acme

ACKNOWLEDGEMENTS

I have been fortunate in having had conversations with several of Walter Handley's contemporaries who were generous with their time and gave me valuable advice and information: Bob Holliday; Sam James; Dick Lewis; Bill Mewis; Harry Perrey; Bert Perrigo; Tyrell Smith; Nigel Spring and written comments from Czech historian Erwin Tragatsch; Pat Driscoll; John Greenwood and Walter's brother, Tom. For access to reports and for his support, my brother Graham Handley. I am also very grateful to my wife, Linda for her interest and patience!

Finally, I would like to thank Ken Nason of Cradley Community Access Point in Herefordshire for his technical assistance with the illustrations and to my publisher, Aspect Design for their close co-operation. Any shortcomings are my responsibility.

Photographs: I am most grateful to Mortons Media Group Archive for their permission to use a selection of the photographs for which they possess copyright and their willingness to assist. Many of the photographs came from the family collection and, to the best of my knowledge, have never been published. I have endeavoured to discover and acknowledge copyright and I apologise if there are any omissions.

ABOUT THE AUTHOR

John Handley is a nephew of Wal Handley and, like his brother Graham, he has held a lifelong interest in motorcycle road racing history, particularly the TT races on the Isle of Man.

A native of Birmingham he was for many years a manager of the business in the city centre that bore the name of its famous founder, W. L. Handley Limited. It was during this period in his life that John developed his interest in motorcycling.

A history and economics graduate, John is an experienced author with several publications on career choice for young people; he has now turned his attention to biographical work and motorcycling with this latest publication *None More Brave.*

BIBLIOGRAPHY

Contemporary written sources

The Motor Cycle, Motor Cycling, The TT Special, The Isle of Man Daily Times, The Belfast Telegraph, The John Bull TT Souvenir Booklets, The Shell-BP Histories of the TT, The Autocar, The Light Car, The Motor, Motor Sport, Sporting Life.

Reports from the national dailies and the Birmingham papers have helped to set the scene.

Motorcycling:

The following list of books does not include all that I have consulted but these were particularly enjoyable and helpful.

Bayley, Dr J., *The Vintage Years at Brooklands* (Goose, 1968).

Davison, G. S., *Racing Through the Century* (The TT Special, 1951).

Davison, G. S., *Racing Reminiscences* (The TT Special, 1948).

Davison, G. S., *The Story of the TT* (The TT Special, 1947).

Davison, G. S., *The Story of the Ulster* (The TT Special, 1949).

Higgins, L. R., *Britain's Racing Motor Cycles* (G. T. Foulis, 1952.

Higgins, L. R., *Fifty Years of TT History* (Shell Mex & BP, 1960).

Holliday, R., *Racing Round the Island* (David & Charles, 1976).

McDiarmid, M., *The Magic of the TT* (Haynes, 2004).

Mellors, E. A., *Continental Circus* (The TT Special, 1949).

Mortimer, C. K., *Brooklands and Beyond* (Goose & Son, 1974).

Mortimer, C. K., *Brooklands Behind the Scenes* (Haynes, 1980).

Reynolds, B., *Don't Trudge It, Rudge It!* (G. T. Foulis, 1977).

Savage, M., *TT Heroes* (Amultree, 1997).

Willoughby, V., *The Racing Motorcycle* (Hamlyn, 1980).

Windrum, N., *The Ulster Grand Prix* (Blackstaff, 1979).

Motor racing:

Birkin, Sir H., *Full Throttle* (G. T. Foulis, 1932).
Howell, J., *Seventy Years of Motor Sport* (Littlebury & Co, 1971).
Lurani, Count, *Nuvolari* (Cassell & Co, 1959).
Lyndon, B., *Combat* (Heinemann, 1933).
Lyndon, B., *Grand Prix* (John Miles, 1935).

Air Transport Auxiliary (ATA):

Cheesman, E. C., *Brief Glory* (Harborough Publishing, 1946).
Curtis, Miss L., *The Forgotten Pilots* (G. T. Foulis, 1971).
Grant, M. and Pratt, D., *Wings Across the Border* (Bridge, 2005).

INDEX